# CLYDE THE GLIDE

## My Life in Basketball

**CLYDE DREXLER** WITH **KERRY EGGERS**

FOREWORD BY **JIM NANTZ**

SPORTS
PUBLISHING

Sports Publishing books may be purchased in bulk at special discounts for sales promotion, corporate gifts, fund-raising, or educational purposes. Special editions can also be created to specifications. For details, contact the Special Sales Department, Sports Publishing, 307 West 36th Street, 11th Floor, New York, NY 10018 or sportspubbooks@skyhorsepublishing.com.

Sports Publishing® is a registered trademark of Skyhorse Publishing, Inc.®, a Delaware corporation.

Visit our website at www.sportspubbooks.com

10 9 8 7 6 5 4 3 2 1

Library of Congress Cataloging-in-Publication Data is available on file.

ISBN: 978-1-61321-042-0

Printed in the United States of America

*To my beautiful wife, Gaynell, who gave me three wonderful children: Austin, Elise and Adam. To my oldest daughter, Erica, whose smile can light up a room.*

*To my mother, Eunice, who brought me into this world and taught me right from wrong; my brother, James, whose love for basketball helped to inspire my passion for the game; my sisters, Debra, Denise, Virginia and Lynn, whose support and encouragement throughout the years have lifted me.*

*To the young men and women who aspire to participate in the great game invented by Dr. Naismith that we call basketball.*

*To Kerry Eggers, a great journalist, for his diligent work on this book. He put in many hours researching my life and career. His genuine interest in the subject shines through in these pages. Together, we made this a successful venture.*

*To the people in the military who fight with courage and conviction to keep this nation free.*

*And to the men and women in the clergy, who contribute to the spiritual well-being of our beloved country.*

*—Clyde Drexler*

*To my high school coaches, Chuck Solberg, Fred Sutherland and Glen Kinney, who taught me the right way. And to youth coaches Bill Wallin, Mike Wantland and Jason Wells, who went the extra mile to help my sons grow as athletes and as human beings.*

*—Kerry Eggers*

# CONTENTS

# FOREWORD

## BY JIM NANTZ

*Glide. Verb (intr.): 1. To move in a smooth, effortless man-
ner: a submarine gliding through the water.*

IT WAS THE FALL OF 1980, my senior year at the
University of Houston. As the student cohost of coach Guy V.
Lewis's weekly TV show, I was a regular at the team's practices. It
was in this context that I first encountered the modest, but enor-
mously gifted, young man who would become a lifelong friend.

The Cougars were in the process of rebuilding after what
was for them a disappointing .500 season. The initial excitement
centered on the celebrated freshman recruit, Michael Young, and
a returning star, sharp-shooting point guard Rob Williams.

Soon, however, those of us who were observing the team's
workouts found it harder and harder to take our eyes off this
unheralded local freshman who was blessed with remarkable all-
court speed, magical ball-handling skills and unearthly swooping
moves to the basket.

From the beginning, Clyde Drexler had a distinctive aura
and a regal presence about him. He was so natural that he made
everything on the court look easy. He showed up with plenty of
"game," as they say, but it was of a different kind: smooth, sub-
lime, and seductive — like jazz set into motion, with faint echoes
of Connie Hawkins, Elgin Baylor, and Julius Erving.

*Glide. Verb (intr.): 2. To fly without propulsion: an aircraft in unpowered flight.*

Yes, Clyde could soar! And when he joined forces with teammates such as Michael Young and Hakeem Olajuwon, the Cougars rose to a pair of Final Four appearances in Drexler's three seasons as a charter member of college basketball's highest-flying fraternity, Phi Slama Jama.

In one of the school's greatest, but often overlooked, triumphs, the Cougars destroyed powerful Louisville 91-84 in the 1983 NCAA national semifinals in Albuquerque. Phi Slama Jama's dunking extravaganza was punctuated by one particularly eye-popping Drexler breakaway in which Clyde double-clutched a pair of pump fakes before slamming the ball through the hole. Even by today's standards, that electrifying high-wire routine still holds up as one of the all-time highlights. (Some dunkologists will argue, and with merit, that Drexler's dunk against Memphis in the Sweet 16 a week earlier might have been more spectacular. Taking off from the foul line, Clyde literally jumped over Tiger guard Andre Turner before twisting, holding on to the rim, and finally jamming.)

The disappointment over being upset by North Carolina State in the 1983 national championship game was compounded a short while later when the Houston Rockets, holding the overall No. 1 and 3 NBA draft choices, selected Ralph Sampson and Rodney McCray (of Louisville!) rather than keeping Clyde at home in Houston.

*Glide. Verb (intr.): 3. To occur or pass imperceptibly.*

Instead, Drexler was selected by Portland. Playing in the Pacific Northwest, he learned the ropes of the professional game.

The Blazers rebuilt their franchise around Drexler, who began to bloom, like the brilliant roses that city is known for, into one of the game's truly great guards.

From time to time, our paths would cross. Clyde would come over from the layup line and we would arrange to get together after a game to catch up and reminisce about our old days in Houston. He would always ask about my folks, and I would get the latest on his wonderful mom, Eunice, who still helps run the family's barbecue restaurant.

Eventually, Clyde returned to Houston, where he and Hakeem helped bring home an NBA championship. By this time, the whole world had already been enthralled by this man of rare athletic and personal grace. Clyde could float through the paint at will. His movement appeared as effortless as Jerry Rice running a slant pass into the end zone or Tiger Woods crushing a 300-yard tee shot.

It was that grace, along with his myriad other divinely ordained physical skills, which would eventually lead him to basketball's ultimate acknowledgement and would bring us together again, in a sense to complete the circle of our relationship.

*Glide. Verb (intr.): 4. Music. To blend one tone into the next.*

Fast-forward to Monday morning, April 5, 2004 (21 years and one day after N.C. State's crushing upset over Houston).

I was standing at the podium in front of a crowded ballroom in the Marriott Riverview Center in San Antonio, some 190 miles from Houston. I had been given the honor of introducing the seven new inductees for the Naismith Memorial Basketball Hall of Fame, but I was not told in advance which of the finalists had been voted in.

I knew that my old college buddy, Clyde Drexler, had a chance for that rarest of honors — to be selected for induction in his first year of eligibility. Silently, I hoped that his name would appear on the list as I thought about the symmetry of our professional careers.

It seemed like just yesterday that I was an eager young announcer, leaning into the public address microphone at Hofheinz Pavilion to give the Cougars' starting lineups on opening night of the 1981 season: "At forward, a freshman from Sterling High School, number 22, Clyde 'The Glide' Drexler!" (Of course, I milked the word "glide" for as long as I could.)

My brief reverie was interrupted when I was handed the script. Dutifully, I read the officially worded introductions for the first six newly elected members of the Hall of Fame Class of 2004. Then I turned to the last page, and there he was! With a thrill in my heart that my voice could not possibly hide, I read the following:

"He burst onto the national basketball scene as an All-America star of one of the most electric college teams of its era. At the University of Houston, he led his team to two Final Four appearances and remains the only player in school history to tally 1,000 points, 900 rebounds, and 300 steals. His NBA career with the Portland Trail Blazers and Houston Rockets included nine All-Star appearances, three NBA Finals appearances and an NBA championship. He was named to the NBA's 50 Greatest Players team and won gold as a member of the Dream Team in the 1992 Olympics. Upon his retirement in 1998, he was one of only three NBA players to collect 20,000 points, 6,000 rebounds, and 6,000 assists and still holds the Blazers' career scoring, rebounding and steals records. Elected to the Hall of Fame as a player, Clyde Drexler!"

The Hall of Fame had asked me not to deviate from its carefully crafted protocol. Believe me, it isn't easy for someone who makes a living out of ad-libbing introductions to stick to the copy. I came within two words of playing it straight. But I couldn't help myself. When I came to the words "Clyde Drexler," I just had to interject "The Glide." (Rumor has it that you can still hear that phrase echoing around the ballroom walls.)

Those words prompted a thunderous ovation, and Clyde Drexler, beaming proudly, emerged from the back of the room and walked up the center aisle. He cut through a sea of assembled basketball royalty and a phalanx of media as seamlessly as he used to drive the lane. Clyde accepted his symbolic Hall of Fame jersey, turned, and came over to the podium to give me a hug.

So now you know how this remarkable basketball journey ends. But on the pages that follow, Clyde will take you along for a wonderful ride from Houston to Portland and back and then on to Springfield, Massachussetts. Enshrined as one of the game's immortals, there are many lessons for basketball and for life that we can all learn from his days as, well, a mere mortal.

No matter how high Clyde could fly, what always impressed me more about him was the fact that he is one of the most grounded athletes I have ever been privileged to call my friend. Now every reader can also get a chance to see the other facets of this warm-hearted superstar. And I think you will agree that there is no single way to define "The Glide," a truly special person whose nickname does more than rhyme; it captures the unique essence of Clyde Drexler.

*(Jim Nantz has been with CBS Sports for nearly 20 years and is recognized as one of sportscasting's biggest names. His credits include anchoring coverage of the Super Bowl, Final Four, the Masters and other major events. He was inducted into the Naismith Memorial Basketball Hall of Fame as recipient of the Curt Gowdy Media Award in 2002.)*

# INTRODUCTION

## by Kerry Eggers

THIS HAS BEEN A PROJECT in the works for more than a decade.

In 1992, the year Clyde Drexler went from being just another great player to an international phenomenon, I was a beat writer with *The Oregonian* covering the Portland Trail Blazers. At the end of the summer, after Clyde's glorious run with the Dream Team in Barcelona, I asked if he would be interested in working on an autobiography together.

"Not until after I retire," he said.

I figured he was making a mistake. He had just finished a year in which he had led the Blazers to the NBA Finals, served as runner-up to Magic Johnson and Michael Jordan as Most Valuable Player of the All-Star Game and the NBA regular season, respectively, and been one of the 12 members of the original Dream Team that won gold in the '92 Olympic Games. He was the most popular athlete in Oregon history at the height of his career, revered for his wholesome lifestyle and accommodating demeanor with fans as much as for his sensational play. Honestly, he could have run for public office and blown away the competition. And his story certainly would have been an easy sell in Houston, his hometown and site of the successes of basketball's most memorable fraternity, Phi Slama Jama.

Clyde said there would be more to tell when his career was completed. Yeah, I thought, but people are more interested now than they will be in the future. Ten years down the road, who knows?

Now I can say it: I sold Clyde the Glide short.

His story is even better now than it would have been then.

From Portland, he moved on to Houston, where he teamed with college frat brother Hakeem Olajuwon to lead the Rockets to the NBA championship. After his retirement as a player, he spent two years coaching at his alma mater, trying to bring the Houston Cougars back to their glory days as one of college basketball's storied programs.

There was inclusion among the NBA's 50 Greatest Players on the league's 50th anniversary in 1997, a fitting tribute to one of the game's most elegant stars. But the coup de grace came in April 2004, when he earned first-ballot selection to the Naismith Memorial Hall of Fame.

You were right, Clyde. There was much more to tell.

Through the nine months we worked on this book, the biggest challenge was to get Clyde to speak his mind on many of the controversial subjects that have been integral to his career and his life. Reporters who have interviewed Drexler grow accustomed to what commonly became known as "Clydespeak" — politically correct statements often averting the truth. There was nothing sinister about Clyde's motives in all of this; he simply didn't want to offend anyone. It is central to his nature. He is a kind, caring person, and if Charles Barkley is outrageous, Clyde Drexler is polite, careful and controlled.

My concerns were alleviated as we spoke and worked on copy throughout the process. For the first time, Clyde is giving the public a no-holds-barred look at his inner thoughts. There is plenty of educated opinion here for the reader to digest.

I spoke with more than 60 family members, friends, former coaches and teammates of Clyde. Their reverence for the man shone through, but the central theme was that despite his success, he has remained the same person. That sounds cliche, but in this case, it is the truth.

Many of his friends and teammates took the opportunity to deliver some verbal jabs. Clyde never flinched, never asked to have the anecdote removed or altered. He took it in good fun and with the affection that it was intended, and he seemed to thoroughly enjoy it all.

Thanks to all who agreed to be interviewed. Special thanks to those who provided assistance via statistical and personal background, including John Simmons, Chuck Charnquist, Mike Hanson and Rich Austin of the Portland Trail Blazers, Rick Poulter of the University of Houston and Matt Rochinski of the Houston Rockets. A tip of the laptop to Fran Blinebury, the outstanding *Houston Chronicle* sports columnist, for information gleaned from his 1995 book, *Believe It! Again!*, which chronicled the Rockets' second of back-to-back NBA titles. And to Peter Knobler for background information provided from his 1996 autobiography with Hakeem Olajuwon, *Living the Dream*.

I am deeply indebted to Clyde's mother, Eunice Drexler Scott, for the extra effort she made to help with this book. Eunice, those scrapbooks and old photos provided historical perspective we wouldn't have had otherwise. Thank you.

Thanks to the good people at Sports Publishing L.L.C., in particular Doug Hoepker and Mike Pearson, whose patience as we cleared the hurdles laid before us is greatly appreciated.

Thanks to my bosses and cohorts at the *Portland Tribune*, Dwight Jaynes and Steve Brandon, who were understanding as I worked to meet the book's press deadline and stayed away from the office even a little more than usual.

Thanks to Gaynell Drexler for sharing her insights, and to her three wonderful children for letting their husband and father spend a little more time away from home working on the book.

And thanks to Clyde, who made this project fun, challenging and nostalgic all in one. We shared many a chuckle in the hours we spent together reminiscing about all those good times in your life. I appreciate your trust, and I hope I earned your respect. You have mine.

# CHAPTER 1

# A CHAMPION AT LAST

For so much of my life — since I was eight or nine or so — I had dreamed of winning an NBA championship. Since I grew up in Houston, the Rockets were my team. So part of the dream was being a member of the Rockets as we won an NBA title.

And there I was. A member of the Rockets. Living out my dream.

The calendar read June 13, 1995. We were so close. After winning Game 3 by a score of 106-103, we were ahead 3-0 in the NBA Championship Series against the Orlando Magic. Now one game separated me from the chance to experience the realization of the ultimate goal of my career.

Game 3 was a pivotal game for us. We thought if we got them down 3-0, no way would they come back to win the series. We exhausted every available source of energy in Game 3. The Magic played well, and we were very fortunate to win. After winning that game and looking at the possibility of a sweep, we were all really eager to get it over with.

It was that time of year when you aren't thinking about what hurts; it is quicker to list the body parts that don't hurt. I had two sprained fingers, one on each hand. I had crooks in my neck that were restricting movement and costing me sleep. I would wake up and couldn't move my head a certain way until I turned my body. During the Finals, our trainer, Ray Melchiorre, had me on this machine to stretch out three or four hours a day. I had no problems with my right knee, thank God. But my right shoulder was hurting. It was hard even to shoot in normal rhythm. And I was dead tired. The mental exhaustion — of trying to stay on top, giving yourself an edge, trying to continue to motivate yourself and your teammates — was overwhelming. We had been playing since October. It was mid-June. Believe me, it is a great thrill, but it is also a trying time. Everyone else is on vacation. You are ready to go on vacation, but you have a little more work to do.

Game 4 was the most difficult game of my career. In everybody's mind, the series was over and the Rockets were champions. It was like sitting over a three-foot putt to close out a match. It was close enough that everybody thought it was in, but it was not in until the ball plunked into the hole. It was not over until we had that fourth win in our hands.

On the night before a game — any game, but especially one this important — I can't afford to have distractions. I have to isolate myself. People have always respected my privacy. I didn't do a lot the night before Game 4. I just had a quiet dinner at home with my wife, Gaynell, and our three kids, watched a little TV, talked to a couple of friends and family on the phone and went to bed about 11:30.

But I didn't get much sleep. Too many things were racing through my mind. I was dead tired, but I had all these thoughts about what had happened and what could happen and what we had to do to win Game 4. We wanted to close the Magic out as soon as possible.

I never eat breakfast, or at least a real breakfast. I grabbed a banana and a glass of grapefruit juice, as I often do, and headed out the door bound for our shootaround at 10 a.m. I jumped into my white four-door Mercedes S500 for the 10-minute drive to The Summit, where the Rockets played in those days.

During the shootaround, our coach, Rudy Tomjanovich, didn't say a whole lot. He talked about not letting the Magic get a win to take over momentum in the series. We didn't want to let them start thinking they had the chance to come back in the series. Mentally the series was over, but if they could eke out a game on our home court, then go back to their place again for Game 5 ... you just never know. And they were a good young team. Shaquille O'Neal was dominant. Penny Hardaway was All-NBA. Nick Anderson, Horace Grant, Dennis Scott ... that was quite a starting five. We went over a few things during the shootaround and headed our separate ways.

I headed out for an early lunch at Drexler's Barbecue, our family restaurant that is located in downtown Houston, not far from what was then known as The Summit. Since I don't eat another meal until after a game, I wanted to put something in my stomach at lunch that was going to last. I had my specialty — the barbecued beef sandwich, potato salad and baked beans.

It was already pretty lively at the restaurant. We had a regular customer base of sports fans, and everybody was into the playoffs. A lot of my buddies were there, talking about the game. "Tonight's the night," everybody was saying. I could feel the excitement in the air. It was a little extra motivation. But mostly, I was thinking I better hurry up and eat, so I could go home and get my rest. My mom, Eunice, was there. She came over and said,

"Clyde, you get home and get off your feet." A mom's job is never done.

My game-day routine includes a nap. It is part of my mental preparation. It seems like I spend half my life taking a nap in preparation for the next game. I got to sleep about 12:30 and napped until about 3:30. I actually slept pretty well. My wife, Gaynell, always made sure the kids were quiet. I was fidgety, but I got to sleep. I rarely have trouble napping. I have a quiet, dark bedroom, but I could sleep in a room flooded with light if necessary. I could nap in an airfield. I am an All-World napper. During the season, I was always so tired, I needed it.

After my nap, I got up and took a shower. Then I had a little snack — some nuts for protein along with some fruit and fruit juice. Then it was back in the car to return to The Summit.

A lot of things went through my mind on the drive that day. My brother, James, and I had always talked about being in the situation I was about to be in. When I was on the schoolyard or in the gym, shooting baskets as a kid, I would put myself into that spot — an NBA championship game on the line. I used to pretend I was Julius Erving, the hero of my youth. Dr. J was the epitome of class. I loved the way he played, how smooth he was, how he seemed to fly when he went up for a dunk or a driving layup. I wanted to be like him. I wanted to be a world champion.

As I drove down the tunnel toward the team parking lot at The Summit, a huge crowd gathered to greet all of the Rockets. There were fans screaming and yelling and rooting us on. Euphoria was in the air. People had their brooms out. "Let's sweep the Magic," they were yelling. I was hoping the Orlando players didn't see that. That placed even more pressure on us. If we didn't win, those fans would have to put those brooms away. We wanted to send them home happy.

I was one of the last players to get to the locker room. Before I get dressed for a game, I read a book. Usually, I am reading until the last minute and then I get dressed. That night, I couldn't read. I was walking around talking to everyone. I felt anxious. It was highly unusual that I didn't have the patience to sit down and read. But I was just excited.

Sam Cassell was his usual self, talking and laughing. What a great guy to have in a locker room. I went over and said a few words to Hakeem Olajuwon, along with Mario Elie and Kenny Smith. The one guy I always talked to was Charles Jones. We just clicked, for some reason. I could talk to that man for hours. I asked Charlie, "What do you think?" He said, "We are gonna take care of business. I will be in D.C. in three or four days." He said stuff like that just to make me laugh. Every team should have a guy like him — an easy-going, stabilizing influence. Chucky Brown was the same sort of guy. We had a great locker room.

I have a routine in the way I put on my gear. I am superstitious. I always put my uniform on in the same order. I put on my socks, the jock, the shorts, and then the jersey, followed by sweatbands on my left arm and an elbow pad on my right arm. Then I put on my Reeboks. Just before that game, Reebok had sent me some new three-quarter-top shoes. I was hesitant to wear them, even though I had worn a pair like them a couple of weeks before. I didn't want to change the rhythm we were in. You win three in a row, you don't want to change anything about your routine.

We knew the Magic were going to come out fighting. It was a matter of pride. They knew they could lose the series, but they really didn't want to get swept.

It was a very tough game and not the best game for me. It was just one of those nights where I wasn't quite in sync. But we had a great team effort. All of our guys played super defense. Actually, the defense was stellar on both ends. It was a defensive struggle until the last period, when we began to open it up offensively.

It was still a close game down to the final minutes. We made a couple of key steals and fast-break conversions to get a little separation. And then it was over. The scoreboard read "Houston 113, Orlando 101." Rockets win! Rockets win! Rockets win!

I will never forget the moment. I just couldn't believe it was over. We had done it — we were world champs. I didn't know what to do with myself. It was not like any other game, where I would shake a hand or two of an opponent and head quickly to the locker room. I saw Mario, with whom I had played in Portland and was now reunited as a teammate in Houston. We hugged. Then Hakeem came over, and we hugged. Those two were happier for me than they were for themselves. They had a ring from the previous season, and I didn't.

Hakeem had told me after I was traded from Portland, "Drex, we will win one this year for you." Now he was saying, "We got you one." That was probably the sweetest conversation we ever had. The look on his face was suitable for framing. I could tell he was physically drained, but he was full of emotion because he saw how much happiness it gave me and the rest of the players to win a championship. He was the consummate teammate.

The confetti was falling down from the rafters, people were celebrating, the music was playing. I thought, this is kind of nice. I am a member of the last team standing — finally.

I had been so close so many times at so many levels. At the University of Houston, we made the Final Four two years in a row but didn't win it. With the Portland Trail Blazers, we made the NBA Finals twice, in 1990 and '92, losing both times. I had been a member of the first Dream Team that won the 1992 Olympic gold medal at Barcelona, but that really didn't count in my mind. Finally I was on a team that was good enough to win it all.

When the trophy presentation by commissioner David Stern was finally over on the court, we went into the locker room.

Rudy didn't talk long to the players, but he talked with emotion. He was in heaven. He was proud of the way we were able to win a title coming into the playoffs as the sixth seed from the Western Conference. Rudy said, "In a lot of ways, this is better than the first one. No one expected us to win. We made the big trade at midseason, and against all odds, we won it. To do this is something from a movie script. I can't believe this is happening." It was sweet.

The locker room scene was pretty chaotic. I had done a lot of interviews on the court and then in the interview room. I didn't get to do all the champagne stuff in the locker room, but Kenny Smith made sure I wasn't left out. While I was doing an interview, he came over with a bottle of bubbly and dumped it on my head. "What are teammates for?" Kenny asked.

I couldn't stop grinning.

Finally I showered and left for a private party we had booked at a downtown restaurant. It was just for my family and close friends, so we could celebrate together in case we happened to win that night. When I was traded to Houston, I had talked with my mom about how I hoped we could win a title in my hometown, so everybody could be part of the celebration. Now it was happening.

As I walked out of the arena toward my car, I was congratulated by the security guards and all the people who worked that season at The Summit. They were as excited as I was, it seemed. There hadn't been any championship teams in Houston over the years. Now the Rockets were champions, back to back!

I got into my car and headed toward the restaurant, which was about five minutes away. The streets were packed with celebrating fans. I made it about two blocks, and people had blocked off certain streets and weren't letting cars get past. All of a sudden, they recognized me, and they rushed over and started rocking my car. I mean, there were hundreds of people surrounding the car. I was literally scared to death. It felt like I was in an airplane, like I was being lifted off the ground. I thought, Lord, this is a hell of a way to go. Then a policeman saw me and rushed over and saved my butt. He cleared the crowd and I was able to get through. People were so happy, and they didn't realize the danger of the situation. It was the funniest thing, yet also the scariest moment of the night.

I reached the restaurant, and as I walked into the place, people were standing and clapping. And then I got to the room where the party was, and there were all the members of my family — my mom, my five brothers and sisters, Gaynell and the kids, everybody. What a scene. It was a celebration.

I was so tired, I didn't have much of an appetite. I am not much of a drinker, but I had a little champagne, maybe half a glass. I didn't want to get drunk. I wanted to have all my faculties, so I could be sure I wasn't dreaming. All I could do was sit there and listen to the stories and soak in the moment.

Mom said, "It is about time we come out on the winning end. We have been to the top a lot of times and come up short. It shows if you continue to persevere, good things happen."

As always, my mother was right.

# CHAPTER 2

# GROWING UP

I was born in Charity Hospital in New Orleans on June 22, 1962. My mother, Eunice, was married to my father, James Drexler, at the time. He worked in a mill. We lived on the outskirts of the city. I don't remember my time in New Orleans at all, because Mom left my father when I was three and moved us to Houston. Mom's sister, Charity, lived in Houston, and it was a city where there were jobs and opportunity. Mom wanted a new beginning.

**EUNICE DREXLER SCOTT:** Clyde's father was really abusive. I couldn't handle it. I had always liked Houston, and I figured we would move there and see how it goes. Within two weeks, I had a job checking groceries at Watkin's. I worked there for about a year and a half and met my second husband, Manuel Scott, who worked at Rice Food Market in South Park. Then I got a job at Rice's, too. I worked there for 15 years and became the head checker there. We took over the family restaurant in 1982.

When we first arrived in Houston, we lived for a few years in some apartments in the southeast part of the city. Then when I was in the third grade, my mom and Manuel — they married when I was six — bought a house. Our first home in Houston was at 5615 Elm Tree Drive, maybe a 10-minute drive from the University of Houston, where I would wind up attending college. It was a small, three-bedroom house with a one-car garage and a good-sized back yard. We had a living room and a family room right off the kitchen, where you could eat and watch TV. When we first moved in, the girls had a room, my parents had a room and the three boys had a room with two bunk beds. There was a back part of the garage where guests could stay. I helped renovate the garage into an extra bedroom when I was in college. Our neighbor was an expert carpenter and he led the way, but I helped, too. It gave us a little extra room, and with three younger sisters, I loved having my own private space.

I was the last of three kids by my father, but Mom had seven children overall, and I was right in the middle. The oldest child was Michael, seven years my senior. Mom was engaged to Michael's father, a police officer, but he was shot and killed in the line of duty. The next child — James Sr.'s first — was Debra, six years older than me. Then came James Jr., four years older. Then me, followed by my younger sisters Denise, Virginia and Lynn. Manuel was their father.

**DEBRA MATHEWS:** I was in eighth grade when we moved to the house on Elm Tree. The neighborhood was better than the one we came out of, the one Michael and I grew up in. It was basically new homes. The neighborhood we moved from was tough. I was always scared to be out by myself there. It wasn't that way at the new house.

All of my schools — Frost Elementary, Albert Thomas Junior High, Sterling High School — were within a 3/4-mile radius. I walked to school in grade school and junior high, which were literally across the street from each other. When I got to high school, there were kids who had cars, so I could always thumb a ride. I would get up early and put my thumb out and hitch a ride to school.

I was a bicycle-riding fool during my early years, and I could get to any place I wanted on my Schwinn. It was a great neighborhood. It was probably classified as lower middle class, but we considered ourselves middle class. Both of my parents were working. We had clothes and food to eat. It was a middle-class upbringing. We had a lot of nice neighbors. They were working-class people — teachers, doctors, police, firemen. When we moved into the neighborhood, it was around 60 percent African American, but over the years it became just about 100 percent black.

Most of my friends were black kids. There were a couple of Hispanic and white kids, too, but to be honest, I didn't and still don't pay much attention to race. That's just the way I was raised. The way I learned about race was talking with people, talking about Martin Luther King, Malcolm X and some of the great black leaders of our time. I remember as a kid being in the room with adults, eavesdropping on philosophical discussions — that was my introduction into racial matters. I didn't experience a lot of racism, if any at all. The people in our neighborhood were all nice people. The schools were integrated, but every year you could see the Caucasians leaving. You didn't think about it. It was just, "I hope someone our age moves in."

My stepfather, Manuel, was a butcher by trade. One of the best. He worked hard. You brought him some raw meat, he would package it and make a lot out of the package, and that is an art. Some weekends, he would be intoxicated and wouldn't make it to work on time. If he overslept, they would come get him — that's how good he was.

Manuel was not affectionate with the kids. His thing was to go to work, come home that evening, then find chores for the kids. If a chore wasn't done, he would ask, "Whose weekend is it to do these dishes?" If he would come home and see six kids watching TV and no dishes done, somebody was going to stop watching TV and do the dishes. That was just the way it was. All kids hate doing chores, right? So did we, but we didn't have a lot of choice. If the yard wasn't cut the way he thought it needed to be cut, he would say, "Get out there and get it done."

Manuel wasn't my dad, but I respected him; he didn't abuse anyone. He was a nice guy, except when he was drinking. Then he could turn into a monster. That happened mostly on the weekend. Monday through Friday, he was a nice guy. If he had been drinking, he became quiet. He wasn't the kind of person to bother you normally. When he had been drinking and I saw him coming, I would go to the other room, because I knew he would have something for me to do. Michael was gone, James was too old — he couldn't tell James to do anything — and the rest of the household were girls. I was the odd guy out. I would hear Manuel say, "Clyde, get in here." I would go the other way and hide to stay out of his way. I would head out for the basketball courts; otherwise he would make me go cut the hedges or do some other chore.

**EUNICE DREXLER SCOTT:** I guess I didn't pick the best fathers for my husbands. Manuel and Clyde didn't have a relationship. Manuel wasn't really a father to any of the kids. He had a job and helped me out financially, but that was it. As I look back, Manuel had no previous children until I gave him three, and I figured he would be involved with raising them. But he wasn't. A lot of stuff he tried to do with Clyde, like make him work, was behind my back. Clyde was really the only one he tried it with — none of the others. But Manuel wouldn't do it when I was home. Uh-uh. I didn't know about it until a long time later. Some things are just that way. There's nothing I could do about it. I don't regret marrying him, but I didn't expect to have to raise the kids myself. We were married for 13 years and then we separated when Clyde was 17. We were separated 26 years and never divorced. He died in 2003.

James Sr., Clyde's father, also had no relationship with Clyde at all. He never was close to any of the kids. He never looked Clyde up or tried to see him once we left New Orleans. Even when Clyde was in high school and college, James would come to Houston to watch Astros games, but he never even called the kids.

As a kid, I didn't even think about my parents splitting up. I knew my father was back in New Orleans and I was in Houston, and I didn't know why they were not together. I know what my life was; that's it.

After we moved to Houston, we would go to Louisiana for much of the summers and hang out there. Mom was one of 11 children in her family, and some of them lived in New Orleans and different parts of Louisiana. We would stay with relatives and hang out, play with our cousins. Our uncles would take us fishing. Sometimes we would cut sugar cane in the fields on their farms, or chase the chickens.

My dad lived in the same town as some of my relatives. It was named Glencoe. It's about an hour from New Orleans, a little ways from Lafayette. Visiting Glencoe was a chance for me to see him and spend some time with grandmothers on both sides, plus my father's dad, who was the nicest guy in the world. We would divide the summer between the families, but spend maybe three-quarters of the time with my dad's mother, Stella Drexler. We called her "Mama Stella." She was a very involved grandmother. I remember we celebrated the holidays, Fourth of July especially. Birthdays were just another day. Cake and ice cream and happy birthday.

My father was not the kind of guy to establish a daily rapport with his kids, for whatever reason. When we went to see him, we would enjoy it and make the best of it. I don't know if it was because he was mad at Mom for leaving or what. When we first went to see him, he was extremely happy to see us. But I saw less of him after he remarried, when I was probably 10 or 11. We would spend most of the time with Mama Stella. He would come over and eat dinner with us and hang out sometimes.

He hardly ever came to Houston to see us. Once in a while he would come into town to see Astros games, but he usually wouldn't even stop by then. We lived right off the freeway, 12 minutes from the Astrodome, and I don't know if he didn't want to see Mom or what. There were a lot of dynamics involved, I guess. Maybe he was just non-confrontational. Maybe he just did the easy thing and stayed away.

We stay in touch now. He is retired and living with full pension in New Orleans. We get along fine. I would have liked to have spent more time with him during my childhood, but it didn't work out that way. I spent more time with him as an adult. He is a very likeable guy and we have a great relationship to this day.

My mother is a great woman who was an awesome influence on all of her children. She didn't give us a whole lot of restriction, but she taught us right from wrong. There were no gray areas. She has a strong personality. She did not bug us to death about little stuff, but she was serious about the things we should be doing, like going to church, taking care of ourselves, coming in at the right hour, and treating people right. Those were the things she harped on. She always worried about how we dressed and that we kept our appearances up.

**EUNICE DREXLER SCOTT:** I tried to keep it simple with the kids. I told them all the time, "Be a good person, treat people right, the sky is the limit. Do your best and you can achieve whatever you want." I have always believed in the saying, "Say what you mean and mean what you say." You can't play with your kids when you are teaching them life skills. You have to make them understand where you are coming from. They all listened pretty well. I didn't have time to do a lot of preaching and whatnot. I was working full-time and doing what I could to keep the household together. What I said, I meant.

Between Mom and Manuel, we all had a lot of chores. James and I took turns cutting the lawn until he left the household; then it was on me. All the kids took turns doing a week of washing the dishes. For a week, you had to wash and dry and put away the dishes. It was the week of hell. The others laughed at you while you were doing it. With such a big family, there were always a lot of dishes to take care of. If my mom wasn't working, she would cook, and sometimes the pots would sit in the sink unwashed and get hard. Ever wash a dirty pot with hard food stains? Man, that was tough. It took a while, trust me.

We also took turns with the refrigerator and the oven. You had to make sure the refrigerator was clean. Wipe it down, take everything out and put it back, make sure it was in good shape. We cleaned the oven once a week, too. And when it was my week to do those things, I still had to cut the yard and tend to the garden, too. Mom always had a rose garden in front of the house. You might be asked to trim the roses.

Taking out the trash was always my responsibility. We had a dog, a German shepherd named Ricky. He was my stepfather's dog. I liked Ricky; I didn't love him. He would always find a way to knock over the trash. I would have to get up every morning and go put it back in the plastic trash bucket, put the lid on it, and place some weight on top of it so he couldn't knock it over. Half the time, he still knocked that sucker over. What a headache.

**EUNICE DREXLER SCOTT:** Clyde was such a good boy. Whatever I told him when he was growing up, he would listen to me, regardless of what I said. The kids had their little ups and downs, like sisters and brothers do. No major fights or anything, I don't think. Today, you can tell it wasn't nothing. They love each other.

The only real arguments in our family took place because of television. There was only one TV in the house, a color TV, which was a big deal, by the way. Some families only had black and white in those days. The older siblings always took liberties with the TV. I would be watching the Cowboys play the Redskins, and somebody else would come in and turn the station. We had some battles over that. I liked other TV shows. I liked *Perry Mason*, *The Beverly Hillbillies*, *The Munsters*, *The Rifleman*. *Speed Racer* was my favorite cartoon. I loved *Popeye*, too. *Fat Albert* and *Soul Train* on Saturdays. And on Sunday night it was *Bonanza*.

My family was always pretty close and involved. The kids were all spaced three or four years apart. That meant we weren't going through the same things at the same time. At least until I got into high school, James wouldn't let me hang out with him; I was too young. My sister, Denise, was four years younger than me. It is like that all the way down.

**DENISE PINK:** I was the oldest of Clyde's younger sisters, and we were very close. He was a quiet person. He didn't have many friends. Me and Virginia, who was younger than me, were his best friends. He was a different kid, but a nice kid.

**DEBRA MATHEWS:** I was Clyde's only big sister. He stayed away from bad influences. He was never in trouble a day in his life as a kid. I was always good to Clyde. When I was a senior in high school, he was in the sixth grade, so he was still a child. I was the big sister to all the kids. When I would come home from school, it was my job to clean up and cook a good dinner. All the kids would be there. My mother would have to work, so I would take responsibility.

Mom did a great job under the circumstances, but we had a lot to do ourselves. Mom was always working, so it was up to me to kind of run things a lot of the time. If I had been the type of child to go around getting in trouble — robbing, stealing, doing drugs, things like that — a lot of things would have happened to the family. The younger kids would have seen that lifestyle, and eventually it would have gotten them, too. But I didn't do those things.

I always thought Clyde was a special type of person. He was an exceptionally smart, gifted child. He liked his books. He liked his sports. He was very energetic. There was just something about him; people liked him.

We were close. If he needed something, he got it. If I had it, he had it. My husband and I moved to Germany for two years when I was 18 years old, and the kids were kind of on their own during that time. Then I got divorced and came back to Houston. And I had an apartment for a while, and he and his friends would come over to my place and use the swimming pool.

**EUNICE DREXLER SCOTT:** Clyde and James Jr. were really close. Clyde still looks up to James, like he is some kind of daddy. I guess he was a father figure, but I didn't see it that way at the time. If I told him something bad about James, you think he was going to agree with me? No sir. James can do no wrong in Clyde's eyes.

**DENISE PINK:** When we were young, the highlight of Clyde's day was when James came home from school.

**JAMES DREXLER JR.:** Clyde and I were always close. He is still my best friend in the world. He's a super person. I love him to death. He reminds me of myself. He is understanding. He can communicate with people of all races. He will talk to you straight without being fake. That is the way our relationship has always been. Truthful. We never hid nothing from each other. We were respectful of our elders. We would never say one bad word to adults. He's still that same way today. "Yes sir," or "no miss." People think that is funny, but it is hard to change that. I see some of the young kids today who don't give adults respect, and it is hard for me to understand.

I was more of a dad to Clyde than a big brother. I took care of him, gave him money, and wouldn't let anybody pick on him. That was just the type of guy I was. I don't pick on younger brothers and sisters. It is like taking advantage of someone. I never picked on him. I protected him.

Clyde could be a bad little kid. He used to stay in trouble with his younger sisters. He picked on them, and I wound up protecting them from him, too. Every day he was harassing them. I don't know how they made it to adulthood. At the same time, I wouldn't let nobody mess with Clyde outside the family.

**VIRGINIA SCOTT-WESTBROOKS:** I am eight years younger than Clyde, next to youngest in our family. We were known to everyone as James's or Clyde's little sisters. Clyde was rough on us girls. Without a doubt, he was the worst. He would bogart everything. We could never watch TV when we wanted because it was always Clyde's television time. I remember we wanted to watch cartoons, but it was always what Clyde wanted to watch. A lot of times it was a baseball game. He always had control of the television.

As we got older, that started not to be the problem. The problem became bathroom time. You always had to wait for Clyde to finish. We had two bathrooms, but my mother's was separate. We had to share the other one, and there were still five of us kids at home — James, Clyde, Denise, myself and Lynn.

Hair was important to Clyde, at least when he got into high school. I would have to stand on the sofa to fix his collar and flatten his hair to make his Afro big. Me and Denise did that a lot.

If Mom and James weren't around, he was the boss of the house. So we were in trouble. We were glad when James was around, because Clyde didn't take over as much. James didn't let him. It was a big-brother thing.

**EUNICE DREXLER SCOTT:** The biggest problem I had with Clyde was that he was a sore loser. He'd be watching the Astros on TV, and he'd be crying. I'd say, "What are you crying about, honey?" He's say, "They are losing." I'd say, "So?" Playing any kind of games — card games, board games, whatever — he would cheat you before he would lose. That is just how he was. He was into winning. It was only when it came to sports and games, mind you. He was just so competitive.

I loved watching pro sports from an early age. I was a bigtime Cowboys fan. They were really good in those days. I could name every starter on their team in the Roger Staubach era. More than half of the kids on the street were Cowboys fans. Until the Oilers got Earl Campbell, nobody paid them much attention. When they got Earl, I became an Oilers fan for a few years.

I liked the Astros big-time. I didn't miss many games, either in person, on TV or on the radio. By the time I was 10 or 11, we would get six or seven friends together and go down to the Astrodome to watch games. We would convince one of the parents to drop us all off, and another parent would pick us up.

**EUNICE DREXLER SCOTT:** From the earliest age, Clyde liked sports. I guess he took that from me. I was the captain of my basketball team at Franklin High School in New Orleans, and I loved the game. I introduced the kids to a lot of sports. I took them skating, bowling, to the park to play baseball. It kept them busy and out of trouble that way.

**VIRGINIA SCOTT-WESTBROOKS:** I played volleyball and tennis. Everybody in the family played sports — around the house, at school, in the streets or parks. It was just in us. That's all we did as kids.

Sports was my life as a kid. It was fun. I liked being competitive. My first organized team sport was baseball. My oldest brother, Michael, had played, and I would go to his games all the time. When I got old enough, maybe fifth grade, I played. I was a first baseman; I could catch and I could hit the ball. I was never an All-Star. I was a hack, really. But I enjoyed it, just being out there on the field with my friends.

**WILL BLACKMON:** Clyde and I became friends when we were both going to Frost Elementary in fifth or sixth grade. I lived just a block down the street from where he grew up. We played Little League baseball together one season. He was a decent player — right close to average, I would say. He was a real quiet, shy kind of guy. Didn't say a lot. Didn't do a whole lot. Kind of went along with everybody else.

**JAMES DREXLER JR.:** Clyde was a good baseball player. At one time, I thought he could have had a career in baseball, before he grew, because he was so good fielding and throwing.

I never did play organized football. I didn't play basketball for a school team until seventh grade. But forget about school-organized stuff. When we got home from school each day, we organized our own neighborhood games. Every day after school, I would be playing football or basketball or baseball just down the street from my house. We lived in an area called Crestmont, at the end of South Park Boulevard, which is now Martin Luther King Boulevard. There were a lot of kids in our area, and we knew everyone. The Watsons, who lived in the house behind us, had four boys close to my age. We always had a place to play and kids to play with.

Whatever the season, that was my favorite sport. Football, basketball, baseball. Every day it was a different activity. In the fall, we would play tackle football without pads on the Albert Thomas grass field after the school team got through practicing. Most of the time, I played with guys from James's age group. Even though I was four years younger, they would let me play if they were short of players. Even as a little kid, I did pretty well. I participated and wasn't bad.

**JAMES DREXLER JR.:** I was a good basketball player as a kid. But from the time I was about 13, I was working in our family restaurant. I was making money every week, so basketball took a back seat. I never played high school ball; I was always working. I preferred to work. I bought my own car at age 18. But I would go into the gym and play against the guys on the team and beat all of them.

Like most little brothers, Clyde wanted to hang around his big brother. My friends and I used to go to the playground to play basketball. Sometimes I would throw a rock at him and say, "Go back home," and wouldn't let him play with me. Sometimes I let him go with me, and a lot of times the guys I was playing with were older than me, so they were way older than Clyde. Sometimes I wouldn't let him play with us because the guys were big and rough. If I did let him, if they would knock him down, they were always looking at me. I was kind of big and strong, and they knew they had to tangle with me if they messed with Clyde. Eventually, when he grew and was so good, he wouldn't let me play with him. He started sending me back home.

I grew to 6'7", and I am not sure where I got my height. Mom is 5'7" and she had brothers 6'2" and 6'3", but none of my brothers or sisters are tall except me. James is bowlegged; if he straightens his legs up he is maybe six feet.

**DENISE PINK:** Really, Clyde's best friend was his basketball, and that's just the way it was. He was always shooting baskets, dribbling a ball from the time he was about eight years old. There was no hoop at the house, so his imaginary hoop was the ledge where the roof came down. He would throw the ball up there enough, and more than likely he would bust a window, as he did a few times. Virginia was interested in basketball. I was into track and cheerleading and the occasional beauty pageant. James was a good basketball player, but he was always working.

**DEBRA MATHEWS:** Clyde liked that basketball from the time he was an itty-bitty boy, six or seven. He would play and bounce that basketball up against the roof, against the window. He just liked to play ball. At that time, it was a little nerve-racking, but he was a child.

**EUNICE DREXLER SCOTT:** When I would go Christmas shopping, I would always get stuck on what to buy for Clyde. Every Christmas, it always came down to a basketball.

By the next Christmas, I would already have worn the last ball out.

**EUNICE DREXLER SCOTT:** He wore out a few window panes, too. The bathroom window, the living room window, the garage windows ... I would hear him out there, and pretty soon there would be the sound of breaking glass. He broke one window three times in three weeks. That was enough. I told him he would have to start paying for those windows.

I learned to dribble on the driveway and on the patio. A lot of times the ball got away from me. I broke the bathroom window four times. It cost $5 each time to have it replaced. I broke the living room window trying to dunk the ball off the roof, and that cost $50 to fix. I broke the garage window twice. It cost $35 each time. I had to work at the restaurant to pay for all of it.

I didn't just play at home. There were a lot of facilities where we could play sports, especially basketball. My buddies and I rode bicycles all over the area. You had to be careful to lock up. Somebody was stealing your bike about once a year, or they would take your front tire or do something stupid. I bought my bike on my own from the time I was about 12 or 13 with money from odd jobs I had. Mom had all those kids. The prevalent thought in our family was, you don't want to have to bug our parents for extra money. They had a lot on their plate. We had to have money to buy basketball nets for the school or park hoops. When I really started playing every day at about 14, somebody had to have a pair of nets. You would bring your own nets. And when you left, you would take them down. That was a big deal. You would keep a stockpile, because if you left them up there, they would be gone the next day.

There were two nearby churches that had basketball courts. I would dribble a ball down and back. You could walk or bike down the street to Crestmont Park. There were six baskets up, and all had chain nets. When I was younger, it was a thrill to get to play with the big kids. You might get chosen last, but at least you got to play. And that helped make you better.

When I was in junior high, every day after school, from four to five o'clock, you could find us at Albert Thomas, shooting on one of the eight outdoor hoops there. You could always find a place to play. Mom knew where to find me — at one of the courts or fields in the area. We would organize games against kids in other areas. There were no gangs or fights. Guys just loved to play sports. Win or lose, you saw them the next day in school, and we were all friends. There were three or four gyms in the area, and we had a lot of good summer programs in the gyms, where you could get a lunch and hang out all day. And as I got older, I expanded my search for good basketball games. I wanted to find good competition daily; that was my goal.

But a lot of the time, it was just shooting baskets on the playground at Albert Thomas. When I was out there by myself, like I was most of the time, I would go one on one — just me and the pole. You have to watch those poles. That is where I learned body control. They will make you back up in midair. And the hoops were a little higher than 10 feet, which had something to do with the trajectory of my shot. On just 10-foot goals, I had to lower my trajectory. That's why I had a line-drive shot during my playing days in college and in the pros. The 10-foot goals seemed shorter. It felt like I was shooting down at the rim.

At Albert Thomas, there wasn't a single straight rim among the outside baskets. I practiced dunking a little bit. I think I bent them all. There was one goal that was my favorite because of the big shade tree near it. It would shield the sun in the afternoon. And boy, did it get hot out there. I had to find a different goal after they cut down the tree to put up some temporary buildings. I would go right out there after school and starting shooting. Sometimes it was so hot I really didn't want to, but I made myself. People used to think I was crazy for doing it.

**VIRGINIA SCOTT-WESTBROOKS:** It is amazing Clyde was a professional athlete, because we always considered him the clumsiest in the family when he was young. We would always reference that to him all the time. "Clyde, you are so clumsy."

But he always had to have something to do. If he was not in the driveway shooting the basketball off the house, you would see him walking down the street with a ball, coming from the park or the school. In the heat of the day, too. It was non-stop. You would just expect to see Clyde coming down the street at a certain time, every day. Whatever he was doing, it always was something having to do with sports.

**JAMES DREXLER JR.:** For a long time, Clyde couldn't jump. He was a skinny, awkward kid. His coordination wasn't that great. He was slow. Then for some reason, he started doing karate and working with the numchucks when he was about 13. He got a lot of coordination by doing that. If you made one wrong turn, those hard things would hit you on the head and knock you out. All of a sudden he grew, improved his coordination, picked up speed, and I was like, "Clyde, who are you, bro'?"

Several years later, during the summer before Clyde's sophomore year at the University of Houston, I went to Dow Park to play basketball. There was this ex-college player, a big guy who was about 6'5", who was giving me a rough time. I was holding my own a little bit, but he was overpowering me.

Clyde just happened to pull up at the park, because he knew I was there all the time. He said, "Let me take your place for five minutes." And he just started dunking over this guy, going crazy. I was on the sidelines, and I said to the guy, "Clyde is doing you like you were doing me."
It was like a scene in a movie or something. Big brother takes care of little brother all his life, and then suddenly one day, we changed roles.

I started martial arts at age 11 or 12 and did it until I was 15 or so, because there were a lot of bullies around who would try to take your basketball, your bicycle, whatever. I wasn't going to have that. I worked too hard mowing lawns to have somebody take my stuff. There was a tae kwon do teacher — Mr. Gant — who had a little studio not far from where I lived. I started going by there, or sometimes he would come by my house and we would practice in the garage. We would be in there for an hour or two, sweating. I never was that good, and I never earned a formal belt, but I loved it. It provided great discipline. He taught me how to train, how to focus, how to develop strength and physical fitness — all virtues of martial arts.

I did a lot of stuff as a kid. During my junior high years, we would go roller skating at the Old Spanish Trail skate park on Saturday mornings. And that was the place to be on Friday and Saturday nights, too. My whole neighborhood was involved. All the guys were into skating. Michael Young — who lived about 10 miles from me and wound up being my good friend and teammate at the University of Houston — used to go there. I could do all kinds of stunts on those roller skates. That helped develop strong ankles. I was a speed skater who could stop on a dime without using a stopper.

I had about 10 friends I saw almost daily. Will Blackmon, Joe Cotton, Glen Gordon, Steve Doucette, Michael Blanton, Darrell Waldrup — and he had four brothers we hung out with sometimes — Reginald Guidry and his two brothers and the Julks brothers, Robert and Darryl. Some of the guys eventually got into trouble, some with drugs, and some wound up in prison. Some of the guys turned out fine. There were guys who earned college degrees and are doing really well in their chosen fields.

**EUNICE DREXLER SCOTT:** We were a religious family. I was raised a Baptist and never let it go. All the kids were baptized. Clyde was baptized when he was 11.

I went to Sunday school from the time I was eight years old. We went to church most Sundays at Bethel Baptist Church, which was just a couple of blocks from our home. I still attend that church. We were supposed to go to Sunday School, and try to make the church service, too. If I could get away with not going to Sunday School, I would do it. Sunday School was from 9:00 to 11:00 and then church from 11:00 to 1:30 p.m. Four or five hours of church on a Sunday was a lot. I used to say, "If I am going to church, I am not going to Sunday School." Mom would usually say, "All right, but you have to go to one of them." It used to drive me nuts, because I wanted to get back to watch the NFL *Game of the Day* on TV.

**EUNICE DREXLER SCOTT:** Clyde was a good student. He made the honor society in eighth grade. You had to make straight As to do that. He was proud of that. He always had the brains. He pretty much stayed out of trouble, as far as I knew, anyway. James's friends used to come over and pick on him, but Clyde handled that pretty well. He was an honest kid. One day in eighth grade, he came home from school crying. I said, "What are you crying for, Clyde?" He said, "The teacher said I didn't return a book to the library, and I know I did, and she won't give me my report card until I pay for the book." I said, "OK, here's some money, go pay for the book and get your card." He said, "No, Mom, I turned that book in. I am not going to pay anything." And he didn't.

The next morning I went to school and talked to the principal. He went into the library and looked and the book was there. He told me, "I told that teacher not to check in the books the way she does. That is how she gets it all mixed up." But she wouldn't even go in there and check. Clyde got his report card that day. I had never heard of a kid crying over a report card. Far as I was concerned, she could have kept it.

I knew I had checked that book in, but I got a late notice, and eventually they said I owed $10. Mom went to the school and was ready to pay the fine, even though I told her not to. And there was that book, sitting on the shelf.

I was a pretty studious kid who, for the most part, did what I was supposed to do. I was always like a teacher's pet. As I got older, into ninth and 10th grade, a B was like a bad grade to me. When I came home with five As and a B, Mom would say, "That's good, honey, but how did you get that B?" It was expected I would do well.

I loved to read. I was into science fiction for a while. I loved autobiographies of people who shaped the course of history. I still read a lot. I have always had a thirst for knowledge. Books keep my attention. And since I lived for sports, I read everything about sports. I would listen to Astros games on the radio and read about them the next day in the newspaper.

**DEBRA MATHEWS:** Clyde was on the honor roll. For a black kid to do that, to be that exceptional, it was rare. He had smarts. He liked school. He went to school every day. He has always been an exceptionally smart person. He was never around trouble. Trouble was in everybody's face, but he never gave in. The thugs in the neighborhood loved him. They respected both Clyde and James. They were like the little nerds on the street, but the thugs didn't mess with them, because they respected them. And these were kids who went around beating everybody up. They left Clyde and James alone, though. They played ball, and everybody looked up to them because they were real good. They played every day after school. They didn't do things to get into trouble with people. They did fun things that guys liked to do. Go play ball, see who can outshoot who, take 'em to the hoop, you know. That's all they did.

The most difficult thing that happened in my childhood was the death of my oldest brother, Michael, when I was 11. He was 18 when he died. He was a very nice guy, a leader, a great big brother for me most of his life.

But he began experimenting with drugs and hanging with the wrong crowd. You could see him deteriorating. He had dropped out of school and gotten a job. He was starting to use drugs more and more. My friends and I would be outside playing baseball, and he would get off the bus and you would see him stumbling down the street. People would be helping him up. It was getting embarrassing.

You saw something happen, but at my age, you weren't sure just what. Really, I had no idea. He died when he was shot by police while trying to rob a pharmacy, probably for more drugs. It was a situation gone bad with a really good kid. When they are on those drugs, there is no logic. It tore my mom apart, and everybody else in the family. We weren't oblivious to what he was doing, but still it was shocking.

**EUNICE DREXLER SCOTT:** I fault myself for not being educated on the subject of drugs. Where we came from in Louisiana, drugs were nowhere around and I knew nothing about them. When I got to Houston, it was a horse of another color. It was bad there, and I didn't even know. The company Michael was keeping, they were using drugs. When I found out, it was just too late.

Mike moved out on me about two weeks after we got our house in Houston, when he was 17. I never went by his place. I was working so much, so busy, but I should have done more tending to him. My husband knew where he was. After Michael died, Manuel told me he went by the apartment and met the lady, and they had drugs. I told him, "I can't believe you waited 'til now to tell me that." I still can't believe it. This woman had guns, she had three men, she kept them drugged up, and she sent them to get more drugs. She was their downfall. I tell you no lie. He was 18.

He was shot by police. The feeling I had back then was that the police were killing a lot of the black and minority kids. I always said, "Let God handle this. It ain't like they are hurting anybody." He was running from them. They could have shot him in the leg. They are trained to do that. A bunch of kids were killed in different incidents.

It was heartbreaking. Michael had a beautiful smile, a beautiful sense of humor. I remember when he was still living with us, if something would come on TV about somebody robbing or doing something illegal, he would laugh and say, "If I ever break the law, they are going to have to kill me, 'cause I ain't going to jail."

**DEBRA MATHEWS:** Michael was one year older than me. We were really close. When he died, I was 17. He lived a different lifestyle than me. I didn't like that lifestyle. He dropped out of school in ninth grade. I didn't really know exactly what he was doing, but I knew he never was at home. I couldn't understand why. He would come home, and we would be so happy to see him. We didn't know what was going on. We all could have wound up the same way as Michael. It was up to us to figure out how we wanted to live our lives. Our mother played a big part, but we played a big part, too. Michael grew up in the same family, but look what happened to him.

Michael and I had an argument on the morning of the day he died. I stayed around the house a lot and listened to music. He used to come in and take my albums. That day, he grabbed some of my albums, and we got into a big argument — you know, silly stuff, sister and brother stuff. I said, "Bring my albums back." He left. That night, he died. I was sick about it. It took me years and years to get over the fact that we had an argument the last time we saw each other. We weren't nice to each other. It tore me up.

**VIRGINIA SCOTT-WESTBROOKS:** Becuase of Michael's situation, it made Mom more conscious of what she needed to say to us kids. I was four years old when he died. All I heard from that point on was her talking about not doing drugs, don't let anybody tell you this and that. At that time, parents weren't preaching to their kids as much about drugs. She put it in our minds as kids that drugs were something we never wanted to do.

**EUNICE DREXLER SCOTT:** After Michael died, I kept a much closer eye on the other kids after that. I blamed myself, and I didn't want to have more problems. I still think about Michael. Every day.

# CHAPTER 3

# A STERLING START

When I was growing up in Houston, our schools had junior high from seventh to ninth grade, then three years of high school. I was starting to fall in love with basketball, but I wasn't any good yet. I was kind of a shrimp, and I hadn't really distinguished myself. I had played seventh- and eighth-grade basketball for our school team at Albert Thomas, and I was on the ninth-grade team, but I never played, and I didn't travel for away games. I was about 5'8", and I was terrible. I didn't really even make the team. Because I had been on the team in seventh and eighth grade, the coach kept me for home games. But we had some really good players, and I don't remember playing at all.

**JOE COTTON:** I have known Clyde since fourth or fifth grade. We lived in the same neighborhood. We played ball together starting in the seventh grade at Albert Thomas Junior high. He was a good guy, a good friend and a pretty good basketball player. We were all pretty good players, though. We had a deep team. Clyde wasn't a starter in middle school. I'm not sure why that was. Coach made those decisions. I was able to get my spot. We used to mess around with Clyde all the time during the games. If the game got out of hand, we told the coach to put Clyde in. Clyde was kind of bashful back then, and sometimes he would tell us not to tell the coach that. He just kind of fit in as another guy on the team.

**WILL BLACKMON:** On the the ninth-grade basketball team at Albert Thomas, Clyde mostly sat on the bench. When we were winning by large margins, the coach put in Clyde. We would tell the coach to, but Clyde would tell us, "Don't say nothing." He was real shy to go in. Once he got in he did OK, but he was maybe nervous about going in.

I was embarrassed to have the guys ask the coach to put me in. If I have to ask to go in, then I don't want to go in. I feel like you should earn playing time on merit. I think the reason I didn't travel was because they didn't have enough uniforms. At home games, if we were way ahead, they might pass me their jersey so I could go in. I think I was the 13th man. But it was still fun.

Maybe I didn't have the confidence to play back then; I don't know. I know I had other interests. I was kind of concentrating on academics, and I had already started working at the family restaurant.

It had opened in 1967 when I was five years old. It was called Green's Barbecue, owned by a man named Harry Green. He had the finances, and my uncle, my mom's brother, Thomas Prevost, had the know-how and ran it. He was my favorite uncle. I spent a lot of time with him. My mom helped out at the restaurant part-time. My brother, James, worked for them for 10 or 12 years until my uncle passed away and he took over the place in 1982. When James was 13 or 14, he started going in four or five days a week. He was cooking by the time he was 15. When somebody 40-something is teaching you, you learn a whole lot. From the time I was about 12 until I graduated from high school, I remember working there three or four times a week. Bussing tables, serving people, whatever was needed. When I wasn't working, I played sports.

**WILL BLACKMON:** I was about 6'3" as a ninth grader. Clyde was probably about the same height. He was just an average talent. He didn't have any type of jump shot, but he was a good athlete; he could run and he could jump. That was a real strong asset.

Will's memory is a little off. I was only 5'8" as a freshman. But from the end of the ninth-grade season to September, I grew six inches. When I got into 10th grade, I was 6'2". All my clothes from my freshman year were now too small. My sleeves were too short. My shoes were too small. My shoe size went from eight and a half to 11 in a six-month period. I had to get new Converse and Pro Keds.

By the end of the school year, I was dunking a volleyball. I was probably 5'10" by then. Sometime that summer, I was able to finally dunk a basketball. The big deal with my friends about that time was, "Can you slam it?" There was a big competition to see who could do it first. It wasn't me — two guys beat me. But I was doing martial arts by that time, and I was getting stronger and bigger. The first time I dunked, it was on the outdoor courts at Albert Thomas, where all the hoops were are a few inches higher than 10 feet. I must have dunked 100 times on each basket that first day. It was euphoria.

Once I started dunking, I was going to figure out a thousand ways to do it. I used to practice doing it so much on the outdoor courts, the older guys would come by and tell me to quit playing on concrete so much. "It is going to mess up your knees." Of course, I never listened.

I was excited to enter Sterling High School in the fall. The student body was about 60 percent black, 25 percent white, 15 percent hispanic. It was a good group of kids. I was a member of the class of '80, ready to play basketball for the Sterling Raiders.

My grades were outstanding as a sophomore, but I did have some trouble in one class. I made my first F, in biology, the first term of my high school career. It was a shocker. I had always done well in school. My mom went ballistic. I tried to sneak the report card by her. I waited until the last minute, and when I handed it to her, I put something over the biology grade and said, "Mom, can you sign this?" She said, "Let me see that. What's this F? When did you start making Fs? Don't you start getting stupid on me."

I had the most beautiful biology teacher in the world, Miss Brown. She looked better than Jayne Kennedy, who was the most beautiful African American woman in the world at that time. Miss Brown was young. Red lipstick, just gorgeous. I would sit in class and stare at her. She was very nice and a good teacher, but I didn't hear a word she was saying. I think she felt bad for me. She said, "Clyde, I looked at your transcripts. You are an excellent student. How can you get an F in my class?" I had never even had a D before. All I could say was, "Well, I'll see if I can do better." I paid more attention to the classwork after that and a little less to the teacher. I got an A the next quarter.

I finished high school with a B grade point average, and I had a good SAT score. I was one of the few guys who went to Houston who could qualify at a major Division-I school without having anything doctored. A lot of the guys had to go to summer school or take their SATs a bunch of times.

**WILL BLACKMON:** One night, Joe Cotton and Glen Gordon and I were going to a party. It was the first night we had ever drunk any alcohol. We got some Boones Farm wine and we picked Clyde up at his house. All of us drank some wine, and we were all having fun — at least it seemed like it. By the time we got to the party, there was Clyde in the back seat, fast asleep. We all laughed about it. He wasn't a party guy at all. I think he had only one girlfriend throughout high school. He was a good student and a well-behaved kid.

**CRAIG "TWIN" LEWIS:** I was a friend of Clyde's older brother James. We were in the same class in school. We used to play Clyde in basketball when he was a little boy. Then one year he grew about eight feet and he was bigger than us all. That's the God's honest truth. James was a much better player than Clyde was for a long time, but James had his work at the barbecue.

Clyde was a clean-cut kid. My friends were always smoking dope and drinking wine. He wouldn't do none of that. He was always playing ball. He would practice every day. I remember when he first beat me one on one in a game at the park. I was 16 and he was 12. He was very diligent. Every day, you would see him walking down the street, tossing his ball into the air. We were going to smoke dope and chase women, and he was always practicing his game. I respect him for that.

As kids, we had choices. Deep down, we knew what was right and wrong. It would have been easy to do some of the things the other kids did. It looked like they had a lot of fun. After what happened with my oldest brother, Michael, a herd of wild bulls couldn't make me do those things. Our family had been torn apart. We were focused on not having any further tragedies. I had three younger sisters to look out for and try to pave the way for a good life for them. There was a sense of responsibility as well.

We had a senior class of almost 500 students, and the beauty of it was, I had known many of them since elementary school. It was a well-run school with an aeronautical program and a link to NASA. We had a lot of kids who became outstanding in their field as adults.

When I was a sophomore, James was still a better basketball player than I was. Every Saturday we would get up early and go to the best gyms in town. James was out of the house by then, but he would come by and pick me up and take me with him. If I couldn't play, at least I could watch. So I would get to play against older guys, which was good for me. By the time I got to playing with kids my age, it made a big difference.

By January of my sophomore year, I was 6'6". And I wasn't playing basketball for the school.

**JOE COTTON:** Clyde was working at his family's restaurant, so he didn't play as a sophomore. He didn't let anybody know about that. As far as we knew, it was a conflict between practice and him having to go to work. He wasn't really hanging around with Will and me after basketball practice.

I had been involved with our restaurant since I was 12. At first, I was the head cashier and I helped prepare meat in the back and waited and bussed tables. I learned how they ordered food and supplies. I learned how profitable beer was for the restaurant. Being around the business and having access to the books, you can see what is happening. I used to take two buses and transfer through a tough part of the city just to go to work every day after school. It took me about an hour and 20 minutes from school to work, and my brother would take me home. Once I started playing basketball at Sterling, I would work on the weekends. And if they needed me, I would work sometimes after practice.

I didn't play basketball as a sophomore, but it wasn't because of my part-time job. I was sick with the flu the week of JV tryouts in the fall. I got back to school and asked my friends, "When are tryouts?" They said, "They were last week. You're too late."

I went to see the varsity coach, Clifford Jackson. I knew a little bit about him. I knew he drove a Cadillac. I knew he taught metal shop, and he liked some of the players to wash his cars or make burglar bars for businesses or homes. I knew he had been the coach when my brother James was in high school. James was one of the better players. I watched him every day in neighborhood games when he was younger, and he killed people on the court. He was the first guy picked. I mean, he put on a clinic, shooting the lights out. But he never played in high school, because he was working. I was thinking Coach Jackson didn't like my brother, so he was probably not going to like me.

I asked, "Can I try out?" He said, "Son, you're too late." I said, "How about JVs?" He said, "OK, come out, and we'll see what you can do." I was probably 6'3" or 6'4", so he probably wanted to see what I could do.

So the first practice I was at — and remember, tryouts had started a week earlier — we were doing calisthentics. I was late getting there, and everybody did 25 push-ups. After we were done with that, Coach Jackson said, "New guy, drop down and give me 25 more for being late."

I was still kind of scrawny, and I could barely do the first 25. Now I was trembling after seven or eight more, and I fell on my face. Coach said, "You come in here late and out of shape? Get out of my gym."

**WILL BLACKMON:** I remember it a little differently. The first 15 to 20 minutes of tryouts, we would do exercises, stretch, push-ups, sit-ups, that sort of thing. Clyde was struggling to do his push-ups. The coach said, "You got to do better than that. Give me 10 more. If you can't give me better push-ups than that, you might as well not play." And Clyde walked out of the gym. He got cut because he couldn't do 10 push-ups. We just kind of let him go. At the time, I didn't think he really wanted to play. I guess he did.

When Coach Jackson threw me out of the gym, I decided man, I can't stand this guy. He didn't even see me play and he threw me out. All the guys who had made the team were there, and they were laughing. I went home, pissed off. I never went to watch the Sterling games that season.

But I didn't stop playing basketball. At lunch every day we played ball. The games were good and we started to develop a crowd in the gym. A lot of good players. Before long, I was getting pretty good. A lot of the time, my team would hold court for five or six games. The guys playing varsity started to get to know me. By this time, I was 6'6", and I was more than holding my own with them. They said, "That's the kid they threw out; he can play. We threw out the wrong guy."

One day in the early spring, they had the coach blend in with the crowd for the noon games. After what had happened a few months earlier, they knew I couldn't stand him. Mention his name, I would go the other way. That day, my teams didn't lose and I scored most of the points. We won the last game and the guys put me on their shoulders and brought me over to the coach. They knew I wouldn't talk to him otherwise. The coach said, "I want you to play for me. You going to play next year?" I said, "No chance." I told him I wouldn't play for him for all the tea in

China. I was not going to play. And the bell rang and I left for my next class.

When I got home that evening, Coach Jackson was at the house talking to my mom. He told Mom I was great, that I was going to be starting for him next year. She said, "You hear what he says?" I went to my room and wouldn't even talk about it. After the coach left, Mom and I did talk about it, and she said, "You know what? You are going to play. I am going to make you play."

**EUNICE SCOTT:** If I told Clyde to play, it was out of character. I am the type of person, if you don't want to do something, it is up to you. You only do your best when you want to do it yourself. I never pushed him into anything. He knows better than that. That's not me. You can't make them. Let them decide.

He came home after that tryout session his sophomore year and said, "I just quit basketball. It's too hard. I am not going to play." I said, "Honey, you have to work for what you get." And I laughed at him. He came out smoking. He was mad. And when he got the chance to play for the school, he was getting after it non-stop.

I was getting some attention from other coaches who were trying to get me to go out for track or play football.

I did go out for baseball as a sophomore and made the varsity as a first baseman. I played a couple of games, but the practices were extremely boring and I was playing a lot of basketball. I decided to focus on basketball, so I quit the baseball team.

I had a pretty good junior season in basketball. I averaged about 15 points and 10 rebounds. Our best player was a 6'5" senior named Kenneth Gordon, who was in his third year on the varsity. He and another senior, Kerry Jones, whose older brother Dwight was on the Houston Rockets at the time, were the team leaders. I played center on defense, but a lot of the time I would be the guy bringing the ball upcourt and getting us into our offense. We had height, but we didn't do much with it. We were a .500 team — an average team. We had a lot of competition, a lot of good teams and plenty of players who went to Division-I schools. Greg Kite played for Madison, which won our league and went on to win the state championship that year.

**WILL BLACKMON:** Clyde and I had started to hang out a little more together. We went to a couple of parties and played a lot of ball in the gym. He had been pretty quiet in junior high, but he was starting to have a little more to say. When he made the basketball team as a junior, he got a little more confidence. We had an OK team. We had a couple of seniors who were pretty good, and then there were us juniors — Joe Cotton was a good wing player, Glen Gordon was a pretty good point guard, and Clyde and I played a double post. Clyde was pretty average. He was a role player. We didn't go to Clyde very often. He got almost all of his points off rebounds and around the basket.

**JOE COTTON:** Clyde was just part of the team as a junior. We had a lot of shooters. The best part of his game was his rebounding, and he played good defense. Clyde was a good player. I think I was maybe looked at as the best player on that team, but Clyde and Will were right there. We were all good players. There wasn't just one best player on the team.

That summer before my senior year was when I first met Moses Malone. The best players in the city — all of the Rockets,

the best college players and so on — would play pickup games at
Fonde Recreation Center. It was a phenomenal experience for a
young kid like me. Of course, no one knew me then. I never got
picked for the games. They would play 10, 11 games and I would
watch every one of them from the sidelines as the older guys held
court. Maybe on the 12th game, a few guys might leave and they
would look for extra people. And then I would get to play.

After that summer, I knew I could be a college player.
Stephen F. Austin was the first college to recruit me. They became
interested in me during my junior year. I was a University of
Houston fan, but they didn't show much interest at that time. I
remember that summer before my senior year, I was thinking,
"What's wrong with the U of H?" They would call, but I could
tell I was not on their "A" list.

We had a better season my senior year. We started five seniors — me, Joe, Will, Glen and Dennis Davis, a 6'4" shooting
guard. We had great size for a high school team and ran a controlled offense. I got some attention when we played in the
Houston Jaycee Tournament at Christmastime. Some of the top
teams in Texas and Louisiana were there. I had a 34-point, 27-
rebound game as we beat Sharpstown. After that was the first
time college coaches really started coming around.

**JOE COTTON:** Our senior year, Clyde was the center, and
Will, who was about 6'6", and I were the forwards. I was
6'2 1/2" and was in my third year on the varsity. You talk
to anybody who saw us play that year, they would say we
were a real good, strong team, but we didn't have a lot of
good coaching. I look back and I can see a lot of things
that should have been done. But we had guys who knew
how to play.

Yates, one of the city teams, was getting most of the
publicity. They had Michael Young, who was regarded

as the best player in the state that year. I always told Clyde he was just as good as those guys. He came to realize that, and once he did, it was trouble for everyone else. I always knew he was good. We played against each other in practice a lot. I knew if I lined up in the first spot and he was in the second spot when someone shot a free throw, I couldn't assume I would get the rebound. He was taller than me and quick on his feet. Even so, Clyde was still just a part of a good team. His emergence as a player really came between high school and college.

**WILL BLACKMON:** Clyde was a better player as a senior. He was an even better rebounder. He had gotten thick and taller and he was real aggressive on the boards. He would easily get 12, 14 boards a game. He still couldn't shoot the ball, but he had athletic skills. He could run and jump and was real quick on his feet. His shooting was always kind of suspect in high school. He was just a garbage-type player, getting 15 or 16 points a game off of layups, tip-ins and dunks.

It's funny, of all of us who played together that year, Clyde was the guy we thought had the least chance to make it to the league. He had athleticism, but he didn't have those real sharp skills. You know — dribbling, jump shooting, real strong defensive play. All he could do was run, jump, block shots and rebound. Guys we played with or against still come up to me all the time and say, "Of all the guys who would have made it off your team, I would have picked you or Joe to go where Clyde went." I never thought he would become the type of player he was during his NBA career. He was never an option in our offense. We would shoot it and leave it to Clyde to clean the boards. I always tease him. I say, "You didn't get good overnight. You had to have competition to get your game to where it was." Those big contracts he got should have been mine. I tell him he was so good because I beat up on him all the time when he was younger. Even at the University of Houston, they didn't have a clue how good he would become.

**CLIFTON JACKSON:** Clyde was the backbone of the 1979-80 team and should have been playing forward. Unfortunately, he was the best big man we had, so he was a 6'6" center. But playing center at Sterling was the best thing that could have happened to Clyde at that stage of his career. It made him a lot stronger and helped him develop as a rebounder and shooter. Clyde had several great games and always seemed to play his best against the good teams.

**VIRGINIA SCOTT-WESTBROOKS:** Clyde's games in high school were a family thing. We tried not to miss any games. Mom would get off work at five o'clock and come home with groceries in her hands, and we would all get ready to go to the game. And by that time, Clyde was so good. I can remember one game his senior year, I saw him do a behind-the-back and up for a layup. I mean, you never saw that in high school. Then when I saw him do the first reverse dunk I had ever seen, his freshman year at Houston, it blew our minds.

**DENISE PINK:** When he got into high school, we never missed a game. The whole family. He was very popular with the student body at Sterling, because he was always making the long shots and the fancy dunks. I kind of figured he was going to be great. I remember the cheerleaders yelling, "Go, Clyde, go!" and I told him, "Hey, brother, you're kind of popular here."

During my senior year, I had a great perk for being tall. I got to escort Jayne Kennedy when she made a visit as a featured speaker at Sterling High. At the time, she was one of the first female sportscasters, but she was more well known for her incredible beauty. She was a tall lady; they were trying to get a guy who was tall enough to be her escort. They wanted someone from the Gentlemen's Club, a boys' honorary of which I was a member. I escorted her from the car to the principal's office to the auditorium, where she spoke. It was my lucky day.

**JOE COTTON:** Clyde deserves to be a Hall of Famer. I am not surprised by what he accomplished. Clyde could always get off his feet quick. He had the ability, but so did a lot of other guys back then. There were a lot of guys who could have been Clyde Drexler. He was the one guy who capitalized on his opportunity.

We finished the season at 18-12 in fourth place in the district, but lost out in the district tournament to Milby. The district champion, Yates, was led by Michael Young, who won the MVP award. They went on to win the state championship.

Maybe I wasn't an all-around player in the eyes of some of the guys I played with, but I averaged 17 points and 14 rebounds, three assists, three blocks and four steals. I got the team MVP and was named to the All-District team. I played an all-around game. I could bring the ball down on the press. I rebounded and went coast to coast. I could start the offense and end it. We needed all of that as a team.

Coach Jackson had seemed like a two-headed monster at the beginning. But after I turned out for the team, he became a great friend. He made high school basketball very pleasurable for me, and I learned a lot from him. He turned out to be a very good coach. I was lucky to have had someone like him for two years. Once I got to know him, he was the nicest guy in the world.

In the back of my mind through the season I was thinking about where I was going to college. Michael Young was a really good friend of mine. I had known him since junior high. We spent a lot of time in the spring and summers playing ball in the parks. We played against each other in high school and we got together as often as we could. He was the state's Player of the Year and a *Parade* All-American, and his team won the state championship our senior year. He was one of the most recruited players in the country, but Houston had the edge with him.

**MICHAEL YOUNG:** In junior high, Clyde was at Albert Thomas and I was at Cullen. We met on the basketball court, playing against each other. We just sort of stuck with each other as friends, even though we went to different high schools. We played a lot of pickup ball at MacGregor Park. We started hanging out together. We would talk and say, "What time are you going to the gym to play?"

When we met, I was a big guy who played center. He was a little bowlegged guy who played guard. I watched him grow — he really sprouted in high school. He was a pretty good player who worked hard at his game. He always talked about being exactly where he wound up — as an NBA All-Star and a member of the Hall of Fame. At that age, of course, you don't know. But he had big dreams. So did I.

I was the No. 1 player in the state of Texas our senior year. Who recruited me? You name it. But in those days recruiting was much more limited. There wasn't the AAU ball where you got a chance to travel and coaches could see you play in the summers. Clyde and I always talked about playing together in college.

At the start of our senior season, Michael and I decided we were going to go to the same school together.

**MICHAEL YOUNG:** I took visits to Washington and New Mexico State. Clyde went on the visit to New Mexico State with me. But the University of Houston is right across the street from my high school. When it came down to it, Clyde and I decided by staying in Houston we could do something special by playing together in our hometown.

**WILL BLACKMON:** The only reason Clyde went to Houston was because he and Michael were real good friends. Houston took Clyde because they wanted Young.

**JOE COTTON:** Clyde and I made a visit to Houston together, and we also visited a couple of junior colleges in Texas. But he developed a relationship with Michael Young that sealed the deal for him with Houston. And then he accepted the challenge in the summer before his freshman year of college. He practiced a lot and really developed his game, and you know the rest of the story.

There weren't a lot of schools interested in me. I visited New Mexico State, Texas Tech and Houston. Texas Tech was giving me the star treatment. Their assistant coach, Rob Evans —who is now Arizona State's head coach — was the guy recruiting me. He basically lived in my yard for a while my senior year. They said, "We have found a diamond in the rough." Their head coach, Gerald Myers, called me the biggest sleeper in the state. It got back to the people at Houston that Tech was going to steal one of the best players in the city right from under their nose.

When the Cougars were recruiting Michael, they asked him who was the best player he played against. He said, "That's easy. The kid at Sterling." They said another player's name. Michael said, "No, not him, Clyde Drexler." They were shocked.

I knew Michael liked Houston. I liked the idea of staying at home and playing where my family could watch me. And Guy Lewis had a great program going. They won 20 games just about every year but had had a couple of subpar seasons, going 16-15 in 1978-79 and 14-14 in 1979-80.

I followed them pretty close and knew their players and had played with a lot of them. They had two really good players in Larry Micheaux, who was 6'9" and mean as a schoolyard bully on the basketball court, and Rob Williams, one of the best point guards in the country. Michael and I said to each other, "You and I could be guard and wing types. All we would need is a center, and we would have an NBA lineup." We decided to go the University of Houston, based upon that and the fact that we liked Guy Lewis. He was honest.

The first time the Cougars invited me for a visit was late in my senior season. You could tell it was kind of an afterthought. I went into Coach Lewis's office and we exchanged pleasantries, and I asked him, "What do you know about my game?" He said, "I know you are a hell of a player, but I don't know a lot. I saw you one time this year, and I left at halftime because you had no points at the half. I went home and had dinner with my wife."

I remembered that game. He came to the game with his two assistants wearing those red University of Houston sweaters. It was a big deal to have them there in our gym. It was a league game, a big game, one of the last games of the year, and I had no points at halftime. Maybe I was pressing a little. I only took about three shots and didn't have many opportunities in the first half, but I probably had six or seven rebounds, four or five assists and some steals. And I got going the second half and finished the game with 26 points.

Coach Lewis told me he saw the box score the next day and said to himself, "Maybe that guy can play for me." And since then, he said, "I have learned a lot more about you. I am going to offer you a scholarship." So I called Michael Young, and he said he had already planned a visit to Washington the next week. He went on the visit, but he decided a couple weeks later on Houston.

The night before letter of intent signing day, Rob Evans told me he would be at the house at 7:30 the next morning. I said to be there at 8:00. When coach Evans arrived, New Mexico State was already there. I told both coaches I was sorry, but I was going to Houston. And not too much later, in came Guy Lewis himself, the great one, to get my signature on the dotted line.

**ROB EVANS:** I never enjoyed recruiting a kid more than Clyde. I told him he made a good choice and I was glad to see him in our league.

# CHAPTER 4

# BECOMING A COUGAR

**A**ttending the University of Houston on a basketball scholarship provided three of the most exciting years of my life. I prepared for my freshman basketball season by practically living in the gym during the summer. Michael and I went to Fonde Center almost every day to play with all the great talent there, including Moses Malone, Robert Reid, Joe "Jellybean" Bryant, Tom Henderson, Calvin Murphy, Alan Leavill and a bunch of good college players.

Moses was with the Rockets and was one of the greatest names in the game. He was the NBA's MVP the previous season — the first of three times he earned that honor — and one of the nicest guys I had ever met. Even though he was about the biggest name in the game at the time, he took time to help me with my game. And he was very supportive. He would always say nice things about my game and encourage me to come out and play.

The Fonde experience was huge. These were NBA players. You got to match your skills against them daily. But getting into a game could be an ordeal. It was all on reputation and your standing in the hierarchy of things. If a guy like Moses lost a game, he would be picked for the next game and you would still be sitting on the sidelines. One day that summer I got in there and impressed somebody. At that point, I still wasn't in the pro group, but they now knew my face. I would get picked for the fourth or fifth game, and I gradually worked my way up from there. After a while, Moses began to like me and started picking me first for his teams.

The first time I was chosen to play in the first game, with all the big-name players, was the summer after my freshman year. Before the game, I was looking around and thinking, "All these great players — what am I doing on the floor?" That meant you were pretty darn good. But once the ball was thrown up, I forgot about that and played. We went on to win eight or 10 games in a row that day. And I felt like I was on my way.

Attending the University of Houston was like living in another city. It was so big, and when I was there I just felt like I was on my own. I had grown up to be a man. It was such a big environment. I was in a home away from home, living in an athletic dorm. Michael Young and I lived on the 16th floor at the Moody Towers. It was awesome, living on campus, going to classes, enjoying the college life. One thing I enjoyed right away was the freedom of having classes two or three hours a day instead of all day. Now I could go to school from 8 to 11 or noon, and the rest of the day was mine.

But I took advantage of my free time a little too much at first. I was on the probation list for the first semester. I had a seven o'clock class on Tuesday and Thursday and missed class for two weeks. I had to drop the class. The guidance counselor called me in and said, "Clyde, we have a problem here. You are not going to class." I said, "It's tough to make that morning class." So he showed me how to drop it.

I barely had enough credits to make the 12-hour minimum to be eligible to play basketball. The funny thing was, I had great academic credentials, with a 3.0 GPA in high school. Guy and the other coaches said, "I didn't think we'd have to do extra tutoring or get you in study hall." I said, "It won't happen again." When you have to mind your own time for the first time, it's not easy. I caught up quickly, though, and was just 30 hours short of graduating after my third year. I took 18 to 20 hours some terms to get there.

Michael and I still had plenty of time to work out and play basketball. We had keys to Robertson Stadium, the practice facility for the basketball and track teams. We would go to the gym or the weight room every chance we got.

Not that we were in the gym 24 hours a day. Michael and I would go out on weekends. A lot of times we would double-date. My freshman year, I didn't have a girlfriend. I saw a lot of beautiful women, though. Went to a few parties on campus and had some good times, and enjoyed college life immensely. I got to know a lot of football and volleyball players and had the full experience of a college freshman.

**MICHAEL YOUNG:** I will never forget coming in a freshmen for fall semester to check into the dorm as Clyde's roommate. Our friendship took off from there. There was never a dull moment. Clyde was the same guy he is today — laid back, straightforward. He was just Clyde, a great guy. We said he always had that Kool-aid smile — conniving-like, sneaky at times. He always liked to joke around.

Michael was the strong, quiet type. He was easy-going. We were alike in a lot of ways. I talked a little bit more than he did. If he knew you, he talked a lot. If not, he was fairly quiet. We basically did everything together for three years. He was my roommate on the road when we traveled. If you saw Mike, you saw Clyde, too. If he had a problem, I had a problem. If somebody was bothering him in practice, they had to see me, and vice versa.

In basketball, he was one of the toughest guys on our team. That was his aura. No one fooled with Michael. He was too strong, too big. But underneath all of that, he was a teddy bear.

**MICHAEL YOUNG:** I got him one time. We were getting ready to go out and have a little fun on the weekend. He had his clothes all ironed and set out. He went home to his mother's house for something. When he got back, his clothes were gone and so was I. We met up later on and there I was, wearing his clothes. That was the first time I had seen him with that kind of anger. I said, "Thanks for ironing my clothes for me." At least he didn't punch me. He never got me back for it, either. I wouldn't let him.

I got him back 100 times; he just never knew it. He would try to pull something on you and then crack up laughing about it. He would eat the cookies your mom sent you. He was a nut.

Michael and I went into fall practice expecting to be starters. I know that sounds brash for a couple of freshmen, especially in those days when most players were staying four years in college. I knew what other players we had, but I knew we could outplay them. I was probably a little overconfident at the time, but I was pretty accurate in my assessment.

I had played pickup games against Micheaux and Williams, and I knew everything about their games, just as they knew mine.

When Michael and I signed with the Cougars, Rob was really happy. The first month of school, all the guys were getting together to play pickup games at our arena, Hofheinz Pavilion.

At the first official practice with the team, I was not playing with the first unit when we scrimmaged at the end of the session. Coach Lewis started the juniors and seniors. But we had a good second unit, and we did pretty well. I had a great day. For the second practice I was up with the first group, and Rob came up and hugged me and said, "Judge, you know you are going to be a starter." To Rob, everybody was "Judge."

We used a box offensive set with a twin post, a point and two wings. Micheaux was a post, Lynden Rose was a wing with me, and Rob was at the point. We had some junior college players coming in, and nobody knew what was going to happen.

After a little while, though, I figured out that with Rob, Larry, Mike and myself, we had four of the positions taken care of.

The one thing missing was a center. Then Hakeem showed up at our doorstep.

**HAKEEM OLAJUWON:** My first sports in Nigeria were soccer, track and field, and team handball. I first picked up a basketball my junior year in high school, and I enjoyed the sport immediately. By my senior year, I was 6'8" and chosen to play in our National Sports Festival in both basketball and team handball. And soon, though I had just learned the game, I was playing for the Nigerian national team. Then, after I played in the African Junior Championships, the coach of the Central Africa team, who was an American, came and talked to me about coming to the United States to play college basketball.

**GUY LEWIS:** I didn't actually recruit Hakeem. A guy I knew in Africa called me and said there was a 6'7" kid over there who could run and jump and wanted to come to the U.S. I said fine, and then I forgot all about it. A couple of months later, I got word that he was on an airplane to America.

Guy's friend was Chris Pond, who had sent him a player or two in the past.

**HAKEEM OLAJUWON:** Christopher Pond had called and arranged for visits to five American colleges — Houston, St. John's, Providence, North Carolina State and Georgia. He said, "You can buy an airplane ticket to visit three or four of them if you want. We don't know which will give you a scholarship, but the one you should definitely visit is Houston. You will like the weather there, and coach Lewis is a good coach and a good friend of mine."

My mother bought me the ticket, which cost around $4,500. She gave me all the money she had. I bought an airplane ticket: Lagos/New York/Houston/Atlanta/Providence/New York/Lagos. I was going to visit St. John's first, and then Houston. I arrived in New York, and it was cold! I had on slacks and a cotton shirt with a button-down collar and no sweater. The way the wind hit me ... I had never felt cold like that ... I walked to the ticket counter and asked, "Can I go to Houston today?" I got on a plane four hours later and was in Houston that night.

**GUY LEWIS:** He had played what amounted to three months of basketball. Most junior high kids would know more about basketball than he did. But he could run and jump and, when they tell you 6'7", you usually get a kid 6'4" or 6'5", but he was a full 6'11".

**HAKEEM OLAJUWON:** I first met Clyde when the taxi brought me from the airport straight to Coach Lewis's office. The team was outside on the field running laps, and he took me outside to meet them. It was October, and practice had just started. The coaches were telling me how happy they had been to sign Clyde and that I would really enjoy having him as my teammate. They were absolutely right.

I was on the welcoming committee when Hakeem arrived. It wasn't such a big deal, except Coach Lewis said this guy is 6'11", and if he can play a little bit, we would have a hell of a squad.

Hakeem had class even then. He spoke decent English but with a thick accent. He looked like he was about seven feet and 190 pounds. He was a stringbean.

As a player, he was really raw, but he had good strong legs even then, probably from all the soccer he had played.

**HAKEEM OLAJUWON:** After practice I was invited to join the players at a pickup game, and there I got to see Clyde's skills. I was impressed with his competitiveness and the fact that his game was not just one-dimensional. He had a complete game — he ran the floor so well, his rebounding and scoring, and one of his specialties was his ability to make steals.

Clyde was, and still is, a very likeable person. I took a liking to him immediately, and after getting to know him, I liked him even more. He was respectful, very close to his family and absolutely charming.

**MICHAEL YOUNG:** Hakeem went up and down the floor a couple of times, and suddenly a shot went up and the ball came out of the basket, and he went up and dunked it back in. Whoa, I knew he had a pretty good upside to him right then from the explosiveness of watching him for 20 minutes.

None of us will ever forget that pickup game. Oh my goodness, he didn't know much about the game. He just took off running. He moved well and he could run, but he just didn't know how to play basketball yet. Then somebody went up for a shot, and he goaltended it, and he got up so high so quickly, we all kind of looked at each other and said, "Hmmm." Based on that one blocked shot, we saw a lot of potential. Then he was trying to shoot this hook shot; it was awkward-looking, but he got so high, he almost dunked it.

Hakeem redshirted that first season. To be honest, we thought Hakeem would be a three-year project. We never thought he would develop so fast. But he was a student of the game, a very quick learner and an extremely intelligent player. He had physical skills like nobody else. After seeing Hakeem for the first time, Coach Lewis marveled, "Shoot, I can teach this guy some things. I can work with him."

I had watched Guy Lewis coach games as a kid growing up, but this was my initial firsthand look at him. I grew to love him during my three seasons playing for him. He was the toughest guy I will ever meet. He had been raised mostly by grandparents on a farm in rural east Texas, and he was a good ol' boy with a mighty thick hide. I could not be faint of heart and play for Guy Lewis. He was going to make me a man, one way or another. The tougher I was mentally, the more he liked me. He challenged me every day. He loved guys to challenge him back, too — at least, in a nice way.

Coach Lewis was the consummate competitor. When I came to him, he was pushing 60 years old, and he thought he could still outrun every player on the team. He knew he could beat me arm wrestling and he thought he could outrun and outplay me, too.

**GUY LEWIS:** I actually got some hate mail from our fans and alumni after signing Clyde. Not because they had anything against him personally, but because we recruited him. They felt he wasn't good enough for us to recruit. It just goes to show you how wrong people can be. Clyde didn't get the publicity a lot of other high school players got, but we knew what he could do for a long time.

**TOMMY BONK:** I was the columnist for the *Houston Post* when Clyde became a Cougar. People were writing the coaches, complaining, "Why waste a scholarship on this twerp?" Clyde never forgot that. He always used it to his advantage. It made him play a little harder.

Enthusiasm for the Cougars had dimmed a little with back-to-back mediocre seasons before my class arrived, but I noticed right away that we had a guy with a pretty good voice handling the public address work at Hofheinz Pavilion. His name was Jim Nantz, and we became quick friends. You could tell he was driven at even that age. For years now, Jim has been a lead voice for CBS television in a number of sports, including golf, college basketball and football. He has become the standard by which others in his industry are measured.

**JIM NANTZ:** I came to the University of Houston to play on the golf team. I lettered one year in golf and played two years for the Cougars. I was the worst player in the

history of our storied program — I am convinced that is
true — from Colt's Neck, N.J., where I was co-captain of
my high school team that went 2-42 my last two years.

But my career goal was to work for CBS. I was a communications major on the golf team with an absolute obses-
sion to broadcast for CBS one day. To help me attain that
goal, my golf coach, Dave Williams, would go around
and tell people in the athletic department, "I have this
kid; one day he is going to work for CBS. Is there any
kind of announcing work he can do?"

Dave talked with Guy Lewis, and the next thing I knew,
I was the PA announcer for games at Hofheinz beginning
with my sophomore year, the 1979-80 season. I did it for
three seasons, until I graduated in the spring of '82. I did
two years of Clyde's games, and I was also the host of the
Guy Lewis television show for three years. In the fall of
'82, I was off to Salt Lake City to take a job there as analyst with Hot Rod Hundley on Utah Jazz simulcasts. I
worked there for two years, then got hired by the net-
work.

The year Clyde and Michael Young came in as freshman,
Michael was the more decorated recruit. It didn't take
long to see that Michael was a gifted player, but it was
clear we also got this other kid from Houston who was
one of those highlight reel kind of players. The whole
program changed right there with that class.

I was the first freshman forward ever to start for coach
Lewis, and he was in his 25th year as Houston's head coach.

Michael moved into the starting lineup, too, but not until the third game of the 1980-81 season. We were a young team, with no senior starters. Our starters were Mike and me at forward, sophomore Larry Micheaux at center and sophomore Rob Williams and junior Lynden Rose at guard. Senior Darryl Brown, a forward, and junior Eric Davis, a guard, were our top reserves. We called the second team "The Cavalry."

I got off to a pretty good start. The very first game of my career was a 112-86 romp past Texas A&I in Hofheinz Pavilion. I played only 12 minutes, but I was five for six from the field and had 12 points and five rebounds.

The Cougars had been mediocre the previous season, but we were in immediate contention with Arkansas for the Southwest Conference championship. We beat the Razorbacks 57-54 at Hofheinz in our first meeting, then got drilled 70-55 at their place three weeks later. Texas A&M had gone to the Elite Eight the previous season, and they were supposed to be the big team in our conference. We won 73-70 at our place and lost a heart-breaker 78-77 over there in our last regular-season game.

And at some point during my first season, Jim Nantz had made my nickname known to everyone.

**JIM NANTZ:** Clyde was an extremely graceful player. It was thrilling to watch him play. He would take shots occasionally from the outside, but he developed his game in Houston as a great penetrator.

When I started doing the PA, they told me to go create some nicknames for the guys. There was a guy who played for the Globetrotters who was called Clyde "The Glide" Austin, so that nickname was out there. For a while, I thought I was the first guy to nickname Clyde

Drexler "The Glide," but it was not an original. Clyde told me I was the first guy to announce him that way, but I think somebody at Sterling High would have given him that name. If it was me, that would mean a lot to me, but I don't claim it.

Jim was the first one to announce it, but they used to call me "Clyde the Glide" in high school. My junior year, my nickname was "Windex." I was a good rebounder. I would clean the glass, and they would say, "Windex." My senior year of high school, I got a lot better, and they had to come up with a better nickname.

I never had the opportunity to shoot 30 times a game at Houston, which is probably the best thing that ever happened to my development. I never wanted to do that, anyway. I scored a lot on fast breaks, dunks, offensive rebounds and steals. You hustle, you get easy layups at the other end — that was my mantra. Every now and then, I would get the chance to drive. If the big man cleared, I would take off.

I was a better than average perimeter shooter. I didn't like to post up guys. I shot over 55 percent. I had a midrange game that was incredible. If I couldn't get to the hole, I was pretty solid with the midrange jumper. That was my game, and if I could finish with a dunk, that was a bonus. The midrange game was how I scored most of my points.

In the Southwest Conference postseason tournament, we easily beat Texas Christian in the semis and caught a break when Texas upset Arkansas on the other side. The Longhorns had a good team led by LaSalle Thompson, but we had beaten them badly twice in the regular season, and we blasted them 84-59 for the postseason title. Rob Williams went for 37 points, making 11 of 11 from the foul line. I had 12 points and 15 rebounds in the game.

Arkansas won the league at 11-5, one game ahead of our 10-6. They advanced to the NCAA Regionals as the conference champion and we entered with an at-large berth, facing Villanova in a first-round game at Charlotte. Everybody was excited; the previous two seasons the Cougars hadn't made it to the NCAA Tournament.

What a letdown the game was. Villanova clobbered us 90-72. The Wildcats hit 33 of 49 shots. I have never seen a game where everything went so right for one team. I guess it was a matter of our team just being glad to be there. We had more talent than they did, but they won. It was a wake-up call for us. It is one thing to get there, but once you get there, you better bring your lunch.

**JIM NANTZ:** I traveled to Charlotte for our TV show and watched the Cougars get dusted by a good Villanova team. But throughout the season there were a lot of chances to watch the team develop and mature into a true national phenomenon. They weren't there yet, but they were coming.

We finished the season 21-9, including 15-1 at home. Williams was named conference MVP and finished the season ranked fifth in the nation in scoring with a 25-point average.

It was a pretty good start to a college career for me. I was voted Southwest Conference Newcomer of the Year. I was third on the team in scoring with an 11.9 average, but I led the team and was second in the conference behind Thompson with 10.5 rebounds a game. I was also second on the team with 78 assists and 58 steals and shot a solid .505 from the field. My weakest area was free throw shooting — .588.

**MICHAEL YOUNG:** Clyde and I were both so competitive. That really helped the team that year. After losing to Villanova, we couldn't wait until the next season. We knew the next year we were going to be loaded up. We had all our starters back, and now we had Hakeem ready to go.

# CHAPTER 5

# CRASHING THE FINAL FOUR

**W**e all vowed to go much deeper into the tournament the next season. Michael and I put a lot of effort into getting prepared during the off season. We lifted a lot of weights. We had a strength coach, a guy who lived on Michael Young's street, named Jesse Hurst. The mere mention of his name today makes me sweat. Hurst was a former strength coach for an NFL team, and he had all this equipment in his one-car garage. We called it "Camp Hurst." We used to bring teammates over to his house to work out with us. I don't remember one of them coming back, ever. If you made it through one time, you were not coming back. It was even more difficult than you could imagine. Mike was there just about every day. I didn't go as often as he did, but I was consistent. And it really paid huge dividends. My strength levels were way higher. My body, which had been pretty scrawny, became well defined.

"Camp Hurst" was incredibly efficient. If you made a session without puking in 110-degree heat with no air blowing through, you were a bad man. I remember planting on my face a couple of times in the dirt yard, totally exhausted, in the middle of the workout. I couldn't finish. Jesse was a tough guy. He was a military man. He would do the workouts with you. He would be sitting there laughing at your pain.

Everyone had a workout partner to spot you on your lifts. If you leaned on the walls, Jesse would look at you with those fierce eyes and say, "Get off my wall." If you didn't listen to him, he would grab you by the collar and make you stand up. He would say, "If you don't want to work, don't come in my garage." It was exactly what we needed. I look back now and really appreciate the guy. If I survived Coach Hurst, I could do anything. The goals I lived by were to be in the best shape, never to be out-hustled, and always to be mentally well prepared.

That summer, I started working as a teller and in the note department at Oak Forest Bank. I was learning the basic principles of being a loan officer. I always wanted to have something to fall back on. Education was a way to pave the road for the rest of your life. I always thought you had to learn some skills to help you survive. I had to have those to get a real job — that was my thought. I wanted to have skills that would help me transition if I didn't make the NBA, or after my career was over. My thought was, people respect bankers because they know all about money. I wanted to know all about banking and all about money. In case I ever had some, I would know what to do with it.

Michael and I didn't live together the second season. We decided to take the university stipend for housing and save a little money. I lived in an apartment with my brother James about 10 minutes from campus. But Michael and I were still spending a lot of time together in the gym.

We also enjoyed the annual Greek shows, where fraternity and sorority groups would provide song-and-dance entertainment. The groups would combine and show off their stuff. Those were fun times. It was a way to support your classmates who were at all the games.

I never pledged a fraternity. I didn't have time for that. I was consumed by basketball. I had no aspirations other than trying to be a good college player. At that point, at least, I never thought I would be a pro basketball player. To compete against the best was my goal — to see how good I could get. Realistically, I thought I would become an investment banker or lawyer.

**MICHAEL YOUNG:** The Villanova game had left a bad taste in our mouths. We both came into our sophomore season really fired up, and we got off to a great start. We pushed each other. We were local guys, so we were more sensitive than most to everyone saying Texas was a football state. Not that it wasn't true, but we played pretty good basketball, too, and we felt like we had something to prove. We gave it 100 percent on the floor. We talked each other through that season. We knew we had the talent to get to the Final Four this time.

The Southwest Conference was tough and getting better each year. The defending champion, Arkansas, had Alvin Robertson, Darrell Walker and Scott Hastings and was the favorite again. Texas had Thompson, Baylor had Terry Teagle; Rice had Ricky Pierce. But we were good, and we knew it.

Our starting lineup was intact — Williams and Rose at guard, Micheaux at center, Michael and me at the forwards.

Hakeem wasn't quite ready to start, but he was a force off the bench. He had to be one of the greatest defensive presences in the nation, even though he was coming off the bench. We didn't know how Hakeem would do, but we were thinking, after winning 21 games the year before, that this year we would make it to the NCAA finals. That was our goal from day one. Guy was adamant about it. He set the tone, Rob and the seniors gave us good leadership, and Michael and I were beginning to take more of a leadership role.

Hakeem played a more prominant role in February and March than in November and December that season. In October, we couldn't even throw him the ball. He was strictly a defensive force, blocking shots and getting rebounds and throwing outlets. He was very good at that. If we threw the ball to him, though, he traveled. Coach would say, "Throw him alley-oops and that's it. Throw him anything else and I will take you out of the game."

**HAKEEM OLAJUWON:** I can't tell you how excited I was to play with a player like Clyde Drexler. Though he was a small forward, about 6'6", he loved to snatch a rebound with one hand, smack it with the other and take off. People said he couldn't shoot because they didn't see him do it very often; most of the time he would push the ball down the floor and go coast to coast. Clyde just wanted to get the rebound and run. That was his first choice: Just go.

I don't know how he did it, but he positioned himself so that every time a shot was blocked it went right into his hands. The ball goes up, everybody fights for it, it gets grabbed by somebody — that's Clyde. When a ball gets swatted away and somebody saves it — that's Clyde.

One day I sat in practice and watched him, just to find out how he did it. He moved around. He moved with the ball on defense. You couldn't really box him out because he kept moving. When someone was driving to the basket, he would see his big man coming in to block it and he would step back. Everybody thinks this guy is going to the basket, everybody on the court is going in ... except Clyde. He moved back. He anticipated the block. He saw where it was likely to be swatted to, and he went right there. And when he got the ball he took off. He would terrorize the opponent, rushing down the court and converting the basket on the other end with a nice dunk. You didn't have to worry about finishing a fast break; Clyde would finish it. Clyde was also a team player and a terrific passer.

Rob had a tough time with injuries that season. He had undergone knee surgery in the summer and missed the first three games. Then through the season he had a wrist problem and a groin strain at different times. He was not at 100 percent, but even so, he was phenomenal — every bit the best point guard in college basketball. No one could touch him. Rob was an excellent athlete. He could run the break and throw down monster dunks as well as anyone. He was extremely hard to guard one on one. We used to play one on one all the time, and he was one of the few players about whom I would say you just could not stop the guy.

We lost in overtime to Seton Hall in the second game of the season, then ran off 10 straight wins to start 11-1 and move into the nation's top 10. In the third game, a 106-74 rout of Biscayne, I went for 30 points on 13-of-16 shooting and also had 16 rebounds, seven assists and four steals. Two games later, I hit nine of 10 shots and collected 21 points, 11 rebounds, five assists and five steals as we outclassed Texas-San Antonio 105-69.

We were running up big scoring numbers — like a 145-78 win over Texas Lutheran — and beginning to show the offensive flash and dash that would characterize us on a national platform over the next 18 months.

But then we hit a rut and lost four games in a row — three of them by a total of five points. And at the midway point of the conference season, we found ourselves 3-5 and in danger of going nowhere but to an early vacation.

We got it together just in time. We won at Southern Methodist 73-71 in overtime, and that started us on our way to winning our last eight SWC games. I began to emerge as a defensive stopper during that time. Coach Lewis saw a certain tenacity in me and the will to compete. He would always challenge me with a tough defensive matchup. I guarded the likes of Walker and Teagle and Pierce and Texas A&M's Claude Riley, who was 6'10" and up for Player of the Year in the conference. Guarding those guys was no easy task. You knew they were going to get at least 25 or 30 shots up. But I didn't back down from the challenge.

Midway through my sophomore year, I had bought a black 1978 Oldsmobile Toronado. It was a great ride, even if Larry Micheaux busted me on it to a reporter before the season: "Clyde's driving is legendary. There isn't much that scares me, but Clyde behind a wheel does. If Clyde played basketball like he drives a car, he would always be out of control."

The truth was, nobody was as bad a driver as Larry. He drove a canary yellow Chrysler New Yorker, and you did not want to get in his way on the road. It was a hog, and he drove it like a sports car.

At least Larry liked my game. He told the reporter, in contrast to my supposedly wild driving habits, "On the court, he is more in control than anybody I have ever seen. Clyde is the type of guy who will always come up with the big play. If we need a steal, he will get it. If we need a rebound, he will be there under the boards. If we need two points, he always wants the ball."

We finished second again at 11-5 in the SWC, a game behind Arkansas. The Razorbacks beat us in the SWC postseason title game 84-69 after we had them tied 32-32 at the half. We had 19 turnovers and just got outplayed in that game.

But we were back in the NCAA Tournament in 1982 with an at-large berth again. They placed us in the Midwest Regionals at Tulsa, where we opened with a 94-84 win over Alcorn State. I was eight for 11 from the floor and had 17 points, four rebounds and five steals. We thought that game was going to be easy, but those guys were tough.

We knew the next game wasn't going to be a cakewalk, either. Our opponent was Tulsa, playing on its home floor. The Hurricanes had Paul Pressey and a loud crowd behind them, but we got by them 78-74 despite 25 turnovers. We were ahead 71-58 with seven minutes to play and then kind of held on. I had 17 points, nine rebounds and three steals.

We advanced to the Midwest regional semifinals at the Checkerdome in St. Louis. We had an extremely tough draw in Missouri, with Steve Stipanovich, Jon Sundvold and Ricky Frazier playing close to home. We knew we would have the crowd against us again. We took control from the start and were able to close out a 79-78 victory. We led by 13 with six minutes to play, then survived what amounted to a replay of the Tulsa game. I had 14 points and 10 boards and made three of four foul shots in the final minute to help ice the win.

Now we were a game away from our goal: The Final Four. All along, Coach Lewis had been telling us, "I am going to the

Final Four, fellas. Y'all can go with me, or you can watch it on TV." We wanted to be there, and after we beat Boston College 99-92, we were in. I had 15 points and nine rebounds, but the story was freshman guard Reid Gettys, who came off our bench to hit 10 of 10 at the line in the final seven minutes. The kid was ice. The Eagles kept fouling him; they didn't think he could make them, I guess. But he made them. He was a good foul shooter and a good passer who made big contributions before he was through with his career at Houston.

What a thrill it was for all of us to go the Final Four that year in New Orleans and play in the Superdome. We had plenty of confidence, but we knew we had our hands full in North Carolina. We went into that game 25-7, and the Tar Heels were 30-2 and favored to win it all. Their leaders were James Worthy and Sam Perkins, and the other front-line player was Matt Doherty. They had great size and skill up front, and we were focusing on them. They also had a freshman guard named — as he was called in those days — Mike Jordan. He was kind of skinny and seemed like a little guy, but we knew he could play.

They jumped us from the get-go, breaking to a 14-0 lead. And that was the game, really. Michael Young had the flu, though he played. He was so weak that day, we knew he couldn't get it done. Hakeem got into early foul trouble. And Rob had the poorest game of his career, I'm sure. He was 0 for 8 from the field and finished with two points. The guy was a 60 percent shooter, and the way he could get to the foul line, he could control a game. But it was left to Larry, Lynden and me to try to keep us in there.

We dominated them on the boards 33-26, and we kind of scratched back in the game in the second half, but they went to the Four Corners offense and shot 59 percent from the field in the second half. We ended up losing 68-63. I had 17 points and nine rebounds, and I guarded Worthy, who had 14 points and four boards, but that was no consolation at all. Afterward, I told reporters, "We could have won it. We should have won it."

**JIM NANTZ:** There were 13 announcers in the arena that night, and I was the youngest. I felt privileged. There were a lot of Basketball Hall of Famers playing in that game. It has been lost in the annals of the great games in Final Four history, but it should be included among them. Houston was going against a North Carolina team that was loaded with talent. After spotting the Tar Heels that 14-0 lead, the Cougars settled down and made it a good game. But they couldn't overcome that 0-for-8 game by the team's star, Rob Williams.

And as they walked off the floor in the cavernous Superdome, Rob took off his wristband and tossed it toward a wastebasket from about 20 feet — and he made it. And I heard him mutter, "Now it goes in."

**MICHAEL YOUNG:** We weren't at full strength. I had the flu. A couple of guys were nicked up with injuries. We played it to the best of our ability, but North Carolina was a better team that night. It was Hakeem's breakout year and in the game against North Carolina, it was like, "Who is this kid?" He stepped up and played well. Clyde had a very good year, too. He got people talking about us, and about him. He took it up to the next level.

Our record was 25-8, including 13-2 at home. I was second on the team in scoring at 15.2 and scored in double figures 26 times. I was second in the SWC in rebounding behind Thompson again at 10.5 and was third in the conference in field-goal percentage at .569. I led the conference and was in the top five nationally with 97 steals, and I improved my free throw percentage to .608. They named me second-team All-SWC, and I was chosen as our team's Most Valuable Player.

Williams, who was a junior, had averaged 21 points and announced he was declaring hardship status for the NBA draft.

During that season, we had NBA scouts at every game. They came to see Rob, who was truly awesome. It was great to have a guy on your team whom all the scouts wanted to see. It made you play a little bit harder.

I remember one game that year, we played Texas A&M at home. The Aggies were tall — 6'11", 6'9" and 6'6" on the front line — and these kids were good. They came into our gym and we beat them handily. I had an incredible game. I was making shots from everywhere and even dunked a few. Afterward, a newspaper report quoted an unnamed Lakers consultant as saying he recommended Rob stay in school, "but I want Drexler now."

Word was that executive was Jerry West. It was the first inkling that I might be able to play in the NBA. Jerry was one of my heroes. I was just mad I didn't see him. I would have gone over to shake his hand.

That spring, I was selected to participate in a national TV promotion cosponsored by the NCAA and the Fiesta Bowl, aimed at the NCAA's antidrug message. The catch: They wanted only underclassmen who weren't turning pro. I told them, "You don't have to worry about me. I won't go hardship. I am having too much fun playing college ball."

And I was. But I was also starting to think about a pro career. I had heard all the big-name players like Williams and Pierce talking about going into the NBA, but I thought I was just as talented as they were. Still, I told one reporter, "I plan to stay my full four years in college."

After getting eliminated by North Carolina, Coach Lewis said to the media, "We will be back in the Final Four. We have a lot of good players returning." We were losing starting guards Williams and Rose, but we did have plenty of talent back for the 1982-83 season. We had Michael and me, and Larry Micheaux would be a senior, and Hakeem was beginning to become Hakeem.

The athletic department staff asked me to live on campus my junior year, and I said thanks but no thanks. I moved back home and lived in the garage apartment. Yeah, I was thrifty, but I still had my privacy, and I enjoyed being around my family more.

**EUNICE DREXLER SCOTT:** My brother, Thomas Prevost, passed away in 1982. So we took over the restaurant and changed the name from Green's to Drexler's Barbecue. I borrowed money to put James into business for himself.

I worked at the restaurant now and then, but I was more interested in the banking industry. I was still working at the bank. And I got a special opportunity that summer. As part of the NCAA's antidrug crusade, I was invited along with other athletes throughout the country to be honored by Nancy Reagan at a White House state dinner. It was super — a great evening. Meeting the president and Mrs. Reagan was a pleasure. I was maybe the youngest person there, and it was a thrill to meet the man in charge of our country.

Over the rest of the summer, I spent a little time playing video games and ping pong. But other than that, I was really into working on my game. And we were getting ready to hit the big time.

# CHAPTER 6

# PHI SLAMA JAMA

The expectations for the 1982-83 Cougars couldn't have been higher. Hakeem moved into the starting lineup, and we were both big and athletic with Hakeem, Larry and me on the front line and Michael switching to the backcourt, at least at the defensive end.

**MICHAEL YOUNG:** We had so much confidence going into that season. The only question was, who would replace Rob Williams? We recruited a freshman named Alvin Franklin, and it worked out well. He did a great job distributing the ball. We knew we were going to have to be good to beat Arkansas, which had Alvin Robertson, Darrell Walker and Joe Kleine. It was a great conference.

At the start of the season, our point guard was Eric Dickens, a sophomore from Houston. But Franklin came on and became the starter in the 16th game, a 98-73 win over Texas Tech. He kept the spot for the rest of the season.

Our key reserves that season were a pair of sophomores, forward Benny Anders and guard Reid Gettys. David Rose, a senior guard, got some time, too, but as we got into league play, the rest of the reserves didn't get a whole lot of minutes.

We were hoping to win the NCAA championship, not only for us but for Coach Lewis. He was 61 years old and in his 27th year as head coach at Houston. He had played for the Cougars' first team in 1946-47, was the first player in school history to score 30 points in a game and averaged 21.1 points that season, which was a whole lot in those days. He served as an assistant coach at Houston for four years and in 1956 took over the program. It took him four years to get his first winning record, and he never had a losing season again. By the time he retired in 1986, he had a record of 592-279 in 30 years, including an 82-50 mark in the postseason. He was twice national Coach of the Year, had 14 20-win seasons and 14 NCAA Tournament teams. He had five Final Four teams, including three in a row in the early '80s. The year after I left, his team finished 32-5 and made the NCAA championship game, losing 84-75 to Patrick Ewing and Georgetown in Seattle.

**HAKEEM OLAJUWON:** Coach Lewis was a mentor for all of us. He demanded the best from his players and he was always very serious about the game. He expected the same attitude from his players, which was the main reason we had so much success. He definitely was a Hall of Fame coach.

Guy was a coach who wasn't easily satisfied. Or at least, he didn't want us to get complacent. Before the season, I had told a reporter I would welcome a move to the backcourt. It had been precipitated by a comment Coach Lewis had made in the press. He said, "I don't think Clyde works hard enough on his shooting, and I have told him that. Of course, Clyde thinks he already has a great jump shot, but he doesn't. That doesn't mean he is not a great player. He is one of the best assist men I have ever seen from the forward spot. He is a great offensive rebounder and he is probably the best anticipator I have ever coached. By that, I mean he is the best I have had at being able to steal the ball. But to be a complete player, he needs to work on his shot. When he squares up to the basket, he is a good shooter. But sometimes he takes a dipsy-do, dumble-de-do shot and they don't go in."

I wasn't sure what to make of all that. I had improved my shot significantly since I came to Houston. I worked at it a lot in the summers. One article about me that came out around that time quoted me this way: "It depends on the need of the team, but small forward is the position I would like to play. Contrary to what some people think, I really don't like to play guard."

That wasn't really true. In another newspaper story, I told a reporter this: "I think I have an adequate jump shot, but as long as coach Lewis keeps playing me at the post, he will never know. I am really a big guard. You have to do whatever it takes to win, but if I am playing the post this year, I am not going to be too happy. He doesn't know that, though. As long as I am in the post, I am never going to shoot, anyway. At the beginning of last year, I was hitting the jumper, but they started moving me more and more inside. You have to prepare yourself for the position you are going to be playing."

The truth was, I was dying to play point guard. I was bringing the ball upcourt a lot, anyway, and starting our offense. Players were getting bigger. I was 6'7" by then, but that wasn't so big for a forward any more. I was a good passer, and I felt I needed to handle the ball and make plays. A couple of years earlier,

Magic Johnson had taken Michigan State to the NCAA championship, and I thought I could do what Magic did. I thought my skills were on that level; I really did. I wanted to be a guard. But I wasn't going to tell Coach Lewis what to do. Nobody was, and I knew that.

We were a true Houston team. Three of our starters — Micheaux, Young and myself — were Houstonians, and the guy who wound up being a fourth starter, Franklin, was from La Marque, Texas, about 20 to 25 minutes from the university. Gettys was from Houston, too. Olajuwon was the only one who had covered any distance to play for the Cougars.

Hakeem was seven feet by then; Larry was 6'9" and Michael, who was now considered our shooting guard, was 6'6". We were all carrying pretty high profiles, and most of us had nicknames. I was "Clyde the Glide." Hakeem became "The Dream." Larry was "Mr. Mean." Somebody called Michael "Unsung" Young at one point, but I don't really remember him having a nickname other than "Seaweed," which is what Moses Malone called him. He said Michael was so strong, he had to be eating seaweed every day. Too bad that one didn't stick.

The previous season, the Houston newspapers had begun including "dunks" in our box scores. It's something I hadn't seen before and I have never seen since. But that was the type of team we were. We played good defense, stole the ball, and created turnovers, which led to dunks the other way. Or we scored off lob passes or power-move dunks at the basket in the halfcourt set. Instead of jump hooks or fadeaway jump shots, our guys would drop-step you and power-dunk.

Dunking is the highest-percentage shot in the game. Our goal was to drive to the basket and throw it down. If every team subscribed to that theory, they would win more games. In practice, our whole thing was somebody taking it to the basket strong. We had a contest to see which player could get the most tip-dunks during a game.

**MICHAEL YOUNG:** We also had bets on who would get the most dunks, period. That is what we loved to do. Style was important to us. We played a fun style. We played the way kids everywhere wanted to play. We played at an up-tempo pace, played good tough defense, rebounded the ball, and pushed it up the court.

Dunking was effective; plus it was creative and got the fans excited. We did want to put on a show for the people watching our games. If you got a breakaway off a steal, it was showtime. Coach Lewis was fine with that, as long as we didn't get careless. He was really concerned with our assist-to-turnover ratio. He told us, "If you guys get steals, you can dunk it all day. But unless you have something sure, bring it out and set it up."

**MICHAEL YOUNG:** Clyde told me once that dunking is like being in an airplane. "When you are up there like that," he said, "you feel as free as a bird."

Somebody at the school tested my vertical leap and had me at 44 inches with a running jump, 33 inches from a standstill jump. I guess Coach Lewis didn't notice. He told a reporter before the season, "I don't think he is a great leaper, but he has such great timing. He always seems to be in the right spot at the right time." I thought I had pretty good elevation, but I am not one to contradict my coach, of course.

**DENISE PINK:** I really thought Clyde was going to be able to make a career out of basketball when he got to University of Houston. He would spontaneously dunk in a way that people had never seen. If I were to say, "OK, Clyde, count to three and do this dunk," he couldn't do it. But put him in a game situation and he would always improvise and execute like no other. It was amazing. I had never seen that before. And I started thinking, "Maybe he can do this one day and get a job in the NBA."

A reporter asked me if I put names to my dunks. I told him, "I don't like to name them. Mine are just plain and simple." Darryl Dawkins was big at that time. He had all those crazy names for his dunks, and that worked for him. People wanted me to name them like Darryl. I couldn't do that. I wanted to be like my hero, Julius Erving — just get it done. Naming dunks didn't fit my personality.

Dunking could be dangerous. When I was in the NBA, I was knocked unconscious in a dunk attempt in one game. It couldn't be helped. There is no room for cowardice in basketball. You can't be intimidated once you commit to the basket.

We weren't just a bunch of dunkers at the University of Houston. Hakeem had become the best shot blocker in the country, and he was slowly adding to his offensive game. Larry was the best guy to have on your team. He was our tough guy, make no mistake. Michael was a dead-eye shooter from 15 to 18 feet and was also good on the break. I did a little bit of everything. I brought the ball up, guarded the best shooting guard or forward of the opponent, rebounded and scored.

We were definitely thinking national championship, even if the media or fans weren't looking at us quite that way. We went into the season ranked 14th in the AP poll and 11th in UPI. I served notice I was ready for a big year when I had 22 points, 11 rebounds and five steals in our season-opening 104-63 rout of Arizona. We moved into the top 10 after we ran off wins in our first six games, including Mississippi State with Jeff Malone and Auburn with Charles Barkley. I had a pretty good game against the Tigers with 19 points, 12 rebounds and three steals. Charles had 14 points and eight boards in that one.

**CHARLES BARKLEY:** It was a scary feeling going up against Houston that season. They had six guys who were unbelievable athletes. It was a remarkable collection of players they could put out there. I don't think I would be going out on a limb to say from a talent standpoint, that Houston team could stack up with any college team in history.

Auburn hung in with us for a half. They were pretty tough. In the second half, we got our running game going and ran right by them. We had heard the hype about this kid who was really heavy but could play. In Auburn's first possession, Charles took a pass at the post, power-dribbled to the basket, turned around and dunked two-handed over Larry Micheaux. I thought, "That was strong. Who is this kid?" But the second half, he kind of ran out of energy.

After going 6-0, we stumbled, dropping from the national rankings after consecutive losses to Syracuse and Virginia. I had a monster game at the Carrier Dome with 28 points, 13 boards and 11 steals, but the Orangemen beat us 92-87 before a crowd of 19,430. We played the Cavaliers in a highly anticipated game at the Suntory Classic in Tokyo. Ralph Sampson had the flu and didn't play, which was a letdown. Everybody was looking forward to a Hakeem-Ralph showdown. When Ralph didn't play, we took the day off and lost 72-63. Their best player besides Sampson was a swing man named Rick Carlisle, who later became the coach of the Detroit Pistons and Indiana Pacers.

After those two games, we never lost again until the national championship game. We were getting our game together and posting some big scores. And pretty soon, Tommy Bonk of the

*Houston Post* hung a nickname on us that became one of the most famous in the history of college sports. We had just beaten Pacific 112-58 and had 10 dunks in the process, inspiring this prose from Bonk:

"As members of the exclusive roundball fraternity Phi Slama Jama, the Houston chapter has learned proper parliamentary procedure. First, while the minutes are being read, you grab hold of the basketball and prepare your opening remarks. Closing remarks should follow immediately, perhaps in the same motion.

"Be careful not to knock down anyone or exceed the speed limit on your way to the rostrum. But make sure your sneakers squeal a little. Always a nice touch. It is permissable to leave your feet. When making travel plans, go by air. Now comes the initiation rite. Forget that freshman-in-a-phone-booth routine. If you're a Phi Slama Jama, you see how many balls you can stuff into a basket.

"Lots. Ten games deep into the season, the Cougars have won eight times and dunked 58 times. Non-conference games have been one long rush party. There have been dunks on the run and straight-up power dunks. Whirling dunks, backward dunks, rebound dunks and one-on-one dunks. Stylin' and profilin', runnin' and gunnin', slammin' and jammin', mercy, what a life.

"'Sure, 15-foot jumpers are fine,' said Clyde Drexler. 'But I like to dunk.'"

**TOMMY BONK:** I was trying to come up with a name for a dunking fraternity, and I came up with Phi Slama Jama. For me, it was just a line in a column. Guy Lewis later told me, "You didn't know you were creating a monster." They flash it every year at the Final Four as a trivia question. I even tried to see if I could copyright it, but I had signed papers giving it to the university.

That was an unbelievable couple of years. Houston practices were a gas. They were about as physical as can be. It was so much fun.

Guy always was criticized for being a coach who just rolled the ball out and let them play. I wrote that very thing one day, and he said, "You come out to a practice." I did, and then I wrote another column, and I wrote that all he said was, "Red ball out." He just them let beat on each other.

**LARRY MICHEAUX:** What were our practices like? Like a boxing match. TKOs every day.

**GUY LEWIS:** I called the fouls. I tried to call a couple every season. I don't think you can be a bunch of sissies and be competitive.

Coach Lewis didn't want to stop practices too much to talk while you were playing. I thought that was pretty smart. I hated coaches who stopped things every couple of minutes. Let the players play while they are sweating and in a flow. When we were through, Coach Lewis would go to the chalkboard and talk about things. He would stop a scrimmage only if it were necessary. Unless you lose a tooth, keep playing. If one got knocked out, he might stop play for a minute.

As a result, our practices got pretty fierce. Our guys were very competitive. We always had such good talent and guys were fighting for positions. Coach Lewis's thing was, you earn your position every day. He set the tone. You had guys on the second string thinking, "I am coming after you now."

**TOMMY BONK:** Larry Micheaux was so tough that he gave himself a tattoo with a ballpoint pen. It was an airplane. I think that is all he could think of. Benny Anders got off the plane in Fayetteville wearing chains around his neck and carrying Louis Vuitton bags. People there thought he was from Mars. Clyde was my favorite. He was such a smooth player, made everything look so easy. He was the perfect player for that team. He could rebound and he could run and he could dunk, and he didn't mind showing off. He was the Michael Jordan of that team. He would soar and dunk and finger roll, and everything he did, he made it look easy.

We climbed back into the top 10 in late January, and we kept moving up. On February 2, I had one of the best games of my career, hitting my first 11 shots from the field and finishing 13 of 16 while going for 29 points and 12 rebounds in an 86-69 win over Baylor. By late February, we found ourselves at No. 2 in the rankings behind Nevada-Las Vegas. When a reporter asked if I would like a shot at playing the Rebels, my response was, "Any time, anywhere. Even five o'clock in the morning on the runway at Hobby Airport."

Then UNLV lost twice within a week's time, and on February 28, Houston became the No. 1 team in the country in both polls. There was a celebration around campus. That was a big deal. We hadn't been ranked No. 1 since the days of Elvin Hayes in the late '60s.

Our next game was at Arkansas, always an incredibly tough place for us to play. Darrell Walker and Alvin Robertson were heralded, but I had a little notoriety, too. The year before, we had them beat in a game at Fayetteville, and they came back and got us. We were determined not to let that happen again. This time, we won 74-66, the first time we had won there in seven years. I didn't have a particularly impressive game, but I did come through with a dunk over my good friend Darrell that impressed even Coach Lewis. He called it a "change-of-direction, sidewinding dunk that was Clyde's best so far. I have never seen anything like it. It was incredible. Walker had him cold. I don't know how Clyde got by him, but he did. Walker couldn't believe it. I couldn't, either." When the writer asked me how I did it, I replied, "Sometimes I surprise myself by how long I stay in the air. It is something that happens in the heat of competition."

A week later, the final poll going into NCAA Tournament had Houston at No. 1, Louisville No. 2, St. John's third, Virginia fourth and Indiana fifth. Our SWC rival, Arkansas, was ninth.

We were rolling. We finished the SWC season 16-0, winning by an average margin of 21.6 points a game. We went into the SWC post-season tournament seeded first. Arkansas, which had gone 14-2 — losing twice to us — was the second seed. But there was no showdown in Dallas. Texas Christian upset Arkansas 61-59 in a semifinal while we blasted Southern Methodist 75-59.

In the final, TCU gave us trouble, but we escaped with a 62-59 win. I had a tough offensive game, making only three of 13 shots and scoring seven points, but I had 11 rebounds and seven steals, plus a big block to seal the win in the final minute.

All throughout my junior year, fans, friends and reporters were asking me if I intended to leave for the NBA after that season. I was beginning to think seriously about it, but I didn't want to bring it up. During an interview in February, I told a writer, "I will be back next year, that's for sure. Mom said she wanted me to be the first in the family to graduate from college." But I did drop a hint when I told the writer the only reason to declare hardship was is if you were going to go in the top five picks in the draft.

The national media paid more attention to us late in the regular season, especially after we got the No. 1 ranking. And I used Rob Williams as an example when one reporter asked me if

I would be turning pro. Williams had come out early and hadn't played much his rookie season with the Denver Nuggets.

"After what happened to Rob, I don't think I will leave after my junior year," I told him. "Getting my degree in finance is important to me. I won't always have basketball to fall back on. I want to continue working in the bank. Who knows? Someday I might be the president."

I meant of the bank, not of the United States.

There was growing interest in our team, and it is fun now to look back on all the feature articles that were written on me and on Phi Slama Jama. Someone asked about my other athletic interests. In one article, I mentioned, "I can easily roll a 200 game" in bowling. Back then I could. Asked about golf, I responded, "I shoot in the high 80s." That was an embellishment. I didn't play a lot and was probably shooting 100 or so back then.

I was getting a lot of attention from fans and the media. People would call me at three, four, five in the morning. Some of them were morning radio talk shows. Some were fans or friends or people I didn't even know.

There were also some female admirers. They called from all around the country. They would say they had seen me on the tube or heard I was a nice guy. And they would say they were coming to Houston and they wanted to look me up. It became annoying. I even had about 10 letters from women proposing marriage that season. Girls would send photos of themselves naked, or in bathing suits.

The attention was flattering, but I tried not to take it too seriously. It was hilarious at that time. I used to die laughing. When I would check into a hotel room on the road, sometimes there would be a bouquet of roses or a box of chocolates, with a note attached from someone I had never met. It was a lot of fun, but not once did I date anyone under those circumstances. I had a serious girlfriend at the time, and I was pretty much into basketball.

There were only two things I worried about: If I was right with God, and if I was right with my mother. As long as I was okay on those two, everything else was all right.

**MICHAEL YOUNG:** Were the women interested in Clyde? Oh, just 24/7. We would go out and about off-campus, and he was pretty much the guy wherever we went. After a game, we would go get something to eat, sit down and talk. You had the little discos you would go to back then. Sometimes we would couple up with a girlfriend, go to the movies, those type of things. Nothing too crazy. But we had a lot of fun.

**EUNICE DREXLER SCOTT:** I was proud of Clyde as a basketball player, of course. By his sophomore year at Houston, I knew he was going to be a great NBA player. But the thing that made me proudest was that he didn't get a big head. He didn't brag. He just played the game and took care of Clyde.

I don't think I missed a game of his in three years. When he first started, he would always come to me and say, "How did I do, Mom? What did I do wrong? What can I do better?" I kind of coached him through a little of that. I pointed out the stuff to him that was more important than scoring in the game. And he listened. He always listened pretty well. He always took my advice on different things.

**VIRGINIA SCOTT-WESTBROOKS:** There was nothing like watching Clyde play basketball. I can't tell you the blessing it has been for us as a family to watch him play at every level. Honestly, it has been more of a blessing for us to see it than it has been for him to play it. Every day, we had something to look forward to when it came to Clyde playing basketball. When he was in college, I was always thinking about the Cougars' next game. It was something I had to look forward to. No matter what was going on in our lives, that was a focus — a fun thing. There was no jealousy among our family, not even an ounce of it. We lived it right along with him.

When Clyde had his pro career, it was like we were living our careers, too. When his team won, we won. When he lost, we lost. When somebody criticized him, they were criticizing us, too. That's the way it was. That's the way it is now, still. I wouldn't trade the experience of following Clyde's career for anything in the world.

**JIM NANTZ:** Clyde was exceedingly polite and thoughtful. He was someone who, the minute you met him, you liked him. He looked you right in the eye. He was a very caring person. His mom was always around at the games. You always saw Mrs. Drexler.

He was incredibly kind to my father. To this day, he hasn't changed. He clearly found stardom in a Hall of Fame career. I really don't think there's anything different about Clyde's character since the first day I met him.

By this time, I had developed a flair for the game, and it was a lot of fun that people seemed to appreciate it. One writer in particular captured my playing style well: "Drexler's soul seems to be the soul of an artist. He does not move with drilled and programmed precision; he really does glide and soar. He does not produce; he creates. He is involved in the game, even intense, but he is not a jerking, grunting 'Charlie Hustle.' He plays with an obvious love for the game, and if you are with him, he makes you think not only of basketball but of things beyond."

I had a good relationship with most of the Houston media, including longtime *Houston Post* columnist Jack Gallagher. In a column during my junior year, he wrote, "In 35 years of the local sports beat, I can't recall a college athlete — and few in the pros — as outgoing, as cooperative, as helpful and as quotable as Clyde Drexler. He was a reporter's, and also a coach's, dream. There isn't a malicious bone in Clyde Drexler's body. You wonder how long he can keep that unspoiled attitude in the NBA."

Jack thought the NBA was going to spoil me. We had an assistant coach, Terrence Kirkpatrick, who said a lot of the same things. He used to say, "Clyde is the greatest commodity since sliced bread. The NBA is going to love this guy." I had a good support base. It is great to have people who believe in you. They were two of those people.

But getting back to the NCAA Tournament... In those days, conference champions got a first-round bye, which was fine with us. We beat Maryland 60-50 in the second round in what amounted to a home game at The Summit. They had Len Bias and Adrian Branch and were a very tough team. I took only seven shots in the game, made five, and contributed 11 points and eight rebounds.

Maryland's coach was Lefty Driesell, and before the game he had pumped us up as the greatest offensive machine in the history of basketball. He obviously knew he couldn't run with us, and he took the air out of the ball, playing a deliberate style throughout the game. We led only 26-24 at the half, and at one point in the second half, Guy Lewis decided to pay them back. We took a turn holding the ball for a two-minute span, making 27 passes before we finally took a shot. We only got one dunk in that one, right at the end of the game.

We moved on to the Midwest Regional semifinals at Kansas City, where our opponent was Memphis State, with Keith Lee and Andre Turner. Their coach, Dana Kirk, jumped on the bandwagon with a little hyperbole about us. He said leading up to the game, "They can beat anybody in the country... maybe I should say the NBA."

It went down to the wire. We led 61-58 with 1:23 left but made some free throws and wound up winning 70-63. Hakeem had a nice game, sinking 10 of 14 shots for 21 points. I took only eight shots, made four, and finished with eight points, seven boards and six steals.

In the regional finals we played Villanova, the same team that had kicked our butts two years earlier in the tournament when Michael and I were freshmen. We wanted to beat them, believe me. They had John Pinone, Ed Pinckney and Harold Pressley. Two years later, the Wildcats would win the NCAA title.

But not this year. We buried then 89-71 for our 25th straight victory in what I called "no question, the best game we have played since I have been here. We have proven we can play with any team in the country."

Our defense led to offense in that game. We had 15 blocks, eight by Hakeem, and nine dunks, five by Hakeem. I guarded Pressley and he went 0 for 9 from the floor, mainly because Hakeem was behind me. Larry was sensational with 30 points and 12 rebounds. He was dominant that game. He was on our team that lost to Villanova in '81 and took on this rematch as a personal challenge. We all wanted a piece of them. Hakeem had 20 and 13 and Michael scored 20 points. I had 12 points, five rebounds and five assists.

An aside to that game: It was the only college game I ever played in which I had six personal fouls. The college rule, of course, mandates disqualification after five fouls. I got my fifth foul with 4:04 to play, but nobody at the scorer's bench — or the referees, or the Wildcats, for that matter — noticed. I stayed in and was allowed to play until I got my sixth foul with 2:57 left. I got a shot off after the fifth foul but didn't score. I was hoping maybe they would let me have seven fouls, but that was too much to ask for. I died laughing on the way to the bench. I was going to stay out there as long as I could.

We went into the Final Four at Albuquerque 30-2 and ranked No. 1. Vendors that week were hawking shirts that read, "Phi Slama Jama — we bad." *Sports Illustrated* proclaimed, "The Phi Slama Jamas have commanded attention as has no team in the recent history of the Final Four." We knew we were good, and so did everyone else. We could smell a national title coming on, and we were close enough to taste it, too.

As luck would have it, we were matched up in one semifinal with Louisville, the nation's No. 2 team. The Cardinals, coached by Denny Crum, were known as the "Doctors of Dunk." They had Milt Wagner, Rodney and Scooter McCray, Lancaster Gordon and Charles Jones. Charles wound up playing a year with me in Portland in the NBA.

Everybody was calling it the true national championship game. We were really juiced, because we loved to play against the best teams, and this was a match made in heaven. Dick Vitale picked Louisville to win, questioning Alvin Franklin as our point guard and what he saw as our weak regular-season schedule.

We really respected the Cardinals, and for a half, they had our number, going into intermission with a 41-36 lead. They were brutalizing us on the boards. Coach Lewis drew a technical when he threw a towel onto the court in frustration. "It slipped out of my hand," he said after the game. But I think he said it with a wink.

Louisville led 57-49 with 13 minutes left, and with Micheaux on the bench disqualified with five fouls, things weren't looking too good for us.

But then we switched from a zone defense to a man to man, a brilliant move by Guy. And suddenly, we were in charge. We went on a 21-1 run that was a thing of beauty, and now we were ahead 70-58. We opened the run when I tossed up a lob pass to Michael, who flushed it. Then I got the ball on the break and dunked myself. We picked up the pressure and it got us going offensively. We turned our defense into offense and had ourselves a dunk-a-thon at Louisville's expense.

During that unforgettable run, I had a double-pump dunk to make it 60-57 that *Sports Illustrated* referred to as "your basic play of the century." I was in transition swinging into the front-court, and I was trying to figure out what the defender — I don't remember who it was — was going to do. I knew I was supposed to keep going at the basket until he cut me off. He never cut me off. And then I went up and dunked it, and it was over. I guess it was special, but I was so intent on winning the game, I never thought about it.

The way we came on with such an explosion was pretty amazing. Some people even today say it was the greatest college game they ever witnessed. We had 11 steals in the game. I had a big game with 21 points, seven rebounds and six assists, and I made 10 of 15 shots from the floor. But Hakeem was the story with 21 points, 22 rebounds and eight blocks. He was just dominant in the second half. A reporter asked me about him after the game and I said, "When he turns pro, Hakeem will be the greatest center in NBA history." I wasn't far off.

North Carolina State beat Georgetown in the other semifinal. The Wolfpack was kind of a Cinderella team, but we never discounted them as a worthy opponent. We knew they were a great team. They had won a lot of games on last-second shots. They were very formidable. They had Thurl Bailey, Lorenzo

Charles, Cozell McQueen and a couple of effective guards in Dereck Whittenburg and Sidney Lowe. The rest of the country thought our semifinal game was the championship game, but I honestly didn't look at it that way.

Jimmy Valvano, NC State's coach, was a character, and he was playing up our reputation after the Louisville game.

"I never saw so many dunks in my life," he said. "I missed the first half, and I wish I had missed the second."

He made it clear he was going to go by the Lefty Driesell slowdown philosophy in the finals: "If the score gets anywhere in the 70s, you can stick the fork in us."

It was awesome to be in the championship game for the first time. But I didn't like the final result. If we had played the championship game on Sunday instead of Monday, we would have been all right. When you are hot, you need to play right away. If you get the day off and sit back and read newspaper clippings about how great you are, it is never a good result.

**JIM NANTZ:** I was working for the CBS affiliate, KSL, in Salt Lake City at the time. Phi Slama Jama was the talk of college hoops. They were a thrill a second; everybody was talking about them. After they beat Louisville, I told my bosses, "I have to go see the championship game to see the coronation of Houston's national championship."

I flew from Salt Lake to Albuquerque and drove to the team hotel. I had a lot of buddies, including George Walker, a grad assistant. I hung out with George and went to Clyde's room at about four in the afternoon to say hello to Clyde and Michael, who were rooming together. The room was very dark, with the curtains closed, and they were lying down, visualizing the game that night. We visited a little, exchanged hugs, caught up on things.

A couple of hours later, I went to the arena on the team bus. I did not have a pass or a credential, but they let me ride on the bus, and I slipped in with the team through the entrance to the arena, sandwiched in between Michael and Hakeem. Then I went up to find a seat in the stands.

**MICHAEL YOUNG:** We were really focused before the game. NC State wasn't a slouch team. You're not a slouch team if you make it to the finals of the NCAA Tournament. We didn't underestimate those guys. We were the No. 1 team in the country, though, and they had nothing to lose.

**TOMMY BONK:** The referees set the tone early in that game. Clyde got a couple of terrible foul calls and had to sit, and that really hurt.

**JIM NANTZ:** It was a heartwrenching night for the Cougars. Clyde picked up three early fouls, was taken out of his game for a few minutes, then went back and drew his fourth foul before halftime. NC State's Terry Gannon, now a broadcaster for ABC, drew a charge that still ranks as one of the worst foul calls in the history of the NCAA Tournament.

Three of those calls were very questionable. On the fourth foul, Gannon tackled me as I went to the basket, and I made the shot, and they called me for an offensive foul. He even told the referee after the call had been made that the foul should have been called on him. Amazing. It took me out of my game completely.

NC State led 33-25 at the half, and I started the second half on the bench. But our guys got hot, and we opened with a 17-2 spurt that put us ahead 42-35. We were in great shape. NC State was getting desperate. It looked like we were going to blow them out. Everybody thought that was going to happen.

It didn't. NC State hung around. With me out, Hakeem had to play the whole way until he was taken out, exhausted, with about 10 minutes left. I hit a couple of free throws to put us ahead 52-46 with 3:19 to play. Then Coach Lewis decided to go into a halfcourt offense, which was designed to get a very good shot or a dunk. Twice we got fouled and missed the front end of one-and-ones that could have pretty much cinched it for us. The Wolfpack tied it up at 52-52 and got to play for the final shot with 44 seconds left.

**JIM NANTZ:** I will never forget the finish. Bailey threw a pass from the left corner to Whittenburg out at the top of the key. Clyde saw the pass coming and leaped out to get it and it very nearly touched his fingertips. I'll bet he felt it. It might have grazed a nail. If he had gotten one-eighth of an inch closer, he would have deflected the ball, caught up to it, and won the national championship with one of his patented dunks at the other end.

The irony of the final possession was that we played great defense. Twice, we almost made steals. Benny Anders got a hand on a Whittenburg pass, but Whittenburg got it back and launched a 30-foot airball. Hakeem was in position to get the rebound had the ball hit the rim, but it landed right in the hands of Charles, who dunked it with two seconds left.

Game over. North Carolina State 54, Houston 52. They had been lucky, but it didn't matter. Fans were storming the court. Valvano was running around, looking for someone to hug. I was completely devastated. We were the better team. You never want to lose when your team is better. But give the Wolfpack credit. They outplayed us that day, and they deserved to win.

We shot .382 from the field in that game, but our biggest fault was that we were 10 of 19 from the foul line. I wound up with four points on one-of-five shooting and two rebounds in 25 minutes. Hakeem had a huge game with 20 points, 16 rebounds and 11 blocks and was named the Final Four MVP. I don't think that made him feel any better.

**TOMMY BONK:** The Cougars were so good and talented, it is a shame they didn't win the championship. But there were two things they couldn't do. They couldn't stall and they couldn't shoot free throws. That's exactly what cost them the game against North Carolina State.

**MICHAEL YOUNG:** We were plagued by not being good free throw shooters. We were ahead; then we slowed the game down by going into a spread, and of course that was a mistake. We were on the verge of blowing those guys out. The momentum changed; we couldn't make free throws and they started making shots. It was a terrible feeling to lose that game. I played professionally for 15 years, and that is the worst loss I have ever suffered. Every day of my life, I talk about it with somebody who remembers how we should have won the title, but didn't.

**HAKEEM OLAJUWON:** Though we didn't win the championship, it didn't take away from the overall success of the team. In our minds, we were still the champions. We were probably the best college team that never won an NCAA title. Clyde was a major factor in our success, and his style was what always got the fans going. Our two seasons with Phi Slama Jama were classic. We had a great time, and I will never forget it.

I was more disappointed for Coach Lewis than for our team. He deserved to win a championship. It would have validated his career body of work on a national level. He didn't have the national respect he deserved at that time. He certainly has had it since.

We ended the season with a 31-3 record, including 14-0 at home. I finished shooting .539 from the field and .737 from the line—all that work in the summer was beginning to pay off—with averages of 15.9 points and 8.8 rebounds. I set a school record and was third in the nation with 113 steals, and also had 129 assists and 55 dunks. I was in the top 10 in the Southwest Conference in just about every category.

I was honored as the conference Player of the Year in two separate polls—one by the players, and one by the sportswriters and sportscasters.

I made the U.S. Basketball Writers Association's first-team All-America squad along with seniors Randy Wittman of Indiana, Ralph Sampson of Virginia, Sidney Green of Nevada-Las Vegas, Dale Ellis of Tennessee, junior Sam Perkins of North Carolina, sophomores Michael (he was no longer Mike) Jordan of North Carolina, Keith Lee of Memphis State and Patrick Ewing of Georgetown and freshman Wayman Tisdale of Oklahoma.

In three years at Houston, I had more than 100 dunks. I was the only player in school history with 1,000 points, 900 rebounds and 300 assists. I had performed pretty well against the best in the country, too. In 11 NCAA Tournament games, I averaged 13.4 points and 7.0 rebounds and shot .573 from the floor. I am still sixth on Houston's career rebound list with a 9.9 average. Not bad for a guy who played the wing. Still, those statistics are OK, but they are not going to scare anyone.

One of the things I was most proud of was our 42-3 record at home over those three seasons, and two of the losses were by a total of three points. We lost to Baylor 70-68 my first year, then

95-83 to Texas and 67-66 to Southern Methodist in back-to-back games my sophomore year. We just weren't going to let a team come into Hofheinz and beat us.

Later that spring, I got to meet one of my favorite players, George "Iceman" Gervin.

**GEORGE GERVIN:** I met Clyde and Hakeem when they came to one of our games in San Antonio. I will never forget them driving up in a limousine to Hemisphair Arena to watch a playoff game. They pulled up in front of the arena and jumped out, and that was when I had a chance to touch Clyde myself for the first time.

In those years, we all had "Iceman" posters in our dorm rooms. It seemed like the Spurs were always in the Western Conference finals playing the Lakers. Hakeem and I went down to San Antonio to watch a game as guests of CBS. It was exciting to meet George and his teammates. He and Artis Gilmore and Mike Mitchell were extremely cordial. George became a good friend. He is quiet, but a real solid guy. And man, could he go to work on the basketball court. He had so much skill, and he could shoot the lights out. I took a lot of my game from watching George and Julius Erving, the finger rolls, the dipsy-dos and all the midrange stuff.

After the 1983 championship game in Albuquerque, when the reporters asked the inevitable question of whether I would returning for my senior season, I answered, "It looks like I will be back. I have got the same views I have always had. I'm not gonna change my mind."

I wasn't being honest. By this point, it was pretty much guaranteed that I was going to go in the top five of the June NBA draft. But I didn't want to draw attention to what I was thinking, and I hadn't decided 100 percent on entering the draft.

The day after the championship game was proclaimed "Clyde Drexler Day" by the city of Houston.

"Whereas the men of Phi Slama Jama dominated the game of basketball in the SWC and the nation like no other team in memory has done, thus winning for themselves a place in history, as well as in the hearts of Houstonians and basketball fans everywhere, I proclaim April 5, 1983, Clyde Drexler Day." It was signed by Kathryn Whitmire, the mayor of Houston.

That was very flattering. But I have to be honest; I don't remember a lot about that. My life was like a blur. I was enrolled for spring term at the university, but there was so much going on. I don't even remember going to class.

**HAKEEM OLAJUWON:** Clyde was thinking seriously about leaving school and declaring himself eligible for the NBA draft. Pro teams had been sending scouts to watch us play, and Clyde wasn't very pleased with what some of them were saying about him — that he couldn't shoot. His jump shot was suspect because all they ever saw was him running the floor and jamming. He had a very good jump shot, but no one knew it because he dunked all the time.

Clyde and I talked about declaring for the draft together. The Houston Rockets had No. 1 and 3 picks, and we talked about coming out as a package deal. The Rockets would get a center and a guard, a young nucleus to build a team around. We could be teammates and play alongside each other and take Phi Slama Jama straight into the pros.

**MICHAEL YOUNG:** Clyde had such a monster junior year, I knew he wasn't coming back. He was trying to get me to go out, too. He said, "We came here together; let's leave together." I knew his was a win-win situation, but I figured I would have a big senior year and then get drafted higher. Looking back at it now, I should have gone out that season. But I liked it at the University of Houston. I had a great time playing there. We had a great team coming back. I just wasn't ready to leave.

I had pretty much decided on declaring for the draft, but I hadn't told anybody except my mom and brother. I was trying to prolong everything because I wanted Hakeem to make the right decision. Even though he was very good, I didn't think he was ready for the NBA. He needed one more year of seasoning, both as a person and a player. Remember, he was not only a relative novice to basketball, but he was in a new country. The next year, I figured there would be no doubt that he would be the No. 1 pick. He wanted to go into the draft with me, and I was afraid he was going to get an agent and make himself ineligible to return to the University of Houston the following season. But he thought he was ready, too. He kept telling me, "Let's do this together." I strongly suggested he stay, but he has always been his own man, and he made his own decision.

Still, right up until we announced what we were going to do, I wasn't sure what Hakeem was going to do. The whole thing became one big mess. We scheduled a dual news conference for May 12. The day before, a radio reporter named Max Edison, who was a friend of my brother James, came by the house. He said, "Look Clyde, I have known you a long time. I know you are going to come out for the draft. Let me record an interview and I promise I won't run it until after your announcement tomorrow morning." So we did it, and he ran it that night.

The next day, the newspapers had the radio report in which I had said I was leaving to do "what is financially best for myself. The main thing I want to do is play with guys who are consid-

ered the best in the world. It is like a dream. If I pass it up, it may
never happen again."

It was my first betrayal by the media — a valuable lesson. I
didn't know what to do. All I could say was that it was a hoax,
that it wasn't my voice. Hakeem and I went into Coach Lewis's
office for 45 minutes before the press conference. We talked and
decided we weren't ready to announce anything. Hakeem and I
went out the back door and left it to Coach Lewis to tell the
media, "They are not ready to make an announcement."
Somebody asked him what he thought we were going to do. He
said he expected both of us to return. "That is my opinion," he
said. "Of course, that and a dollar and a quarter will get you a cup
of coffee."

The next day — Friday the 13th — we made the announcement. I was leaving. Hakeem was staying. We both made the
right decision.

"I hope to be a lifelong member of Phi Slama Jama," I told
the reporters. "But in my heart, this is what I want to do. ...It's
hard to go out second fiddle, but when the opportunity comes,
why wait? It was hard to concentrate on basketball with all the
distractions the last few weeks. There were agents trying to talk to
me every day."

Jerry Bonney, a family lawyer and advisor who had played
basketball at the University of Houston, had helped me with
arrangements in the months leading up to my decision.

"I am not sure I will have an agent," I told the reporters. "I
may just let Jerry handle it, if he can do it. An agent wants 10 or
20 percent of the gross. That's ridiculous An attorney works for
a fee."

I was passing up an opportunity to play for the 1984
Olympic team — it was strictly an amateur proposition at the
time — after I got a letter from a guy named Bobby Knight say-

he wanted me and Michael Jordan to head up his Olympic team. I wish I had kept that letter.

I felt a lot of pride for what I had done at the University of Houston. We hadn't won an NCAA title. But we took a team that was .500 when I got there and thrust it back into national prominance and a spot in the Final Four three straight times before they were through. I would miss my teammates and Guy Lewis, whom I really admired. But it was time to move on.

# CHAPTER 7

# HELLO, CITY OF ROSES

**W**hen I decided I was going to come out for the NBA draft, one of the major reasons was that I had been given strong indications that I would be taken by the hometown Houston Rockets. They had the first and the third picks, and I was pretty sure they would take me, probably with the third pick.

But after the season, they had a coaching change. Del Harris was fired and replaced by Bill Fitch. And not long after that, probably two weeks before the draft, I got called into the office of Rockets' general manager Ray Patterson.

"Clyde, we promised we would take you, but sometimes things happen," Patterson said. "We have a new coach, and if he wants to go in another direction, don't be surprised. ...We just want you to know of the possibility."

It was the last thing I wanted to hear. I had turned down a lot of teams for personal workouts because I really thought I would be going to Houston. It was such a lock; I was telling everybody that. I figured people had seen me enough and I had done enough to prove myself; it didn't matter who their coach was.

**CARROLL DAWSON:** I was the reason Clyde had the feeling that Houston was going to take him in the draft. I was working as an assistant coach for the Rockets when Clyde was playing at the University of Houston, and I had seen him and Olajuwon play a lot of times. I was paying Clyde a lot of attention. If I hadn't been a scout, I would have gone over and paid to watch that team. If you liked basketball, you liked Phi Slama Jama. Holy cow, that was a team.

When Del got fired, I was retained. Rudy Tomjanovich had just retired as a player and was going to start scouting, learning his craft. In the interim, I had researched the draft for us, and I had let Clyde know that I liked him a lot. So it was probably my fault he got that impression.

Then we hired Fitch, who had already done his homework on the draft. He of course wanted Ralph Sampson, and he liked Rodney McCray. It wasn't that Bill didn't like Clyde; he just he didn't like Clyde better than those two players.

Carroll Dawson is a great friend of mine to this day. I don't hold anything against him, but I was pretty upset about it at the time. I considered it my second instance of betrayal, and I wasn't even in the NBA yet. But that is part of the business. You learn fast.

After my conversation with Ray Patterson, I wasn't sure what to do. There really wasn't any time to visit a lot of places. I only went to one team for a workout — Portland. The Blazers had the 14th pick. Bucky Buckwalter, who was Jack Ramsay's only assistant and the Blazers' chief scout at the time, arranged the visit.

**BUCKY BUCKWALTER:** I started watching Clyde play during his freshman year at Houston. When Clyde was a junior, I spent some time watching Hakeem Olajuwon, and the more I watched the Cougars, I realized how important an ingredient Clyde was to their success.

The athleticism was the thing that first attracted me. We were very unathletic, and we decided we had to change that. I was adamant that we get more quickness. The teams winning were the teams that had the speed up and down the floor and played the quick game. We were doing too much setup stuff. Stu Inman, our general manager/director of player personnel, Harry Glickman, our executive vice president, and I talked a lot about it. When we figured we had a chance to get Clyde with our pick. We decided he would be the guy to build around if we could get him. We had never had an open-court player like him in franchise history.

**STU INMAN:** When we did our research on that draft, I was fortunate to know almost every coach in the Southwest Conference on a reasonably intimate basis. The thing that came through from conversations with all of them was that Clyde was the glue on that team. I was taken by the almost unanimous reaction from other coaches in that league. They said he did what he had to do to win a game. His ego never interfered with his will to win.

When we brought him in for a personal workout and an interview, he impressed everybody with his intelligence. He was a straight shooter, a no-nonsense guy, and had his life together. I remember noting in our pre-draft material he was working at a bank in the summers, a job that related to the course of study he was involved in at the university.

As a player, he was very athletic — more athletic than a great basketball player. We saw him as a player dedicated to winning, a fierce competitor who wasn't in any way dirty. He saw the game in an artistic form, and that was pretty much the way he played the game.

**JACK RAMSAY:** I wasn't involved heavily in the draft. My role was to indicate where we needed help, and Stu would tell me the best players available at that position. We did not have a need at either small forward or shooting guard, but he and Bucky were very high on Clyde. He was simply the best player available. It was Stu's pick, and he chose Clyde.

**BUCKY BUCKWALTER:** When we found out Houston was looking elsewhere, we figured Clyde might slide to our pick at No. 14. There was some reluctance from teams to take him any any higher than that. A lot of NBA people felt there was an inadequacy in the shooting department. He was not a great shooter, and at his size, he had to play the two or the three spot. We felt he would learn to shoot from the perimeter, or somehow make up for it with his other talents.

During my visit to Portland, Jack and Bucky were saying, "We can't believe you will be there at 14, but if you are, we are going to take you." Some people thought they were going to take Randy Breuer, the 7'3" center from Minnesota, and the Blazers had brought Breuer and Louisiana State guard Howard Carter to Portland for pre-draft physical exams and interviews along with me. But I think more than anything, they were putting out misinformation on purpose to throw other teams off.

Meanwhile, all of the pros I was playing with in the summer were saying, "This guy is going to be awesome in the NBA." They told me it was a given the Rockets were going to take me. At least that's what we thought. But I had a sneaking suspicion it wasn't going to happen after my conversation with Ray Patterson.

The league invited me along with the top 10 or 12 prospects to New York for the draft. Houston took Ralph Sampson first and then Rodney McCray third. I was disappointed, but I was thinking, "I hope some other team has faith enough to pick me pretty soon." Dallas had two picks, No. 9 and 11, and took Detlef Schrempf and Derek Harper. I thought, "Damn, that's a Texas team. They had to have seen me in a lot of games, and they pass on me, too?" Later, the Mavericks said something about not expecting me to be around, but I was — so why didn't they take me?

When it came to New York's pick at No. 12, the fans in the audience started chanting "Drexler! Drexler!" And the Knicks took my old foe from Arkansas, Darrell Walker.

At No. 13, Sacramento chose Ennis Whatley. I was thinking, "These are all guys I was supposed to be taken ahead of."

Finally it was Portland's pick, and the Blazers took me. "Tell them we are pledging Phi Slama Jama fraternity," Harry Glickman said to the Blazer representatives at Madison Square Garden. My bad feelings went away quickly. I was happy. I was an NBA player at last.

**JIM NANTZ:** The Rockets should have drafted him. I couldn't believe they passed on Clyde Drexler.

**CARROLL DAWSON:** It goes without saying all of us with the Rockets regret not taking Clyde. I noticed over the years, when Clyde played one of Fitch's teams, he averaged about 40 points a game. I have kidded him about that. Maybe it was just a coincidence.

I remember Fitch telling some people I knew that I would be another Charles Bradley, that I would play a couple of years and then fizzle out. "Clyde's skills are not good enough," Fitch told others. Just about every time I played against him, I wanted to let him know my skills were indeed good enough.

**BUCKY BUCKWALTER:** I don't think anybody could have projected Clyde to be as good as he turned out to be. You knew he would be a good defender who would get after the loose ball, give you energy plays, but he turned out to be a more skilled player driving to the hoop and dumping off than I would have expected. He could dunk, but everybody could do a little of that. The thing about Clyde was, he did it so quickly. He was up and the ball was down through the net before the defender could react.

**STU INMAN:** As part of our draft process in those days, we did a psychological profile on each of our potential draftees — at least, the ones who would cooperate. A few of them didn't want to do it. Bill Walton was one of those guys. That was just Bill at the time. He didn't want us to know that much about him, or at least, that is how I interpreted it. I am sure Bill would have scored very highly had he taken it. Some of our other players didn't.

The test was put together by Bruce Ogilvie, a premier sports psychologist during those years, and we had grown up together in San Jose and were good friends. He had worked for years with the San Francisco 49ers and Dallas Cowboys and had written a great deal on the area of evaluation.

**JACK RAMSAY:** I had met Bruce when I was coaching Philadelphia from 1968-72. I used him my last year when we had a mixed bag of players. I thought it would be good to get a psychological background on them. After he was finished, I remember sitting with him and he looked across at me, and I didn't know him that well, and he said, "If you can win with these players, it will be a miracle." I said, "Really?" I didn't think they were that bad. He said, "The psychological makeup of this team is a disaster." And as it turned out, we went 30-52 that year.

When I got to Portland four years later, Bruce had been with the Blazers since their beginning. I found his evaluations were right on the money. They weren't basketball-related. These had to do with the intangibles — leadership, coachability, mental toughness.

**STU INMAN:** This was not a pass/fail test. It was a chance to provide some insight into what the person is really like. In Bruce's evaluation process, there were 13 dimensions to the inside of a champion. Nobody has all of them. There were questions that dealt with coachability, the appetite to know more, persistence in achieving a goal, character, things like that. It was an incredibly accurate test. Other NBA teams were taking psychological looks at draftable players, but none to the degree that we used it and trusted it. Mind you, we didn't draft people solely on the results of this test. I mean, a spastic could score well on this test. You had to like the talent before you would consider it in your evaluation. But it provided a clear barometer as to whether the guy would fulfill his potential.

When Clyde arrived at our office for the test, he was wearing a suit and tie. He was a class act from day one.

Bruce called me after Clyde had taken the test, and he asked me — it was meant as a joke — is there any way he could have gotten the answers ahead of time?

**HARRY GLICKMAN:** Stu said, "Absolutely not." And Bruce said, "Clyde came out with the best-looking profile I have seen since Roger Staubach." That was pretty good company.

I thought it would be about five or six questions. The test took two or three hours to complete. There were a lot of questions about common sense, sports situational questions and that sort of thing. They were like rocket scientists in their evaluation of a player's mental state. And I thought I was done with school. But I guess I did pretty well. Maybe I was ready to surprise some people.

# CHAPTER 8

# GROWING PAINS

I chose Fred Slaughter as the representative to help negotiate my first contract with the Trail Blazers. It might not be accurate to call him my agent. My mom had strongly suggested I get someone in the business to help me out. Fred was a former player and a former dean at the UCLA Law School. He was reputable and came highly recommended. He represented a lot of players at the time, including Norm Nixon and Michael Cooper.

I called him and asked if he would represent me. Back then, agents were commanding around a 10 percent cut of a contract. We worked out the logistics of an agreement where his cut was a whole lot less than that. I told him, "And you have to teach me how to do it myself, too." I wanted to learn about his business. He was a great mentor for that.

I was disillusioned by the agent thing. Starting about my sophomore year at Houston, I began receiving a lot of phone calls from people I didn't know. There was something sleazy about it, and I didn't like it. These guys were talking at me, and I didn't know anything about them at all. I mean, come on. If I was hiring an agent, I am going to pick someone I feel comfortable with, not someone who cold-calls out of the blue, right? They were all trying to see if they could get a leg up in the recruiting game.

There were some unscrupulous things about that business. A lot of the agents wanted to give you money to sign with them, but you know that comes with a payback. A player takes money from somebody he doesn't even know, this guy owns them and tricks them out of money in the future.

Then there is the issue of eligibility in college ball. Technically, student athletes couldn't talk to agents. They would call, or talk to my friends to try to get me to go out and eat with them. I did go to dinners with friends, only to find out there were agents there. But I was a big boy. They couldn't trick me. I never took anything from an agent. I didn't want to feel obligated.

My rookie salary was pretty much predetermined. It was dependent upon what the player at my spot in the draft the year before had received, and maybe I would obtain a slight increase above that. More than that, it depended on what the players drafted immediately ahead of me and behind me in my draft year were being offered. So as we got into negotiations, there wasn't a whole lot of money we were fighting for — maybe $20,000 to $40,000 over a three-year period. But that was a lot of money to me at the time.

I felt the Blazers were lowballing me a little. We wanted to start at about $170,000. The Blazers were offering maybe $150,000. We were fighting over nickels. If I had known then what I did a little later in my career, I would have gone into the office of our owner, Larry Weinberg, and just completed the deal.

When I talked with Fred, he told me worst-case scenario was that we don't sign and sit out a year, then I go back into the 1984 draft. I could have gone to Europe and played. I really didn't want to do that. Still, I didn't want to just give in. I was doing what I thought was right, and eventually I was going to come to some kind of agreement.

As summer league began at Loyola-Marymount in Los Angeles, I was unsigned. We decided I would go to summer league and practice with the team, but not play in the games. That was insurance in case I got hurt. It was, "Give me a contract and I will play." That didn't make our coach, Jack Ramsay, too happy. But I thought I was operating in good faith, learning his system even while I wasn't being paid.

There were four young veterans in camp — Fat Lever, Audie Norris, Jeff Lamp and Petur Gudmundsson. We had a great time getting to know each other. But it was tough to skip out on the games. I went to watch every one of them. Everybody there wanted to see me play, and I wanted to play. I was nineteen, 20 years old — I wanted to display my game. But I was instructed by Fred not to play.

At summer league, I started to get to know a man who played a colossal part in my career — Rick Adelman. He joined the Blazers' family about a week before I did. He was having a press conference announcing his hiring as an assistant coach the day I came in for my pre-draft workout. It was, "Nice to meet you." I couldn't tell we were going to have a special thing between us down the line. He was just an assistant coach with Bucky Buckwalter, who also became a good friend.

Rick was an original Blazer. He was point guard and captain of the very first Portland team back in 1970-71, and he played seven years in the NBA. He was very knowledgable, nice and supportive. But we did have one blow-up that first season.

**RICK ADELMAN:** We stayed in San Diego during the All-Star break that season. The players were scrimmaging, and as an assistant, you always have to officiate. One of the best things about being a head coach is I don't have to ref any more. Clyde was a strong-minded individual. I didn't make a couple of calls, and Clyde got all over me and said some things I didn't appreciate. We got into it.

Things were getting pretty physical in the scrimmage. He wouldn't call a foul when somebody kept hacking me. He was giving the other team too much of an advantage. I said, "All right, Rick, you are making some really bad calls here." That didn't sit too well with him.

**RICK ADELMAN:** Jack was watching from the sidelines. He never said anything. He wanted to see how it was going to play out.

Rick and I were about to throw blows. We were going at it. Things were said in the heat of battle. Finally he said, "You can't talk to me like that." I said, "Hey, can you call 'em better than that? Damn." The other guys were dying laughing, because Rick was quiet. I said, "You are terrible today, Rick." Finally Jack came by and said, "You guys cut that out."

**RICK ADELMAN:** I ran into Clyde in the hotel lobby that night and I said something to him, and he kind of apologized and said he was probably frustrated from not playing as much in games as he wanted. I think that moment kind of helped solidify our relationship in the long run.

I know Rick appreciated my competitive spirit. He proved to be a great coach, but I would never have hired the guy to be an official.

After summer league ended in July, I went back to Houston. I stayed there until late October, when I finally signed. Negotiations dragged on. I let Fred handle it. I worked out and played a lot of ball, but I wasn't where I wanted to be — in Portland with the guys who were going to be my teammates. Or at least I hoped.

Once October rolled around, I was going to the Cougars' practices. The guys were all going, "Hey Clyde, what's up? You going to play in Portland or not?" It was embarrassing. People were saying maybe I had made a mistake coming out for the draft. And I started thinking maybe they were right. I was starting to second-guess myself.

Sometime early that fall, I signed a five-year contract to endorse Kangaroo shoes my first year. They were based in St. Louis and were competing with Nike in those days. They outbid Nike for me. They had Walter Payton in football and me in basketball. They wanted a player with great jumping ability to be their basketball guy. (Kangaroos—get it?) I loved those red shoes.

Finally, on October 21, one week before the first regular-season game, we got the contract hammered out with Harry Glickman, the team's executive vice president. I got $165,000 the first year, with increases to $175,000 and $200,000. I think I was the last of the league's first-round picks to get a contract settled. I was just glad to have it over with.

I never had a full-fledged agent throughout my career. After my second season in Portland, I used a local guy who was a friend and an agent, Marc Caplan, to renegotiate my contract. After another three years, I negotiated an extension through Kiki Vandeweghe's uncle, Gary, who was an attorney and one of the nicest guys you would ever want to meet. Gary and his wife, Barbara, define what a married couple should be. Gary handled the legal side for me. I don't believe he ever took a dime for it, other than to have me pay secretary's costs. Later, when I got my final deal in Portland that included the big $8 million balloon payment, I handled negotiations by myself but had Gary look over the contract from the legal side.

I had begun to meet people in the organization, most of whom I would be associated with the next 11 1/2 years. It was a mom-and-pop business in those days. There were Jack, Rick and Bucky on the coaching staff. Harry and Stu Inman were in the front office. Ron Culp, the longtime trainer, had been with the team since 1974. There was Steve Jones, the former player who was a TV analyst and acted as a big brother to me during my first four or five years in Portland. I could always call him and bounce ideas off him, and just converse about things. He was a good friend and regular tennis partner. And there was the legendary broadcaster Bill Schonely, who had been there since the first day of the franchise. Schonz was a joy to be around. I got to know him quickly, and he became a good friend. He was one of my favorite guys to see on a daily basis. Just before game time, he was at his best. He wanted the Blazers to win. He would look you in the eye and say, "How do we feel today, Big One? Let's do it." He would give you a handshake and he would be off to the announcer's table. I looked forward to having conversations with him before games.

**BILL SCHONELY:** You knew from the start that Clyde Drexler was going to be special. He had that flair about him, and he had all the tools. I just loved his game, the way he approached it. He came to play. He was a great athlete, a thoroughbred, a Jerry West type. He was into the game, he was not one-dimensional and he was definitely a team player. When things weren't going good, though, he could take the game over a la Michael Jordan or Jerry West. The guy had it all.

I liked Clyde from the first time I met him. I never had a problem with him, even though he stiffed me a couple of times on postgame shows. And he knows that, too. When he was a young whippersnapper, he might have had a little bit of a chip on his shoulder, because he felt he should be playing more — especially that first year.

He was always very nice to people. But if Clyde didn't want to do something, he didn't do it. Clyde played to the beat of his own drummer. He did his thing when he wanted to. He wasn't always on time. Jack was concerned about his work ethic for awhile. But he was always ready for the games. Clyde was a big-time gamer.

When I got to training camp, I was way behind. I knew it and everybody else knew it too. There was a lot of catching up to do. They had already played seven of their eight exhibition games. Training camp was pretty much over.

I had gotten a taste of Jack's system in summer league, which was good. But Guy Lewis didn't have 200 plays. He probably had 10. Jack had a bunch of offensive sets and a variation off of all of them, and you had to know them all. "Duck in," the "pin down," all this new terminology. It was a lot to take in. And everybody else already knew it.

That first day of practice, Jack said to me, "Glad to have you. Give us your full attention. We will be patient. Before you hit the floor for me, though, you have to know the plays."

I basically teamed up with the two point guards, Fat and Darnell Valentine, and got to know each and every play. They would stay late after practice and help me out. Or I would follow them home and have them go over the plays with me. They used to laugh at me. I would say, "I have to learn these plays!" And those guys were very gracious about it. I can't say enough about how great those guys were. That is why every team needs good veterans to help the young players.

We had good veterans. Mychal Thompson was the funny guy. I felt comfortable coming to Portland in part because of him. My teammate at Houston, Lynden Rose, was from the Bahamas, as was Mychal. When the Blazers had played the Rockets in Houston, the three of us got together for dinner. Mychal was a very nice guy, and when Portland drafted me, I was thinking, "I will get to play with Mychal." After I got to town, Mychal took great care of me. "Whatever you need, come by the house. Get some food. Need a car?" I didn't know anybody. I had just turned 20 and I was now in a different world, by myself. Mychal made it easier for me.

> **MYCHAL THOMPSON:** Clyde was cocky, but in a good way. He just knew he was going to be a star in the league. He knew how good he was. His rookie year, I told Jack, "Even though we have a lot of veterans, this is Clyde's team." Jack just rolled his eyes. He never believed anything I said. But he could tell by the second year that Clyde was the best player on the team.

> **RON CULP:** Clyde may have lacked in a couple of areas, but self-confidence was not one of them. The old line about talking the talk and walking the walk? Well, Clyde was right there. When it came down to nut-cutting time, Magic and Michael and Larry Bird and Dr. J wanted that ball, and Clyde was in that group with them. When it was time to step forward, Clyde wanted the ball. That was a rare commodity.

I was getting adjusted to living in a new city, a new environment and a new climate. I found an apartment downtown in the

Madison Towers. I wanted to be right in the heart of the action, close to Memorial Coliseum and to the Jewish Community Center, where we practiced. Having lived in a big city my whole life, I was surprised. The city of Portland closed down around 10 or 11 at night. I would go somewhere for dinner after games and the place would be closed. I couldn't believe it. I felt like I was in a different world or something. Everything stayed open late in Houston.

Still, Portland was a great city for a player to live in. The people are very nice and supportive. The Blazers are the only game in town, and a lot of former players choose to make their home there when they retire. It was just a great environment to learn the NBA game. The rainy climate didn't bother me; I was there for basketball. When you are traveling as much as you do in the NBA, when you come home, you want to rest, anyway.

I was getting acclimated to the NBA game, and to my new teammates. We had a good group of young veteran players. There was Darnell at point guard. Calvin Natt was an All-Star-caliber forward. We also had Mychal Thompson, Kenny Carr and Wayne Cooper on the front line, and a shooting guard who had been an All-Star the previous season, Jim Paxson.

**KENNY CARR:** I had played at North Carolina State, and Clyde took grief from me that entire first season over the Wolfpack beating the Cougars in the national championship game. Guy Lewis went to the Four Corners late in that game with a team whose free throw percentage was like 40 percent. It was beautiful.

We were undersized that season. I was a power forward at 6'7". Mychal was the center at 6'10". We made up for it in quickness. We competed well. But to win the West, you had to beat the Lakers, and you weren't going to go to the Finals with them around.

The year before I arrived, the Blazers had won 46 games and a first-round playoff series over Seattle, then lost to the Lakers in the Western Conference semifinals. They were pretty good, with a chance to get better now that I was on board.

The *Oregonian*'s sports columnist, George Pasero, wrote after watching me play, "There is a certain charisma about the new man. He is quick and seems to move with great ease."

And Jack Ramsay had his say: "Like all collegians, he has a lot to learn."

I wonder how Jack would have dealt with all the high school kids coming into the NBA today?

**RICK ADELMAN:** Clyde and I were together for 11 seasons. When we started, he was a rookie and I was a first-time NBA assistant coach. I watched him mature as a player. He had such great athletic ability. He could make phenomenal plays. He had incredible quickness. From day one, you always noticed what a great passer he was, especially in the open court. He could always find the open guy at the right time.

His outside shot was not consistent, though. He shot it differently every time. Jack talked to him and got him to think about working on his shot a little more.

Even though I was a late arrival, I never received any rookie treatment from any of the veterans. Some of them kidded me when I got there. "'Bout time," that sort of thing. A couple of guys tried to get me to carry their bag. Of course, I looked at them like they were crazy. They said, "You get here late and you don't do what you're supposed to do?" I did have to get the ball bags after practice and put them on the bus — especially on the road. That probably happened three or four times. But I didn't mind. And it didn't happen very often.

**MYCHAL THOMPSON:** Even as a rookie, Clyde wasn't in awe of anybody. He fit in with the veterans. Every rookie goes through some hazing, but he took it all in stride. Clyde was so confident in himself. You could tease him about anything; he would just laugh it off.

**KENNY CARR:** Clyde joined in quickly with the group. He was fun-loving. He didn't put on any airs that he thought he was a superstar. He laughed and joked and talked. He always impressed me as a team player. He was one of the guys.

As for rookie hazing, he was too smart for that. He was too savvy. The next year, I worked Jerome Kersey over pretty good. I had Jerome get me the paper and carry the luggage for me, until somebody told him he didn't have to do that. You come out of Longwood, Virginia, you don't know much.

I loved Jack Ramsay, but we didn't have an easy beginning. Jack had his way of doing things. He was quite different from Guy Lewis. We had the same goals in mind, but we gave each other a hard time about that. If I saw him in a pool getting a swim workout, I would go over and say, "Man, is that all you got?" He would crack up laughing. Consequently in practice, if he saw me getting beat at something, he would say, "Is that all you got?"

Jack was a real mentor, which is what a coach is supposed to be. He gave you good guidance on how to eat right, how to take care of your body, how to work out right, how to work on different skill aspects of the game. The guy was an amazing physical specimen who always kept in great shape. In his 70s, Jack was still competing in triathlons. That kind of attitude and dedication was motivation for me.

Looking back on it, Jack was a great coach for me. I knew it at the time. But as a rookie coming into the league, you think you know it all. In reality, there is so much you don't know.

**STU INMAN:** Clyde got off to a little rocky start in the eyes of Jack. Jack didn't know exactly how he should play him. Jack would have a game plan, and sometimes Clyde would go off on his own a little bit in the early years. This was a very difficult time for Clyde. I can remember talking to him on the road somewhere that first year, and he came over to me and said, "Stu, I don't know what to do." I told him, "Time will heal this problem." And it did.

One thing: There is a competitive speed we use in practice and in games, and it is a highly competitive speed. Clyde was always the epitome of that. There was not an ounce of dog in the guy.

**RON CULP:** Clyde didn't particularly like to practice. That wasn't one of his strong points. Jack's thing was, if you practice hard, you carry that over and play hard in the games, so Clyde was a frustrating player at times for Jack.

Jack was very organized, and when he called a certain play, he expected that play to be run through. Clyde was a bit of a free spirit on the court, and if he could see other avenues for getting it done, he would choose them rather than carrying the play to fruition. But the bottom line was, the guy produced.

Jack wanted everyone to be a practice player. My first season, I could have a good practice, and the next game I would only play five minutes. So the next practice, I would be pissed off, so I might take it a little easy. And Jack would say, "What's wrong? Yesterday, you had a really good practice." And I would say, "But you didn't play me in the game." And he would say, "It doesn't work that way."

And I would tell him, "I thought if you do it in practice, you would get a chance to do it in a game." I wanted immediate gratification. His deal was to show it over a period of time. I didn't get that. If there were any crossed hairs between us early in my career, that's where it came from.

**RICK ADELMAN:** Jack knew the players he had. Jim Paxson was an All-Star shooting guard. Jack saw the talent in Clyde, who had only played three years of college ball and was still learning how to play the game, becoming a player as well as a great athlete. He was a young player who wanted to play now.

Clyde always had a great belief in his ability. Jack saw a guy with tremendous talent who needed to work on his game. It was a situation where a coach was trying to win games, and the player was somewhat impatient to succeed in the league.

Clyde became a good shooter and great free throw shooter. All great players end up doing that. Jack saw that in him, a great athlete who only needed to hone his skills.

I still see it in players coming into the league today. They feel the games are work. If you just come in and play the game and don't worry about anything else, that's fine. That is how Clyde perceived things as a rookie. Don't get me wrong — it is pretty obvious Clyde worked at his game. But as a coach, you have to find a way to reach a guy and make him understand what he can do to become a better player. Sometimes the player's perception of what he should do and the coach's perception don't coincide. You try to get on the same plane.

Think about it. I was 20 years old. I wanted to play. And I knew from practice I could compete with my teammates. I had a lot of respect for them, but I was ready to help the team, and I knew I couldn't do that sitting on the bench. To Jack's credit, he played me every game my rookie season. There wasn't one game I didn't get in. I had a bunch of five or 10-minute performances, especially during the first half of the season, but he always got me in.

I thought I was a shooting guard from day one, or a point guard. But the way I played, it really didn't matter what position I was at. If I got a rebound, I would bring the ball downcourt. Jack wasn't okay with that. He became okay with that, but initially, he was used to guys getting the ball to the point guard. Darnell used to die laughing. "You can't just take off with the ball like that," he would say. And I responded, "Why not? I am going to go down to the other end and dunk."

Jack and I butted heads. It wasn't a real bad situation, but we had to iron things out. Sometimes he would say, "Don't do it that way. Meet me tomorrow at 7 a.m. and we will work on it."

**JACK RAMSAY:** Clyde was very athletic, but his basket-ball skills needed a lot of work. He got by on his athleticism in college, and to some extent in the NBA, too. He was just quicker and stronger and could jump higher than everyone. But he dribbled with his head down, he dribbled only with his right hand, he brought his jump shot down below his waist before he brought it up to shoot it, and he was not a good perimeter shooter.

**MYCHAL THOMPSON:** Clyde was a little inconsistent shooting the ball, but he wasn't terrible. He wasn't like the guys are today. Clyde did things his own way, different from just about everybody else, but he got them done. He had a shot kind of like Dick Barnett with the old Knicks, kicking his legs behind him.

**JACK RAMSAY:** I made him do a lot of drill work on things like coming off a screen, catching the ball and shooting it; catching the ball, showing it and driving it in both directions;  working on the post-up; working on passing out of double-teams.

Clyde didn't think he needed work on those things. He kind of resented that I made him do it. He didn't think it was necessary. After having a high level of exposure and popularity as a college player, coming into the NBA and not having immediate success was very hard on him. But he was very determined he was going to be a great player. Maybe he thought he was a great player from the beginning. I don't think he ever admitted to the things that I saw in him as shortcomings. But that was okay. That is just part of coaching. Initially, Clyde was a tough guy to coach, but he had such great athletic skills, he overcame all of his shortcomings and became a great player.

**STEVE JONES:** Jack chafed Clyde. Clyde didn't think he should be sitting on the bench — ever. In his mind, he was ready to play in the NBA from the day he arrived in Portland. He said, "I did not come out of school to sit down." But Ramsay could see all the raw skills that would make his system easier for Clyde. Clyde made some adjustments and started to understand at least what the system was. Guy Lewis liked his players to get up and down and play in the open court, and he thrived with great athletes. Jack's system was different, and Clyde had to live with it.

Right away, I was thinking I needed to be traded. After the preseason game, we had a week before the season started. I didn't get in to do much at practice. I didn't know the plays. I thought, "How can I learn the plays if I don't get in during practice?" I was pissed off that whole first week. Jack said, "You have to learn the plays."

I was a member of the second unit with guys like Fat, Audie, Lamp and Wayne Cooper. We were really competitive with that first unit, which included Thompson, Natt, Carr, Paxson and Valentine. A lot of times, the second unit would kill the first unit. To be fair, part of that is the starters would have played a lot the night before and they were tired while we were fresh.

Jack sometimes used our group together to pressure an opponent full-court in the second quarter, or early in the fourth. He wanted to speed up the game and make the opponent get tired. We had a lot of success with it. Mychal called our group the "the Jackrabbits." Somebody else came up with something even more clever: "The Blazer Press Corps."

My first NBA game was at home against the San Diego Clippers. It was a thrill to be in uniform. I was kind of in a daze, trying to be cool, when in reality I was pretty much excited out of my mind. I did okay. I played 11 minutes, made the only shot I took, scored two points and had two rebounds. And I also had three personal fouls. A little over-eager, maybe.

The next game was our first road game at Golden State, and I had a more significant role. I made the most of my 13 minutes, making three of five shots from the field, six of eight from the line for 12 points and five rebounds. I had two steals and four fouls — at this rate, I was going to set an NBA record for fouls per minutes played.

So now I am thinking I am working my way into bigger minutes, right? In our next game, at San Antonio, I played four minutes. Four minutes! Maybe Jack was sending a message; I don't know.

**JIM PAXSON:** Clyde was one of the most physically gifted athletes I have ever been around as far as athleticism, strength and build. When he came into the NBA, he was more of an athlete than a basketball player, but he was very confident. Jack was fair with him, but he demanded a lot out of him. He tried to teach him how to be a pro. It was a tough transition for Clyde. It was hard for him not to play as much as he had in college, but we saw Clyde's abilities and that he had the makings of a great NBA player.

**DARNELL VALENTINE:** Jimmy Paxson was such a professional. His game was so different from Clyde's. Jimmy's game could fit into any kind of style, because he was a great shooter and he moved so well without the ball. He didn't have to have the ball to be effective. Clyde needed the ball a little more and was incredibly athletic and creative.

Back in those days, the Blazer formula was trying to duplicate the same kind of patterns and players they had during the '77 championship team. Mychal was kind of like Bill Walton had been. Jimmy kind of moved around picks like Bobby Gross did. Kenny and Calvin were like Maurice Lucas. When Clyde came along, there wasn't a team plan and a formula that matched the kind of player he was. It was a new formula, and very soon it was he and Terry Porter, as opposed to a frontcourt-dominated system. That provided some of the impetus behind Jack moving on after the 1985-86 season. He had trouble adjusting to it.

I played double-figure minutes in the next seven games and had a couple of great performances. Against Phoenix, I went eight for 10 shooting and had 18 points, four rebounds, two assists and two steals (along with five fouls) in 22 minutes. Against Atlanta, I reached my peak up until that point in minutes played — 27 — and was seven for 10 from the field, six for nine from the line for 20 points along with three rebounds, three assists and two steals. Three games later, I was on top of my game against Denver. In only 16 minutes, I scored 20 on 10-of-13 shooting to go with six boards, three assists and two steals.

All my big games so far were in Portland's Memorial Coliseum, my home arena for the next 11 1/2 years. The fans were already taking to me. I figured it was only a matter of time before Jack saw the light and started me. I had another thing coming.

As the season moved along, my minutes were irregular. I would play 20 minutes one night, then five the next. I thought, "What do I have to do?" I would play really well most of the time. But five minutes in a whole game? I just wasn't used to that. It wasn't a good motivator as far as I was concerned. I felt if I was able to come in and disrupt practice — I mean, play so well that everyone noticed — how could Coach keep me on the bench during the game? I would get six or seven steals in practice, my team would win, and Fat would say, "He has to play you now." Next game, I would get five minutes.

**JACK RAMSAY:** That was a pretty good team. Clyde didn't like being asked to come off the bench at all. In some games where we won in a blowout, he would get in for 20 minutes. He might score 20 points, and then he expected the next game he was going to start. He couldn't understand why I didn't start him over Natt or Paxson if he did well in those kinds of games.

Jack was diplomatic. You could respect what he had to say. He would look at you through those big thick eyebrows and say, "Clyde, you know you have a couple of All-Stars [Natt and Paxson] ahead of you. I can't just put you in front of them." I said, "Why not?"

He tried to play me behind Calvin, but I wanted to handle the ball, too. I didn't care who I guarded defensively; I felt like I needed the ball in my hands. Don't get me wrong — Natt and Paxson were really good. I couldn't argue with that. That is the one thing Jack used to keep me quiet. He would say, "Which guy am I going to put on the bench?"

But I figured all three of us could start. Put me at point guard. Calvin was so strong, he would touch you and you would be sore for three weeks. Pax was so smart. He was always on the move, flashing around screens and Mychal would hit him for layup after layup. I learned a lot playing against those guys in practice and really competing. I couldn't help but learn. I got beat up and schooled and had to live and learn.

After I learned the plays, my thinking was, "Jack has to at least bump my minutes up to 20 or so a game." I knew I wouldn't be happy if I didn't play. He said, "You learn the plays and we'll go from there."

Jack kept that carrot out there for me, but I wasn't seeing a lot of time.

**DARNELL VALENTINE:** Jack tried to shoehorn Clyde's game. Jack didn't allow his players a lot of freedom. This is not an indictment against Jack or anything, because he was a very successful coach, a Hall of Fame coach. But he didn't allow for a lot of flexibility, especially individual flexibility with the kind of talent Clyde had.

**KENNY CARR:** Clyde he had a tough year coming off the bench behind Pax, but it did give him some time to develop. Clyde was a raw talent. Jack didn't change his system; you fit into it, or you didn't. Still, Clyde was impressive. Portland might have been the only team he wouldn't have started for that first year.

**DARNELL VALENTINE:** You didn't need two good eyes to see you had to utilize Clyde's ability. He came into the league as a small forward, but it was obvious he was going to be a better fit in the backcourt, because nobody could match up with him. He was still improving as a perimeter shooter, but the thing is, he could take you to the block. He was always taking defenders down low, doing a little spin move and flipping the ball up and under guys and off the glass. If he got a step on you, he was going to dunk on you. And if you laid off him, he was going to knock down his jump shot, as ugly as it was. I mean, he wasn't a shooter, he was a scorer. But he became a pretty solid shooter, too, with time.

In early December, after I started a road trip by playing five and four minutes against Kansas City and Cleveland, respectively, I approached Jack before our next game in Boston. I said, "Jack, this is not good. I practice hard every day. You have seen what I can do. I can defend anybody, I can run the break. I can even handle the ball at the point. I can play center, if you want me to."

At that point, he cracked up laughing. He couldn't help it. But I was dead serious. He saw the determination I had. He wanted to work with me. I said, "If you don't give me at least 25 or 30 minutes a game after the All-Star break, I have to ask for a trade. I want to play. I mean, people are going to think I can't play." He said, "If you show me you can do some things on the court when it counts, I will give you more time."

**DARNELL VALENTINE:** The thing that really stands out in my mind was how tremendously confident Clyde was. He was playing behind two All-Star players, Calvin and Jimmy. Every day at practice, Clyde would be there on the block, battling Calvin and Kenny. He never backed down, not one iota. Then he would challenge Dr. Jack and Stu Inman, telling them if they didn't play him and play him soon, to trade him.

**JACK RAMSAY:** Clyde did ask for a trade at one point. We were struggling through a part of the season, and I sensed some resentment among some of the players. I said, "If any of you don't want to be here, tell me."

After practice, Clyde came in and said, "I think I would like to be traded. Nothing against you, but I think I would do better somewhere else." I said, "Clyde, I am not going to trade you, because you are too good. That is not an option. We will just have to work it out, you and I." He got a little better about it after that.

**DARNELL VALENTINE:** One day at practice Clyde threw a behind-the-back pass. That wasn't a part of Jack Ramsay's philosophy about the game. In fact, that was the exact opposite of how Jack felt basketball should be played. Jack said something to Clyde about it. The very next play, Clyde came down and threw another behind-the-back pass. I mean, the rest of us all kind of looked at Clyde like, "Whoa." Nobody dared to do that with the Doctor. But Clyde had enormous self-confidence, and most of the time could back it up, and I always admired that in him. He believed in himself so much, believed so much in his abilities, that he was not going to be denied.

**WAYNE COOPER:** Jack wanted us to be serious about our layups when we shot them during pregame warmups. Clyde liked to be cool, and he would sometimes just go in and throw the ball up all fancy-like. One day Jack said, "Come on, Clyde, make the shot." Clyde smiled and said, "Come on, Chief. When I am in the game, I am automatic." We started calling Clyde "Automatic" after that.

**JIM PAXSON:** Mychal, who was always on top of everything, started that one. Pretty soon it got shortened to "Auto" or "Auto Man." Actually, I think that started in practice one day. Jack always had us do halfcourt work on offense and team defense. One team would have possession, and if you missed the shot, you went to the other end and you continued until you scored. One time,

Clyde went to the other end, and instead of making sure of a basket, he flipped it up in the air. Jack said, "Clyde, you have to finish that play." And Clyde said, "Don't worry, Coach, it's automatic."

**KENNY CARR:** It was a little tense at times between Jack and Clyde. There were times when we were walking on eggshells. Clyde thought he should be out there playing and starting right away. It wasn't all that pretty, but they got through it. In the end, it helped Clyde in his discipline and made him more humble. Maybe it was better for him to pay his dues a little bit, instead of jumping in there as the man right away.

**JACK RAMSAY:** Players like Clyde are always contentious to some degree. It is not that he would stick out in that regard, but in the NBA, you have all kinds of personalities. And as a coach, you just deal with them, that's all. While you give full consideration to what they are saying and what they want to do, your job is to determine what is best for the team. Then you just fight the battle. You may have to fight it every day.

Personally, I liked Clyde. What's not to like about the guy? He is very intelligent, gregarious, gracious, and articulate.

**MYCHAL THOMPSON:** Jack tolerated Clyde because Clyde had a good demeanor. He listened. But Clyde has his own way of playing, and Jack eventually accepted it. You can't turn Secretariat into a plowhorse. Even though Jack wanted Clyde to be a disciplined player, his talent and athleticism would make up for his mistakes. He could recover quicker than anybody his size that I ever saw play the game. He was kind of like basketball's version of Deion Sanders.

**JIM NANTZ:** Utah played 11 of its home games in Las Vegas at the Thomas & Mack Center, and one of them was against the Trail Blazers, so Clyde and I were able to get together. I saw him before the game in the layup line, we hugged and said, "Hey, let's get together after the game." We went out and hit the strip — two young kids who didn't know anything yet. We went out to Caesar's Palace and walked around, played some blackjack, and I remember Wayne Cooper hit a nickel slot machine for three grand.

**STEVE JONES:** Clyde was extremely athletic and competitive. Those are the two outstanding qualities he carried with him throughout his career. He had a different style of play than anyone who had been in Portland before he arrived. He came from a college team that ran, and Clyde played above the rim. Very few players played above the rim like Clyde. To do it on a consistent basis like he did was extraordinary.

He had great hands defensively. He was a different type of on-ball defender. It would look like he was going to get beat sometimes, and he would somehow reach around and grab the ball. It was amazing. He was a very good rebounder.

He liked winning. Whatever it took, he would find a way to accomplish it. Clyde would improvise at any moment, and the improv was what set him apart. There was never any room for improv in Jack's system, but Clyde would make his way. Ramsay knew this kid was going to be a great player.

I enjoyed my new teammates, including Mychal. He was the team's resident comedian. He would do some good impersonations of Jack on the bus. Jack wasn't aware of it, of course. Jack would have killed Mychal if he had had seen it.

**MYCHAL THOMPSON:** One thing about Clyde, in a discussion with somebody, he was never wrong about anything. I know I never heard him admit to me being right and him wrong in an argument. We called him the Shell Answer Man. He sticks by his guns. A stubborn young fella.

I was asked to participate in the dunk contest during All-Star Weekend in Denver, the first time the NBA held the event. There were some great dunkers — Dominique Wilkins, Darrell Griffith. I didn't do that well; I didn't make it out of the first round. I wasn't that good in dunk contests. I was always better in a game situation than being a show dunker, I guess. The dunk contest was fun, but my goal was to make it in the real game and prove I was an All-Star.

Larry Nance beat Julius Erving in the finals. I had met Julius in college. I knew Moses Malone from playing at Fonde Recreation Center in the summers. When the 76ers came to Houston, he introduced us and told Julius, "This guy has a little bit of you in him. He is gonna be a nice player some day."

It was fun to be around Julius that weekend in Denver. Every chance I got, I went over and talked to him. He was the guy I emulated most early in my career. If Dr. J was playing on TV, I was glued to my set.

Through the All-Star break, I averaged only about 15 minutes a game. After the All-Star break, my playing time increased to more than 20 minutes. In only one game after the break did I play fewer than double-digit minutes. I got to start three games, and in two of them I played more than 30 minutes. In a March 6 game at Kansas City, I had my rookie year-high 21 points and six rebounds — all off the offensive glass — along with three steals in 36 minutes. On March 27 against Seattle, I had 13 points, 13 rebounds and seven assists in 37 minutes. But all in all, I never did get the time I felt I deserved that season.

**DARNELL VALENTINE:** Clyde was a good teammate; he was just young. During your early years in the leagues, you mature, and he matured with his game and as a person. He was probably a much better teammate later in his career, because he was so eager to prove how good he was early on. He was looking at Michael Jordan and, the next year, watching Hakeem Olajuwon do his thing, and he wanted his time in the sun. I don't think he was a very patient person. It didn't matter that he had two All-Stars playing in front of him; he wanted it now.

We made the playoffs with a 48-34 record, but that was deceiving. We won eight in a row in late March to climb to 47-28, then floundered at the end, losing six of our last seven to finish second in the Pacific Division, six games back of the Lakers. That set us up for a first-round matchup with Phoenix, a mediocre team that was fourth in the division at 41-41.

My introduction into playoff basketball was not a happy one. We lost the opener of the five-game series 113-106 at home, then wound up losing Game 5 at home, too, to lose the series 3-2. The first four games, I played between 14 and 18 minutes and didn't make much of an impact. In Game 5, I got to play 24 minutes and contributed 12 points, 10 rebounds and three assists. But we lost, and we never should have lost to that team. It was the way things were going to go in the postseason for us, at least for awhile. But at least we made the playoffs for the second straight year. It was the start of a 21-year consecutive run of play-off appearances by the Blazers that didn't end until the 2003-04 season.

My rookie season had been very much up and down. I averaged 7.7 points and almost three rebounds in 17.7 minutes a game. Kenny Carr and I were the only players to play in all 87 regular-season and postseason games. I shot .451 from the field and .728 from the line, and I had 107 steals, third on the team despite my limited playing time.

The whole year was a learning experience. I missed almost all of training camp, so I got off to a slow start. There were good players at my position, so it wasn't like I was coming in and had a spot. I had to work my way into a position. It was more difficult than I expected, but I was willing to pay the price.

**JACK RAMSAY:** Clyde and I had a lot of encounters after I left coaching. In 1995, I was working for ESPN when he won a championship with the Rockets. I interviewed him after the final game and said, "Clyde, remember all that drill work I made you do? It was so you could have a night like this." He said, "I know that now."

# CHAPTER 9

# START ME UP

I got an apartment at Mountain Park in Lake Oswego during the summer of 1984 before my second season. A lot of the older guys on the team lived out there. It was great, but it was all about convenience. It was close to our practice sites at the Jewish Community Center and Portland Community College. It was just a place to go to change clothes and sleep and get ready for the next practice or game. I was really focusing on my craft.

I had proved to myself that I could play in the league if given the opportunity. I was more concerned now about what kind of opportunity I would have going forward. The Blazers had made one of the biggest trades in franchise history, giving up Calvin Natt, Fat Lever, Wayne Cooper and a pair of draft choices for Kiki Vandeweghe.

We all knew Kiki was a great player, but a lot of people thought we gave away too much for him. But with the players we were going to have, we had a chance to compete for a title. I was pretty excited.

Sports fans everywhere know the story of that draft. Hakeem Olajuwon and Michael Jordan both came out of college a year early. Houston and Portland had a coin flip for the No. 1 pick. The Rockets won and took my old college buddy, Hakeem. With the second pick, we took Sam Bowie, the 7'1" center from Kentucky. Chicago drafted third and chose Jordan.

Looking back, I go crazy thinking about it. Think if we had won that coin flip. We would have selected Hakeem, and the course of the franchise's future would have been changed. But we lost the flip. So it was a no-brainer to take Michael Jordan with the second pick, right? Well, somehow Sam Bowie snuck into the equation.

I understood the logic. Michael was a good player, but he and I were considered to be similar. We were both athletic, 6'6" or 6'7", and could do the same things on the basketball court. The Blazers' front office was thinking, why should we get two of the same kind of players? I remember Mychal telling me, "We don't need a seven-footer. We should have taken Jordan." But the prevailing thought was, we were a big man away from being a championship team. Sam was a very good player. The Lakers' Kareem Abdul-Jabbar was a dominant center in the West. We needed someone to neutralize him. The biggest problem was, Sam had missed two straight seasons with leg problems at Kentucky, and he wound up having an injury-plagued career. He was a great guy and wanted to play. I felt bad that he was injured so much during his career. He had a lot of desire and a lot of talent. He could pass the ball, he could really block shots and he could run the court when he was healthy. If he hadn't been hurt so often, he would have been a top-tier center.

Later in the first round of the draft, we chose Bernard Thompson, a 6'6" shooting guard out of Fresno State, with the 19th pick. That was interesting, because the Blazers knew I wanted to be traded, so I wondered if they were considering trading me for a big man. I think that was their original idea. Bernard was a left-hander who could shoot the ball. He wasn't the athlete I was, but he could shoot and he could certainly play. I wondered if they got him to kind of fill my spot on the team if I was traded.

In the second round, we chose Steve Colter, a point guard from New Mexico State. He was a good player, Jack Ramsay liked him a lot, and he wound up playing a lot and starting 22 games for us that season. The last of our three second-rounders that year, the 46th selection in the draft, was Jerome Kersey, a small forward out of Longwood (Virginia) College, an NAIA school that had been a women's institution until recently. None of us knew anything about him, but he wound up being one of the great draft picks in franchise history.

I went to the Southern California Pro Summer League, played with the guys, did everything Jack wanted. I thought, "All right, I am going to play this year." But the biggest story of the summer and early fall was the Jim Paxson situation.

Paxson had been an All-Star the previous two seasons but had just completed the final year of a contract that paid him $125,000 during that season. Jim was a great player at the top of his game, but he was underpaid and had gone through an acrimonious situation when he wanted an extension the previous season but didn't get it. He wanted a big contract, and Blazers management was balking.

So when training camp began in October, Paxson was a holdout, and I moved into his spot in the starting lineup through the preseason. I don't know what would have occurred if Paxson hadn't have held out. I do know it gave me the opportunity. I came in and started at two guard with Kiki as the starter at small forward.

Now we were running. We had Darnell pushing the ball and a real good transition game. The first three games of the preseason, I averaged more than 20 points, eight assists and seven rebounds, and people were saying, "You should have been playing more to begin with." Kiki said, "I can't see Pax starting in front of this guy when he gets back." Like Kiki said, Jack had some decisions to make, and that was the general consensus.

**KIKI VANDEWEGHE:** Clyde was a great player looking for a position. That is the way I viewed it. Initially, coach Ramsay had him behind me at small forward, which was not his position. Clyde was a two guard. When Jim Paxson held out for a new contract, it gave Clyde a chance to come in and flourish.

We played very well together. We saw basketball the same way. We were both a running type of player. We both viewed basketball as an attacking game on both offense and defense.

Before a lot of people had respect for Clyde's game, I knew what he could do. I can remember quite clearly talking to Jack, who had just traded what amounted to five players for me. I said, "Look, you need to play Clyde. He is the best player on this team." Jack looked at me like I was crazy. He said, "I just traded five players for you, and you are telling me Clyde is a better player?"

But he was. He was a unique player. Like very few other superstars, he could control the game in all aspects — defensively, offensively, the transition game, blocking shots. I saw him do it. I saw him totally take over games. I thought he was a superstar even then.

It wasn't as if Clyde and coach Ramsay didn't get along. The way I saw it, they got along pretty well.

Pax signed a six-year contract on October 15, in time for the last few preseason games.

**JIM PAXSON:** By that time, Kiki and Clyde developed a good relationship, and maybe they both thought Clyde should already be starting, but it wasn't anything that carried into the game. As Clyde's game was starting to emerge and he was becoming a better player than me, maybe I didn't like it much, but I was never jealous of him. I thought he was a great talent and a good player.

My only sense was I had signed a big contract, a six-year deal, and he was just starting to emerge as player, and he was thinking, "I am going to be better than him; I need to make that kind of money." But I never had any real issues with him. He is a pretty classy guy as far as how he handles himself. He must have had a good upbringing.

With everybody on board, we had plenty of talent. Think about it. We had Mychal Thompson, who had been the No. 1 pick in the 1978 draft. We had Sam Bowie, the No. 2 pick in the 1983 draft. Kiki averaged 22.4 points that season. Pax had been an All-Star the previous two years. Darnell was a very good point guard, just a half-step below an All-Star. With either Pax or myself, Kenny, Steve, Jerome and Audie Norris coming off the bench, that is a hell of a team.

Sam wasn't healthy to start the season. So I started the first three games of the regular season at small forward, with Darnell at the point, Pax at the two guard, Kiki at power forward and Mychal center. We were small but we could run. I had 19 points and seven rebounds in 31 minutes in the opener at Kansas City; 12 points, six rebounds and five assists in 27 minutes against Seattle; and 21 points and 10 boards against Phoenix. I was shooting better than 50 percent from the field.

Then I was back to the bench. Jack decided to start Sam, Mychal, Kiki, Pax and Darnell and tried to sell me on the sixth-man role. He told me, "I have Kiki and Pax, two All-Stars; Mychal, a great power forward, and Sam Bowie, a young center who can block shots, with Darnell at the point. You can be the spark off the bench. You could win the NBA's Sixth Man Award."

What was I supposed to say — no? I said, "All right, I will try, if we are winning. But if we start losing, try something else." That was my attitude. He said, "I promise I will try to get you 30 minutes a game."

That sounded real good. I was happy with that. I knew we had quality players. It was a strong starting lineup that didn't include me, Kenny and Jerome, who made some good contributions with pretty consistent minutes for a rookie. Kenny was very strong, very solid, and could drive to the basket like a two guard. But he got hurt and played only 48 games that year.

**KIKI VANDEWEGHE:** Sam missed only six games that year, but Kenny was out a lot. If we had both of those guys healthy, we would have been pretty interesting. They had drafted Arvydas Sabonis the previous summer, but it took years for them to sign him. Had Sabonis come in... I have always wondered how we would have done. They needed an inside presence. It was proven in 1989 when Buck Williams came in. If we'd had Buck during our years, he would have been the perfect fit for that team.

I wound up starting 42 games and played a lot of point guard that year. Pax was still one of the better shooting guards in the game, and Jack tried to find a way to play us together. I enjoyed it when we did. I had to chase some of those little guys sometimes, but it was great.

On November 24, I played against Michael Jordan for the first time as an NBA player when we played the Bulls at home. I didn't start and played only 22 minutes, but I had a decent game with 19 points and six assists in a wild 141-131 victory. Michael scored 30 points, but was only 10 of 24 from the field. He was 10 for 10 from the line, though, and also had six rebounds and eight assists. We weren't out there at the same time much and didn't guard each other, but it was the start of a rivalry that continued for almost 15 years and hit its zenith in the early '90s when the Blazers and Bulls were the two best teams in basketball.

**DARNELL VALENTINE:** Early in the careers of Jordan and Drexler, Portland was a much better team than Chicago. We had our way with the Bulls for a few years until Jordan and the Bulls began emerging. If it weren't for the fact that Clyde came along in the Jordan era, the national media would have been talking even more about Clyde Drexler. But he came along at the same time as the best player in the history of the game at his position.

There are few who ever played shooting guard who could challenge those two. I mean, Clyde was so big and strong — good grief. I have heard former teammates of Jordan say he took it as a personal challenge every time he played against Clyde. He knew Clyde was really his only peer. It would be foolish to say they didn't have some individual competition. Each was out to prove who was the superior player, though I don't think it really developed until later in their careers, when both of their teams were playing at a very high caliber.

Pax got hurt and I started seven games in late December and early January and had some monster games. In my first start at Phoenix, I went for 28 points, eight rebounds, eight assists and six steals in 44 minutes in a 110-108 loss. The next game, a 106-97 win over Golden State on Christmas Day, I played 44 minutes again and contributed 26 points, 11 boards, eight assists and three steals. In those seven games, I averaged 21 points, six rebounds, 5.4 assists and 2.6 steals.

But then Pax was back and I went back to a reserve role for the next three weeks. During that span, we went 4-7, and I was getting restless. Well, really, I was kind of pissed off. I told Jack, "I want to play more. I can help us win. I can give so much more, Jack, if you will let me start."

He said, "What do you expect me to do with Pax?" I said, "You have some decisions to make. That is your job, but I want you to know I am ready." I liked Pax, I respected his game, and it was nothing personal. Truth be told, I thought Jack should have started the two of us along with Kiki at the three perimeter positions. And a lot of times that season, the three of us were in the game together during the fourth quarter. I could pass and rebound, and Jack knew I could defend.

You have no idea how hard it was for me to come off the bench. I had started every game I had ever played since I was a junior in high school. When the game starts, I am ready to go. To have to go back to the bench and sit after warmups? Oh my goodness, it was a difficult experience. I remember one game, out of habit, I took off my warmups and got ready to take the floor and Fat came over and said, "Clyde, you aren't starting this game. Relax."

**KENNY CARR:** Paxson was an All-Star, but Clyde's talent shone through. You couldn't keep him on the bench any longer. He blossomed so quickly. You could see he had the athletic ability, and on top of that, he knew how to play. He had good basketball sense. He made a lot of things happen on the court, and we started running more. We were quicker at the guard positions now. Jerome came in that season, and then Terry Porter the next year, and they started building that team for the early '90s run at a title.

**RON CULP:** Clyde took a brutal fall in a game in New York. He went up for a dunk and was undercut, and it was a vicious collision with the floor. We carried him off the floor in a stretcher and transported him via ambulance to Lennox Hill Hospital. Clyde never stopped talking to me the whole time until we got to the hospital. I was to tell Jack he could go back in the game, he was ready to play, he was okay. He had such a severe concussion, he wasn't totally aware of what was going on.

We made it to the emergency room, and Clyde was finally [knocked] out. We had Dr. Cook on the phone back in Portland, and Clyde woke up and said, "Ron, what are we doing here? What's going on?" It was probably a good half-hour after we arrived at the hospital, and he didn't have a clue where we were.

He was a pretty sore puppy. He had hurt his knee and his back, too. He was mad he missed the rest of the game — he had 25 points and 12 rebounds before he got injured in the third quarter. He missed the next game but returned to action after that. Clyde was just a competitor. He competed at every level, in every aspect of the game.

**STEVE JONES:** The one thing I always marveled at about Clyde was his belief in himself. It really crystallized for me after that game in New York. Clyde tried to dunk the ball,  got knocked down and fell hard to the court. He was a guy who always wanted to bounce right back up after getting knocked down; he never wanted people to know he was hurt. This time he laid there for awhile, had a deep cut on his head, and everybody was concerned about him. The next time we talked, I told him, "Clyde, you can't always jump over everybody." He responded, "Why not?" I said, "You saw what happened to you." He said, "I take what I want." The very next game, he got a similar opportunity and went in with the same determination and dunked. I mean, wow.

**GEORGE GERVIN:** When I was with San Antonio, every time we went up to Portland when Clyde was with the Blazers, they had a great team and we had to come ready to play to beat them. Clyde dunked on me quite a few times when we played against them. He became one of the dominant big guards to come into the league after guys like Magic, myself and Dennis Johnson. He showed he had the confidence to compete. That was the key. He had a lot of confidence when he came into the league. That is what made him the player he was — that confidence in his ability. And he was a great athlete. I loved him because he loved to pass before he would shoot. That was an important aspect of the game, and it showed that he loved basketball. That guy, man, he would pass up a layup to give somebody else a layup. That is what made him special in my eyes.

He was a big-shot shooter. He didn't mind taking that last shot that would beat you. And if it didn't go in, it wasn't something he would sulk over. That is where that confidence comes in. He felt he could make big shots,

and he did over the years. That combined with his drive
to win was important to his success.

I was starting to become a close friend to Kiki. He became
like a brother to me. We were both single. We were both gym rats.
We developed a lot of common interests. After practice, we would
get something to eat and hang out. A lot of times we would go to
RiverPlace Athletic Club and get in another workout, a massage,
maybe take an exercise class. It was a daily routine when the
Blazers were at home. On the road, we would have dinner together, maybe catch a movie.

**DARNELL VALENTINE:** Kiki was really conservative, a
down-to-earth but very connected person. Everybody
respected Kiki. He and Clyde became like partners.

**BOB COOK:** I remember some referred to them as Rexler
and Vaneweghe — no "D" in either one of them. That
wasn't really true, with Clyde at least. They were just so
spectacular at the offensive end, people missed the other
parts of their game.

**STEVE JONES:** They were the NBA's odd couple. You
would have never thought they would be lifelong friends,
let alone that they might be able to coexist on the same
floor. They were both offensive players, but Kiki was
more of a traditional fundamental jump shooter. Clyde
was whatever it takes. As quiet as Kiki was, he liked winning. That was the bond for them. They both liked winning.

Clyde had never been a really outspoken person. Off the
court, Clyde was kind of quiet, went his own way, had his
own thoughts. Kiki was much the same way. In those

days, you would never have suspected Kiki would become a very good general manager, because he never said anything. Clyde didn't say a lot of things other than the obvious, either. For the record, he was always going to say the right thing for the right reason. That is what endeared him to his teammates. Clyde could be real hard on people, but in public he was never going to take any teammate apart.

Kiki was just a great guy. His teammate in Denver, Rob Williams, had played with me in college. Rob and I would talk on the phone and he would say, "This Kiki V, he is the baddest white boy you will ever see. This dude can play." Rob was worse than Charles Barkley — he would say anything. He said, "Kiki will kick anyone's rear end."

I knew Kiki was a hell of a player. He was so efficient as an offensive player. He was versatile. A great passer. He shot 55 percent, had good range and was one of the best foul shooters in the game. He was also a very underrated dunker. He had a lot of hop, and with those big hands he was always dunking on guys. He could do most of the things I did, and we both loved the running style of play. We had given up a lot to get him, but I thought it was worth it. He could put up a lot of points in a hurry.

**KIKI VANDEWEGHE:** I got to know Clyde through Rob Williams, and I liked him a lot. Clyde is one of the most honest guys that I have met in my life, and he could really play basketball, which I respected.

I respected him as an individual, too. When I came to Portland, he was one of the few guys on the team who didn't hold anything against me. I was traded for three

Portland players, some very popular guys on that team. All those guys missed their friends. He was one of the few guys who said, "You can play; let's go play." Clyde sought me out, and welcomed me. We hit it off.

We played a lot of basketball together. That was initially our common interest. We spent a lot of time together, not necessarily at the official practices, but at the RiverPlace Athletic Club. We would go there at night, in the mornings, before practice. We would shoot, play one-on-one or horse, talk, just enjoy each other.

**BUCKY BUCKWALTER:** Clyde made himself into a shooter. The guy who really helped him was Kiki. Clyde always felt he was a good shooter. He would always say that. You would talk to him about working on it, and he would say, "Nah." Kiki finally convinced him he needed to improve his shooting, and one summer Kiki and Geoff Petrie worked with him, and Clyde came back a much better shooter.

To be a good shooter, you just have to shoot more. I did work on it. I shot more jumpers that summer. As a result, I became a more efficient shooter. But I never looked at myself as a guy who was going to stand around and just shoot open jumpers. I was the kind of player who was always moving. I was a playmaker and I was setting up the shooters. I never had the luxury of being out there spotted up, waiting for the ball to arrive.

**BUCKY BUCKWALTER:** Clyde was a real competitor. His need to win was very important. A lot of guys could have gotten by with their athleticism, but he worked on different parts of his game. He was a wonderful passer and became a decent shooter. It was a need to be as good as anybody.

Julius Erving was his hero. When you were talking to Clyde about improving his game, you would try to slip in Dr. J to motivate him. He wanted to be like Julius.

I started on February 2 against Milwaukee, collecting 17 points and nine assists in 39 minutes. Then I came off the bench for two more games before moving into a starting role that I never again relinquished. I started the last 32 regular-season games and all nine games in the postseason.

**JACK RAMSAY:** Clyde went out and just earned that starting spot. Listen, he was already among the best two-guards in the league. He had become a very good passer. He was somewhat unorthodox, but he could see the floor. If somebody was open, he would find a way to get him the ball. And he was very, very competitive.

**JIM PAXSON:** In the NBA, you have to earn your minutes. The better players play. Jack wasn't going to play guys because they were his favorite; he would play you if he thought you could help him win. I ended up coming off the bench at some point that year. That is the nature of the business.

After Paxson moved into the sixth-man role, Mychal started calling him "Wally Pipp."

**JIM PAXSON:** Nothing against Kiki, but I thought we had a different type of team before we made the trade. Management felt they needed another scorer with me. After that trade, we weren't as tough as we were before. But it wasn't a Clyde vs. Jim Paxson issue. It was more the dynamics of our team had changed.

I was asked to be a participant in the dunk contest at All-Star Weekend again. I finished last — Dominique beat Michael in the finals — but it was still fun just to be there. I was hoping to make the real game pretty soon, though.

In the 32 regular-season starts at the end of the season, I scored in double figures 30 times and scored 20 or more points 14 times. On February 24, I had my best game to date, going for 37 points, 10 rebounds, nine assists and three steals in a 137-121 win over San Antonio. On March 1, I had my first career triple-double, getting 19 points, 10 rebounds and 10 assists in a 111-109 loss. I would get 21 triple-doubles during my time with Portland, a franchise record. Sidney Wicks and Terry Porter are tied for second with seven apiece.

In the final regular-season game against Denver, I was in a zone. I made 14 of 18 shots from the floor and seven of eight from the line en route to a 35-point night. It was a great way to roll into the playoffs on a high.

We matched up against Dallas in a best-of-five first-round playoff series. We finished 42-40 and were fifth in the West. The Mavericks finished 44-38 in fourth place, so they had home-court advantage. They had Mark Aguirre, a small forward who averaged 25.7 points and could score on anyone, a nifty point guard in Brad Davis, two of the league's top five three-point shooters in Davis and Dale Ellis, one of the game's best young shooting guards in Rolando Blackman, and Sam Perkins inside. We lost the opener in a wild one, 139-131, but came back to win three straight and advance to the second round. I played well in my first playoff series as a starter, showing consistency with scoring games of 18, 19, 20 and 18. I averaged 18.8 points, 7.3 rebounds, 9.3 assists and 2.0 steals in the four games. My best average, however, was 40.5 minutes. I went the route in the opener. It felt good. Kiki was awesome in that series and showed why he was worth the five-player trade.

Then it was on to the dreaded Lakers and the Western Conference semifinals. They had won the season series 5-1, but we felt we were getting closer. In the final two games, we beat them 116-113 in overtime on March 26 at our place; less than two weeks later, they beat us 135-133 in overtime at the Forum.

They were still an intimidating presence, with all the key components of the team that had lost in seven games to Boston for the NBA title the year before. With Kareem Abdul-Jabbar, Magic Johnson and James Worthy, they were the heavy favorites.

L.A. won the first three games of the series. We came back to win Game 4 at home 115-107, but they closed us out with a 139-120 rout at the Forum and our season was done. The Lakers went on to get revenge against the Celtics, beating them in six games to claim the NBA crown.

I had a terrible game in the opener of the Laker series, making one of 10 shots and finishing with four points, five rebounds and four assists in 19 minutes. I played pretty well in the final four games, averaging 17.8 points, 5.3 rebounds and 10.0 assists. Jack was making sure the ball was in my hands quite a bit, and I was producing. I think I showed in that series that I could play Portland's style of ball against the best team in the league. People were saying, "The Blazers have to make Drexler the center point of that team and build around him."

All around, it was a successful season. In my last 26 games, I averaged 18.9 points, 7.3 rebounds and 7.7 assists. I finished eighth in the league in steals with 2.21 per game. I more than doubled my season averages from my rookie year for scoring (17.2), rebounds (5.9) and assists (5.5). I had improved my shooting percentages, on field goals (.494 up from .451) and free throws (.759 up from .728). And I averaged 32 minutes a game, which was more to my liking. Even though we were bounced out in the second round, things were looking up.

# CHAPTER 10

# COMING INTO
# MY OWN

During the summer before the 1985-86 season, I signed a two-year contract extension. It gave me a little security, and Blazers management liked it because it tied me up through 1988.

I was working out at a gym in Houston in the late spring when I did something that would affect my entire third season with the Blazers. I was lifting weights with my legs — apparently too much weight — when I heard something pop in my left leg. It hurt like heck. I went to see Dr. Bob Cook, the Blazers' team doctor for 20 years and through all but the last half-season of my time in Portland. He said it was a stress fracture of the fibula.

Just what I needed. It was strange, though. I didn't have to have surgery or a cast put on it. I don't even remember laying off it for a major period of time. I quit lifting weights for awhile, but I could run okay. The doctor gave me this bone-stimulating machine that was supposed to speed the healing process. I slept with that thing strapped to my leg all summer. It made a loud humming noise, which made it harder to get to sleep. But anybody who knows me understands that a purring machine is not going to keep me from catching a few Zs.

**BOB COOK:** The machine is fairly standard treatment for healing stress fractures or traumatic fractures as a means of augmenting the healing process. Since Clyde was never sidelined, he probably stopped short of actually rupturing the bone. Sometimes the associated tendinitis would give lingering symptoms long after the bone has healed. He wasn't playing with a totally broken bone, but with a stress facture. If a pro athlete can gut it out, so to speak, he can play through it.

By the time training camp started in October, it was better but not 100 percent. Running was fine. If I tried to plant and jump, there was pain. I had to alter my game significantly because of the injury. I didn't do a whole lot of dunks early that season. I was staying grounded, because if I jumped, it hurt.

I didn't make it an issue with the coaches. I wanted to play. So I played that season under doctor's supervision. Bob said I wouldn't injure my leg further by playing. He said it would heal over time, but that it might take a year or two. And it did.

It was funny the way things evolved. I couldn't jump without some pain, so I attempted fewer dunks. And the party line was, "Clyde has settled down. Clyde is more mature. He is more under control." Not really. I just had to play on the ground more because of the leg. Most of my dunks that season were with the left hand, because I could jump off the right leg.

**BOB COOK:** I scoped Clyde's knee twice, the first time after the 1992 Olympic Games and then again in 1996, when he was playing for the Rockets.

I just felt comfortable with Dr. Cook, so I had him do the surgery when I was with Houston, too. He was an expert surgeon, and I also learned a lot from him about nutrition and health habits that helped to prolong my career. After my first surgery, I would meet him in the morning or evening and he would run with me. He is a salt-of-the-earth guy, one of my very good friends.

**BOB COOK:** After a surgery or injury, Clyde was always eager to get back and play. He never had a physical complaint before a game, like a lot of guys would. "That's an excuse for failure," he would say. He never played the injury card, and I always admired that. He would never come off the court and say a sore knee was affecting his play. That is increasingly rare amongst NBA athletes. He was tough as an alligator.

I didn't have to go to summer league that summer. I worked out on my own, and I made sure that I got my workout in every day. By the time the season began, I had bought a house in Mountain Park. It was time. I wanted to get an investment going. It was a 4,000 square-foot, four-bedroom home that had a great view of the city. It cost $160,000, and I thought I had hit the big time.

The Blazers were the same team with two exceptions: We added veteran forward/center Caldwell Jones, and we drafted Terry Porter with the 23rd pick of the first round. Like Jerome Kersey the year before, it would prove to be one of the very best draft selections in the history of the franchise.

**TERRY PORTER:** My rookie year was a blur, in part because I was so much in awe of Clyde because of his days at the University of Houston. I found myself watching what he did in practice, to see how he handled himself. He was one of the most competitive guys I had ever been around. It didn't matter what he was doing; he was determined to be the best he could be.

At first, he wasn't that much of an outside shooter. Even in his later years, he got it done, but it was that line drive, imperfect jump shot. But it was an area of his game that he needed to improve to reach that top level as a player, and he was always willing to do what it took. His drive to be successful was his best trait. And of course, his athleticism was sensational. He was so big, 6'7" and 230 — there weren't many guards like that. He was also strong, so he could outmuscle most guys he went up against.

**CALDWELL JONES:** That was actually a pretty good team. We were on the brink of coming together, but we still had a few pieces missing. Clyde was a high-energy guy with a ton of talent who could play both ends of the floor. The game came easy to him. He could score, he could shoot from the outside, he could post up the smaller guards. Coach Ramsay, and later Mike Schuler, both ran a lot of post-ups and isolations for him down low, and he was able to take advantage of that. He did a good job of improving his shooting percentage each year. He worked on that. He wanted to be a complete player.

I was able to play, but my leg wasn't right and my game wasn't, either. I had some big games but some bad ones, too, and I wasn't able to play a ton of minutes. On November 17, in our 13th game of the season, I had 24 points, 10 assists and six rebounds in a loss to Milwaukee. I sat out the next six games.

When I came back, I was better — not 100 percent, but better. I gradually got my health and my game back together.

On January 10, I came as close as I came in my career to a quadruple-double. I had 26 points, 11 assists, 10 steals and nine rebounds. Usually steals is the category that is hardest to get into double figures.

**RON CULP:** Clyde was a time management challenge. He was Superman. He could leap tall buildings and stop speeding locomotives and miss flights regularly. But he always came to play. He always had what I thought was a sleepy demeanor. Not disinterested, but a kind of, "Don't worry about this, we'll get it done." I honestly believe he was always surprised when we didn't win. He just left it all out there on the floor.

**JACK RAMSAY:** Clyde was often late. He had a lot of tardies on his record, but very few absences.

**JEROME KERSEY:** Clyde was a little late sometimes, but almost always, he eventually got there.

**BOB COOK:** Clyde was usually the last guy on the bus. If we were playing golf, he was the last guy to the first tee. He came up with his shoes untied. We always refer to it as "Clyde time."

**RON CULP:** I never remember Clyde making an excuse on the basketball court. I can never remember him saying, "I got screened" or "I got fouled and they didn't call it." I can remember him saying, "It didn't work. The shot didn't go in."

He is right up there with the best players I have ever worked with. I have the utmost respect for his game, how he played the game, and for the quality of person he is. I have less respect for how he managed his time, however.

I was never late. At the same time, I was never early. If the bus was to leave at 11, I would get there at 10:59 and 30 seconds. That was my mindset when I was a player because I was always so tired. I would try to get as much rest as possible, squeeze out those extra 10 minutes.

**STEVE JONES:** I can say a lot of things about Clyde. Was he a great practice player? No. Was he always on time? No. But any time the game started, he wanted desperately to win. His style was, if you don't want to do it, get out of the way and I will do it. A lot of times it looked like he was playing out of control, trying to do too much. I did the radio talk show in those days, and callers were saying, "This guy is never going to make it; he tries to do too much." But that was his nature. "If you didn't want to step up, step back and I will do it," was Clyde's philosophy. If that meant taking a bad shot, his thought was, "Fair enough, because I believe my bad shot is better than your good shot."

You know how many times he started that corkscrew spin to the basket, and everybody was saying, "Oh no, what is this?" But he would always make it. That was the most amazing thing about him. It didn't make any difference who he was playing with. He felt he was the leader, and his attitude was, "We are going to win the game."

**HARRY GLICKMAN:** This will sound crazy. I am not much of a ballet fan, but nobody ever did a pirouette to the basket like Clyde did. It was something to behold.

**STEVE JONES:** By his third year with Portland, he had become the leader. There was a little resistence to Clyde, that he couldn't make his teammates better. But he could do things other players couldn't do.

**KENNY CARR:** Clyde was already beginning to lose his hair. I used to pick at him. I would bring a bag with me to practice or to the airport. He would say, "What's in that?" I would say, "Your hair." I told him, "It's only a matter of time before you don't have any at all."

By the time I was 22 or 23, my hair was starting to thin. I didn't really lose it until about '92. In the Dream Team pictures, I still had hair. I didn't go all the way bald until '93. That's when I shaved my head and quit fighting it.

**JIM PAXSON:** We went into Boston in December to play one of the best Celtics teams, a team that would go on to win 67 games and the NBA championship. The Celtics went 40-1 at the Boston Garden that year — and we beat them 121-103. Clyde scored only 19 points in that game, but he was just dominant in the second half, making some unbelievably athletic plays. With Clyde, it was a matter of learning the NBA game and how to use his athletic ability, because early on we knew he had a chance to be a special player.

We were red-hot that night against Boston. Jerome and Steve Colter had big games. We were just running by the Celtics. We must have caught them on a bad night. It was our claim to fame for the year.

I made the All-Star team for the first time this season. I had been in the dunk contest the previous two years, but to make the real game was a thrill. The game was in Dallas. All of my family came for the game. It was a great event. Imagine, I went from being a center in high school to an All-Star guard. It was quite a dramatic turn.

Playing in an All-Star Game with the guys I had grown up watching—and had a lot of respect for—was a dream come true. I didn't get to wear my No. 22, though. Rolando Blackman was also 22 and they went by seniority. It didn't matter; I was just happy to be there. I played 15 minutes and put up good numbers, hitting five of seven shots and collecting 10 points, four rebounds, four assists and three steals.

**KIKI VANDEWEGHE:** Clyde was a great teammate. The measure of a great player is you never worry about him in big games. He comes to play. You never worried with Clyde if he was going to play well that night, or at least try to. You never worried about any of that stuff. You knew he was going to bring it every single night once he stepped on the court.

**CALDWELL JONES:** Clyde would play in spurts during practice, like most of the guys. He was so much better than everyone else, he didn't have to play that hard. He could coast sometimes. And he would get bored in practice. But he enoyed the game, the competition against other players.

**MYCHAL THOMPSON:** As a player, Clyde could go anywhere and do anything on the court. He was just a notch below Michael Jordan in athleticism, and that is saying a lot. Actually, Jordan might have been a more polished player, but as an athlete, Clyde was just as good or even better. He could play any sport and do anything required of him on the basketball court.

**STEVE JONES:** Clyde loved to play games. Any game. No matter what game it was, he always thought he could win. Even if he lost, he would say, "Nah, you didn't beat me." Any game that he picked up, he would get into it and swear that he was the best at it. Even though he might be real bad, he was going to be better. I played him quite a bit in tennis; he still can't beat me. But had Clyde put the same amount of work into tennis as a high school kid as he did in basketball, he would have made a terrific pro. He had size, he had quickness, he could jump. The men's tennis tour would have never been the same if Clyde had played the sport as a young man, because he had all the athletic gifts that make you a fantastic player. And the bottom line is, he was a true competitor.

I can't beat Steve Jones in tennis? Probably not that he can remember. His memory is getting shorter as he gets older. He was a pretty good player, though. It just kills him that I never acknowledged the fact that he owns me in tennis. I know I beat him in golf quite often.

**CALDWELL JONES:** During the 1985-86 season, we played Dallas and Clyde had 41 points, 15 assists and eight rebounds. He was doing everything — dunking, offensive rebounding, making flashy passes for a layup.

He just had it going. When he was like that — in a zone — it was a joy to watch. He always enjoyed playing against the Mavericks because of Rolando Blackman. And, of course, against Michael Jordan and the Bulls. He relished that. Competing with the best shooting guards, he looked forward to it. He wanted to display his skills and let everyone know he was in the same class as those guys.

I enjoyed my four years playing with Clyde. He pushed everybody else. He wanted to win. It was like, "Come on, we can beat these guys." He was that kind of leader. You could always see that competitive fire in his eyes.

**MYCHAL THOMPSON:** Clyde was always so cool. Unflappable. Nothing got to him. He always reminded me of the lead singer of Kool and the Gang. They looked alike and had the same sort of temperament. Nothing flustered Clyde, unless it was the sight of Jake O'Donnell with a whistle on the basketball court.

Clyde was one of the professional athletes who understood and accepted his role. He understood his place on the team and in the community. He and Magic Johnson were the two most accessible superstars I was ever around. Anybody could come up to either of them — any place, any time — and they would both take the time to treat that person respectfully and make them feel welcome. Clyde and Magic should write a textbook for NBA players on how to deal with the fans.

Clyde is the fourth best player I played with behind Kareem, Magic and James Worthy. James is probably the most underrated great player in history. Look at it this way: We had Kareem and Magic, and Worthy was nor-

mally our No. 1 option on offense. You put great back-
courts out there, you start with Michael Jordan and
Magic, then Jerry West and Oscar Robertson. For the
third team, you could make a case for Clyde and Isiah
Thomas. At least you're not crazy if you throw those two
guys in there.

**JACK RAMSAY:** Clyde was always swimming against the
current because he played at the same time as Michael
Jordan. Michael was a better player, and Clyde was
always compared to Michael. So Clyde had that battle to
fight. He is certainly among the best players I have
coached. Of the guys I had, I would put him in a lineup
with Bill Walton, Maurice Lucas, Billy Cunningham and
Hal Greer. That would be an exceptional starting lineup
against anybody.

We had a meltdown at the end of the 1985-86 regular season. We lost 12 straight games to fall to 29-34, then finished at
40-42 on the season, 22 games behind the Lakers. Sam Bowie
was out for a spell and we lost a ton of close games. I was still trying to figure out my role and how to fit in with what Jack wanted me to do. We played poorly in the playoffs and lost to Denver.
That Nuggets team was led by such players as Calvin Natt, Fat
Lever and Wayne Cooper — guys we had traded to Denver in the
deal that brought us Kiki. They played out of their minds, especially Calvin and Fat. They were determined to let Blazers management know they had made a mistake.

After the season, the Blazers made an important trade, sending Mychal Thompson to San Antonio for Steve Johnson. Steve
had played his college ball down the road at Oregon State and
was a terrific inside scorer and one of the best percentage shooters in NBA history. He was probably the last guy in the game
other than Kareem Abdul-Jabbar to shoot a true skyhook.

I not only lost one of my favorite teammates in Mychal, I also lost my first NBA coach. The Blazers fired Jack after a 10-year run as the team's coach.

**JACK RAMSAY:** We had a rash of injuries — it wasn't just Bowie — and a tough road schedule. But I didn't feel good about the way the season turned out. I didn't think I did a good job coaching the team. The Nuggets were good, but I felt we should have beaten them.

After the last playoff game, Larry Weinberg came into the locker room. At one point, I was in the trainer's room by myself. Larry came in, we chatted a little, and he said, "You know, I may want to change coaches." I said, "Larry, that is your prerogative. In fact, I'm not sure I would want to stay here, anyway."

The Portland years were a great period of time for me. I liked the city and the people. At the beginning, it was still a small organization. There were a few key staff people like Harry, Stu, George Rickles and then three or four others in the office. It was a very congenial group, a family. As time went by during the 10 years I was there, it grew into a large business organization. It lost its closeness with the new employees who came in. A lot of things kind of spilled into my area — the promotions people, the business people, "marketing genius" Jon Spoelstra... it wasn't the same atmosphere. People were kind of interjecting their business into my business. There were people working for us who were doing statistical analysis and trying to tell me which players to use. I didn't like that.

On May 28, 1986, they named Mike Schuler as Jack's replacement. Mike had been an assistant coach under Larry Brown in New Jersey and Don Nelson in Milwaukee prior to coming to Portland, but we knew each other from way back.

**STEVE JOHNSON:** Clyde is a very loyal person. And if you crossed him, he has a very long memory. Something happened with him and Mike Schuler at Rice, and he never forgot it.

Schuler had been the head coach at Rice from 1977-81, which was in the Southwest Conference. We had played against him my freshman season at Houston.

Rice was a school Guy Lewis loved to beat. Guy had attended Rice for a short time before transferring to Houston as an undergraduate in the '40s, so he saw it as a special game. We had tough games with Rice my freshman year but beat them both times. The year before, my senior year in high school, I remember watching on TV as Rice upset Houston on the Owls' home court. Afterward, Schuler was running around the court, yelling, "We beat them!" as if they had won the national championship. The next year, Guy showed us that tape about 1,000 times. That was all the motivation we needed. We knew Guy wanted to cream them.

So Mike knew about me and I knew about him, but I really didn't know a thing about his coaching style or what he would bring to the table in Portland. As it turned out, he opened up the offense, which was a good thing. Mike retained Rick Adelman as an assistant coach and hired on Jack Schalow as an assistant coach and chief scout, which were also good things. Jack was one of the most positive, supportive assistant coaches I ever had. He was with you every step of the way.

Even so, there were some turbulent waters ahead.

# CHAPTER 11

# MARRIAGE, AND THE RIGHT COACH

**A**fter wearing Kangaroos the first few years of my career, I switched to Avia beginning with the 1986-87 season. The representative I dealt with from Avia was Tim Haney.

**TIM HANEY:** When I was sports marketing director at Avia, we were a major sponsor of the Blazers. We signed Clyde, and I was there to do a lot of things with him. He never had anybody step in to handle any of his business negotiations with us. We negotiated the business points of his deals with him directly.

Clyde was always a little contrary. He got an offer from Nike, but didn't want to be in the same shoes as everybody else. Plus, he was a dollars and cents guy, and we made the best offer. He had been wearing the Kangaroo shoes; nobody else was wearing those. When he switched to Avia, we spent a lot of time together as we were shoot-ing commercials or doing camps. I took the initiative of going to his home at Military Drive, picking him up, doing the event with him and taking him home.

Over the years, I have worked with a lot of pro athletes, and he was the only guy I became friends with. He was by far the best guy I dealt with. People don't remember Avia. We had three Dream Teamers — Scottie Pippen, John Stockton and Drexler — along with about 40 other players that season. The other two became so pricey, they moved on to Nike. We kept Clyde. I think he liked being our only guy.

Clyde was a different breed. He was the easiest guy to deal with in endorsement situations. He understood what our expectations were. He followed through on clinics and camps and appearances. We weren't making him a bazillionnaire. But when he said he was going to do something, he did it. We did a kids' basketball camp for years in northeast Portland. Most pro athletes with their name on camps show up the last day. Clyde showed up Monday morning and he stayed all day every day through the week. He was out there teaching kids, and it was great to watch. There would be adults trying to get to him during that week, but he made sure that didn't get in the way of his responsibility to the kids. He was really good that way.

It was amazing how good he was with the public. We ran a reading program for kids, called BASIC, and he was the spokesperson. I would get him out of bed and drive him down there, still groggy. As soon as we opened the door to a roomful of kids, his face brightened and it was like,

"Hi kids. How are you?" He would answer every question, take every picture and give every autograph until I was the bad guy who got him out of there. People were mesmerized.

It is important to have a presence in your community and to give back. I wanted to get to know the people. They support what I do. I don't care what anybody says, a pro athlete is going to be a role model. I tried to use that as a positive influence, to let kids know we are regular people. They can do the same thing we are doing if they do the right things and continue to work hard. I always felt it was my civic responsibility to try to do good, to touch the lives of the children, and maybe some adults, in my community.

**JEROME KERSEY:** Clyde got a fair amount of attention when he was out in public, but it wasn't like it was with Jordan — unless we were in Houston. Then it was like the president had arrived. But normally, he didn't have to sneak out the back door of a hotel or restaurant. He was very cordial to fans, and graceful — always graceful. At games, he would sign autographs and talk with the fans. He was the consummate professional.

I spent my summer traveling between Los Angeles, Las Vegas, New York and Houston, a couple of weeks at a time in each place. It was a chance to experience life in different cities. When I was in L.A., I would stay with Kiki. When I was in Houston, I would play ball every day at Fonde Recreation Center.

I was never a big disco guy, but I would go out with the guys, go to dinner, and maybe go somewhere afterward. L.A. was a good singles town. You could have a lot of fun. I took out some starlets, but I am not going to mention any names here. When I was young and single, I was in the experimentation stage. I got to discover what I liked and didn't like in women. I liked beautiful girls, and I am not going to lie like some guys and tell you that I was celibate.

**TIM HANEY:** I was down in L.A. a lot when Clyde was spending a lot of his summers there, hanging out with Magic Johnson a lot. I am not going to tell any secrets. All I will say is the good times were had by all.

But if I was going to get up and work out the next day, I couldn't stay up all night. I have always been a guy who likes to sleep in. In the summers, I would sleep until 11 a.m. or so. I remember staying at the Vandeweghe's house. They would all be gone by the time I woke up.

The next year, I became a father for the first time. Erica Drexler was born in Houston. I had known her mother for a couple of years and began seeing her when I split up with my girlfriend, but we were not dating seriously. It was quite a shock when I learned she was going to have a baby. As it turned out, it was one of the best things that has happened in my life. I got a wonderful daughter from the relationship.

For the first seven or eight years of Erica's life, we saw little of each other. When I was in Houston to play against the Rockets, her mother would bring her to a game and I would get to hang out with her a little. But I was literally afraid to see her, never knowing what was going to happen. There were hard feelings between her mother and me over her continued efforts to obtain more child support. Of course, that should have had nothing to do with my relationship with my little girl, and I regret that now.

In 1994, about a year before I was traded from Portland to Houston, her mother and I became conversational again. All I wanted to do was see my daughter and not be in court every year. By this time, I was married — Gaynell and I wed in 1988 — and Erica began coming to stay with us, to take vacations with us, and so on. Gaynell has been an excellent stepmother to Erica. She includes Erica in everything our family does if she is with us, and she's very encouraging and supportive.

Erica just graduated from East High School and is a unique young lady. She's a little like I was as a teenager. She does what she is supposed to do. I love her dearly. No headaches, just a good kid.

I had plenty of headaches ahead of me that basketball season, though. Mike Schuler looked at our talent before his first season as head coach and decided we were not going to beat anybody up physically. If we were going to win, we were going to outrun opponents like a bunch of greyhounds.

We had young colts in Jerome Kersey and Terry Porter — Jerome in his third year, Terry in his second. We had Steve Johnson in the middle. When we posted up, we went to Steve, who was in his prime and I thought was our team MVP that season. We still had Kenny Carr, and we had Kiki and me out on the wings running. Everything was more up-tempo. By this time, I was strictly a two guard, and I played the most minutes on the team. Terry started at the point. He was young, but he was ready.

This was the style of offense I was born to play. We used our defense to create offense. We would get a turnover or rebound and take off to the other end. If we didn't get a basket off the fast break, we would set it up, go inside to Steve and see what he could do. Talk about triple-threat offense. With Kiki, Steve and me, we could score in a lot of ways. Jerome and Terry were both becoming terrific players and giving us a lot of energy.

**STEVE JOHNSON:** I was excited about the makeup of the team. We had a good young point guard in Terry, great scoring from a lot of spots, outside shooting with Kiki and the athleticism of Clyde. We had a lot of talent. The thing we were missing was a power forward. During the 1986-87 season, with Kenny Carr hurt most of the time, our power forwards were Caldwell Jones and Fernando Martin. If we had a better power forward, we could have been a very good team. As an undersized center, I needed a strong power forward alongside me.

When we were playing Houston, for instance, we could compete with them, but they had Hakeem Olajuwon, Ralph Sampson and Jim Petersen rotating inside. We had no answer. We acquired Kevin Duckworth that season, but Duck and I had similar games. We were offensive players, not great rebounders or defenders. Once the Blazers got Buck Williams in 1989, that was the final piece. Buck gave them all the things they needed — rebounding, strong defense, all the dirty work.

Kiki and Steve were the guys I spent the most time with off the floor.

**STEVE JOHNSON:** We hung out quite a bit. Clyde, Kiki and I weren't partiers or late-night people. We were always kind of low-profile. Movies and dinner on the road. Clyde and I would play video games — "Karate Champ," for instance. When the guy got knocked out, a $1,000 graphic would appear over his head. We played that game for hours. Or we would go to the movies. A couple of times, we would be the only ones in the theater. It must have been either an afternoon showing or a horrible movie.

Steve is Stu Inman's son-in-law. He and his wife, Janice, would have me over to their home for dinner quite often.

They are a great family, and Steve was a class guy and super teammate. We did have fun playing Karate Champ. We took turns knocking each other out. We used to have tournaments while playing that game — too much time on our hands on the road, I guess.

We started the season 0-4, then won 22 of the next 32 to get into the thick of the race for the Pacific Division title. In December, we made one of the great trades in the history of the franchise. We sent Walter Berry to San Antonio for Kevin Duckworth.

Berry didn't play much for us, but he was a player. He came to us from St. John's as the College Player of the Year, and whenever he got in during practice, he would do things that would make you think, "Wow, this kid can play." He had the misfortune of coming along when we already had a guy named Jerome at small forward.

Berry arrived in Portland before training camp, we were waiting to see how good he was. In one of his first practices, he drove the lane, switched the ball and reverse dunked with about three guys trying to block his shot. It let you know he had big-time talent. But Walter wasn't much of the mind to come off the bench, and he and Schuler didn't get along so well. And soon he was gone. Walter had one pretty good year with the Spurs before going to Europe and fading out of sight. If he had gone to the right team, he could have been awesome.

Duck was big and too heavy at 300 pounds, but he had a lot of good post moves. He was seven feet tall, had some serious talent and was very effective at using both hands with jump hooks. He had post moves and could hit the short jumper with precision. And he ran the court pretty well for a big guy. We were thinking, if we can just get this guy in shape... and the next year, he slimmed down, won the Most Improved Player Award, got the big contract and became a bona fide starting center.

It was a good thing, because we lost Sam Bowie to a fractured tibia in the fifth game of the season. He was gone all season. It was frustrating, because we were thinking one of these years, Sam was going to stay healthy and we were going to realize our full potential. We needed a big guy to compete against players like Kareem, Hakeem and Ralph Sampson. Steve Johnson was devastating around the basket, but he was only 6'10" and not much of a shot blocker.

The first season, when we were watching video or going over scouting reports, we would ask Schuler, "Coach, how should we play this?" His favorite phrase was, "Can't tell you that." He could have told us, but he wanted us to figure it out on our own. We used to laugh about it so hard. But it made some sense, because it made us think.

But the next year, after he won the NBA's Coach of the Year award the previous season, things went sour. All of a sudden, he was a guru. He had a plan for everything. He didn't need us to figure things out on our own any more.

**STEVE JOHNSON:** Schuler became really controlling. He tried to dictate everything. We were viewing tape one day and on the tape Clyde had lost his man. Schuler was asking, "Clyde, what happened here?" Clyde kept denying he had done anything wrong. Mike rewound it backward and played it over again and again. Finally Clyde said, "I don't care what that tape shows; I didn't do that."

**JACK SCHALOW:** Most great players are not easy to coach. They never think they take a bad shot. Maybe Mike would say, "We are taking some bad shots," and Clyde was the one he was talking about, and it would tick Clyde off.

**STEVE JOHNSON:** Before games, each player was asked to give a scouting report on the guy he was guarding. Clyde and Kiki would say the same thing every night. I don't care if they were going against Larry Smith or Larry Bird, the report was the same: "Good player, works hard, got to box him out, just don't let him have a big night." They were kind of rebelling against Schuler in a mild way.

Eventually, it became a problem. We went from a team where Mike put us in a system and left the system up to us to one where he tried to control everything. He sat up nights watching tape on the VCR, and the next day would try to tell us how to do everything. He wore on the players. Schuler ended up being his own worst enemy.

**JACK SCHALOW:** Mike was a coach who wanted to control a lot of the offense and defense, especially the offense. Clyde liked to just play. "Let's just play," he would say. Mike was more controlling, and Clyde just didn't like it. With Mike, it was, "You are going to do it this way."

The main problem I had with Schuler: We would play four games in five nights, and on the off day he wanted to have a two-hour practice. I was playing big minutes, and midway through an NBA season, my body is fatigued. I couldn't keep up that rigorous schedule, playing all those games and practicing my ass off, too. I asked him, "Do you want me now, or do you want me during the games?" He wasn't too forgiving. He would say, "I want you for both." That was the only rift we ever had. I would come to practice in sandals, grab a newspaper and put some ice on my ankle. The look on his face was priceless. The players would start snickering and talking to each other, saying, "Watch this, a showdown."

Mike would come over and say, "You can't practice like the rest of us?" I would say, "Mike, I could, but I don't think it would be beneficial." He would say, "Your teammates are out there. Don't you feel like you should be out there, too?" I would say, "Not the starters. Half of these guys didn't hardly play the last four games. Let them go at it with you."

Mike's style was to pit guys against each other. He used a couple of hustlers to make you look bad, because those guys were hustling at practice. That is not the right way to do it. We are all teammates. Don't do it just for the sake of practice. That was his biggest downfall.

Mike promoted team unity. He was a rah-rah guy and wanted everybody else to be a rah-rah guy. He liked guys who hustled in practice. I say that's all well and good, but let's bring that to the game. Don't do it just in practice and not in games. When I practiced, I played hard. But if it is the only day off in a period of four games in five days, you are not going to get much out of me. I had to guard the toughest guy, rebound, run the lanes on the fast break, set people up and score. I played my ass off. I think most people would tell you that.

I don't mean to sound like a prima donna here. I don't want to take away from the team concept. At training camp, in the preseason, during the periods in the season when we had some down time, I practiced as hard as anybody. But Mike clearly didn't understand when a guy is putting in big minutes, he can't continue to work him that hard, especially in March and April. Every coach in the NBA understands that concept now.

If I keep sleeping through my alarm clock, my body is trying to tell me something. I was always the kind of guy who would listen to his body. If I couldn't move the next day, I had to let the coach know. As a coach, Mike needed to find a way to get his starters some rest so they could stay healthy. He was pretty much uncompromising in that area. Rick Adelman saw all this and learned a lot that would benefit him during what would turn out to be a very successful career as a head coach in the NBA.

There was one other thing that bothered me about Schuler. Sometimes at the end of close games, if we were down one or two points with the last possession and the game on the line, he would try to surprise an opponent by calling a play for someone like Richard Anderson or Caldwell Jones — good players, but they didn't want the ball at that time in the game. They would say, "Drex, come get the ball."

Now I was stuck between a rock and a hard place. I wanted the ball, but the play wasn't called for me. If I got it, and we didn't score, I'd get blamed because I didn't follow the play. But my thinking was, we've either got to get it to me, to a good shooter or to someone in a good shooting rhythm at the time in order to give ourselves a chance to win. If we lost that game, I might hold it against him for weeks just for making that call. It happened three or four times that season, and I was really pissed off about that. As a result I might be late for the bus the next morning, or maybe not show up at all. And I probably wouldn't talk to him for a week or two. It was an immature, rebellious act because of what had happened the night before.

**JEROME KERSEY:** I got my break from Schuler, but I don't put that as a premise for liking him as a coach. Mike was a guy who wanted players to earn playing time through working hard in practice. That wasn't Clyde's cup of tea. He always said, "I know what I can do. You know what I can do. Why would I kill myself in practice?" I couldn't play any other way but 100 percent. Terry was much like me. We brought game nights to practice.

Schuler wanted everyone to practice hard, and he was more confrontational about it than Rick would be. With

Mike, everything was basketball. He lived and breathed it 24 hours a day. If we went out to dinner, he would always want to talk basketball. He didn't even know who the president of the United States was.

**DWIGHT JAYNES:** I was the Blazers beat writer for *The Oregonian* during the Schuler years. Mike used to brag about his devotion to basketball. If I tried to steer the conversation away from basketball he would say things like, "Dwight, I don't have any idea what Watergate is. I can't pay that any attention. I don't have time for that."

**MIKE SCHULER:** You have to understand, I was very excited to be a head coach in the NBA. When I look back on it, coaching the Trail Blazers of that era was a piece of cake compared to coaching the players of today. In my head coaching career, I never experienced anything like the difficulties of what NBA coaches go through today.

**DWIGHT JAYNES:** After he left Portland, Mike became an assistant coach in Minnesota during the time J.R. Rider played for the Timberwolves. Mike told me, "I used to think Clyde was a tough guy to coach. By today's standards, he is a choir boy."

**MIKE SCHULER:** I have told people, if I were going to coach Clyde today, it would be like coaching Jesus. It would be a piece of cake.

Mike and I had a little rift at midseason. After making the All-Star Game the previous season under Jack Ramsay, I didn't make it this time, and Mike didn't speak up for me. Coaches vote on the seven reserves from both the Western and Eastern

Conference teams, and typically a coach will lobby for his deserv-
ing players. All my statistics were better at midseason this year
than they had been the previous year except assists, and that figure was very close. I was averaging better than 21 points a game,
shooting better than 50 percent and had numbers comparable to
any guard in the league. But I was told by a very good source that
Mike had said something negative about me.

It didn't bother me not to make the team; it bothered me
that my coach didn't say something positive on my behalf. I went
to Mike and told him, "If you have something to say about me,
say it to my face. No need to talk behind someone's back." Of
course, he denied it, and it was over. I was professional about it.
He was entitled to his opinion. Kiki didn't make the All-Star
team, either, despite averaging more than 25 points a game. And
it wasn't as if we were a bad team. We were 30-19 at the All-Star
break that season. Mike just wasn't going to promote his guys.

I did participate in the dunk contest, and this time I made
the semifinals. I was figuring out a little bit about what the judges
liked. Michael beat my teammate and buddy, Jerome, in the
finals.

We finished the season 49-33, but we were better than that.
We had a lot of close losses. We were 34-7 at home, and we finished second in the Pacific behind the Lakers again. But we
weren't good enough to beat the elites — or even the also-rans.
We certainly weren't good enough to beat Houston in the first
round. The Rockets had Hakeem and Ralph Sampson, the Twin
Towers, but had finished only 42-40 in the regular season. Part of
that was Sampson was injured and played only 43 games. Ralph
was available for the playoffs, though, and Hakeem was overpowering. The Rockets beat us in Portland in the opener and eliminated us 3-1 in the best-of-five series.

Still, we had made strides. We had transformed ourselves
from a team that had no identity to one on the verge of great

things. I averaged career highs in scoring (21.7) and rebounds (6.3) along with 6.9 assists and ranked fifth in the league in steals. I figured a lot of good things were ahead.

We improved to a 53-win team in 1987-88, tying Dallas for the third best record in the West. Unfortunately, we were still looking up at the Lakers, and they were pretty much invincible, it seemed. They finished 62-20 and wound up beating Detroit for the championship in seven games.

We could have challenged them if we had stayed healthy, but that didn't happen. Kiki hurt his back and was able to play only 37 games. He was still very good when he was able to play, averaging 20.2 points and giving us pop off the bench after Jerome moved into the starting lineup. Jerome had a terrific year and averaged 19.2 points, the highest scoring average of his 16-year NBA career.

We also added Maurice Lucas, the veteran enforcer who gave us some muscle off the bench.

**MAURICE LUCAS:** That was a tough year for us. We had all that talent in place, and we actually should have won something. It was not good for coach Schuler to have that on his resume.

If we had everybody healthy, we were pretty imposing. But Steve Johnson got hurt, too, and played only 43 games. What it meant was we were missing both Kiki and Steve for about half the season. And Sam Bowie never played all year due to complications from his injury the previous season.

Fortunately, Kevin Duckworth emerged quickly as our starting center and did a marvelous job, averaging 15.8 points and 7.3 rebounds and earning the Most Improved Player Award. And in his second year as our starting point guard, Terry Porter

**What a gentleman!** That's me on the right escorting Jayne Kennedy, one of the first female sportscasters hired by CBS, when she visited Sterling High School as a guest speaker in 1980. My teammate and friend, Will Blackmon, is on the left.

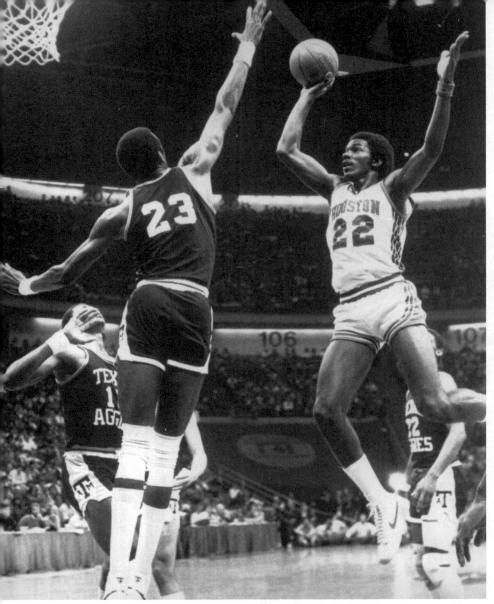

During my three years as a Cougar, my nickname
**"The Glide"** became a permanent addition thanks to
then-public address announcer Jim Nantz. Sure beats
my original nickname, "Windex."

AP/WWP

Attending the University of Houston and playing for Coach Guy Lewis shaped me into the consummate competitor I am today. In the **NCAA Tournament Final Four** in 1982, we nearly beat an amazing North Carolina team that featured Michael Jordan (23), Matt Doherty (44), James Worthy and Sam Perkins. In the end, my 17 points and nine rebounds weren't quite enough to carry us to the NCAA championship game, which North Carolina won.

**Watch your head!** Doing what I did best against the rival Lakers in 1988. During the 1988-89 season, I set my career-best scoring average of 27.2 points per game.

During my days as a Blazer, Magic Johnson and the Lakers

were always **our No. 1 rival** and a road block to the Finals.

As a Trail Blazer, **Houston homecomings** were always something to look forward to. Little did I know I would eventually call Houston my home team once again.

Nathaniel S. Butler/NBAE/Getty Images

**Hakeem and I were reunited** as All-Star Game teammates

a few times before I was traded to Houston. Here we are

in 1992.

**Coming at ya!** Over the course of my career, I was a 10-time All-Star, including eight times as a Trail Blazer, an Olympic Gold Medalist and one of the 50 Greatest Players in NBA History.

I made a few new friends during my time with the original

**Olympic Dream Team,** photographed in Barcelona, Spain

in 1996.

**Some of the best teammates I could ask for:** (left to right) Jerome Kersey, Terry Porter, Kevin Duckworth, and me. Along with Buck Williams, Cliff Robinson, and Danny Ainge, we gave the Lakers and the rest of the NBA all that they could handle during the 1989-90, 1990-91, and 1991-92 seasons.

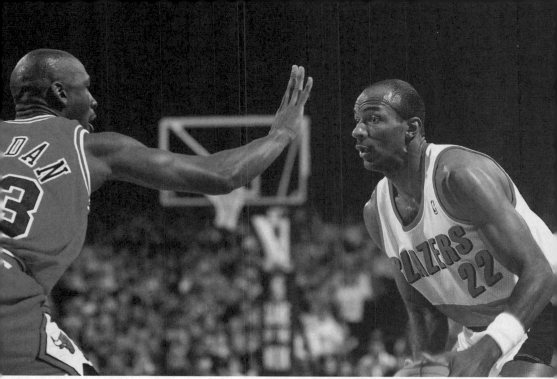

The media loved to play up **Michael Jordan vs.
Clyde Drexler,** and we did our part in making sure
the duels were unforgettable. But we all know it
takes 12 players to win a game.

**Finally—a champion!** Hakeem and I celebrate after we swept the Orlando Magic for my first championship in 1995. It was the second of back-to-back titles for the Rockets.

**Changing of the guard:** Old school meets new school as I squared off against Kobe Bryant and the new Lakers dynasty during my final season.

Coming back to the University of Houston to coach after my NBA retirement brought me full-circle in more ways than one. I got the opportunity to coach Gee Gervin, the

son of George Gervin, whom I had idolized as a young basketball player. Here we are in my **first victory as head coach,** a 71-69 win over Texas at Hofheinz Pavillion.

Since I first met **Julius Erving,** the player whom I most admired growing up, he has become a wonderful friend of mine.

**Thanks to the NBA Legends Tour,** I got a chance to hang out with some of my childhood heroes, including Moses Malone, center, and George Gervin, right.

**My mother, Eunice Drexler Scott,** means the world to me. She blessed my life by always showing me the right way.

Me and my 18-year-old daughter Erica, a unique young lady and a great daughter.

My wife Gaynell, daughter Elise, 13, and sons Austin, 14, and Adam, 11.

took a significant step forward with his game, too. Blazers fans look back and recognize this season as the start of the nucleus that carried us to a pair of Western Conference championships in the early '90s. It was the point where Duck, Terry, Jerome and I began our time together.

**KEVIN DUCKWORTH:** Every week, Clyde would do something that would surprise you. There would be times when the game was close at the end, and Clyde would make a turnover at a crucial moment. "Dang, we lost." And he would usually turn right around and make up for it in some way.

That year, we were down by five or six points with less than a minute to go in Seattle. Schuler took the starters out of the game, and Clyde told him, "Man, don't take us out. We can still win this game." That is when I realized the game isn't over until the clock shows zero. There were a lot of times when we would be down by seven or eight and Clyde and Terry would hit back-to-back threes and we would be right back in it. We came back and won that game in Seattle.

With Steve and Kiki out, Mike asked me to carry more of the offensive load. That worked out well. I averaged 27.0 points and was still able to shoot better than 50 percent from the field and 80 percent from the line. And I was improving as an outside threat.

**STEVE JOHNSON:** Clyde did get better at perimeter shooting. When I first got to Portland, he still relied a lot on his athleticism. It was funny. He had all those whirling moves to the hoop. He would do one of them, get caught up in the air, and then have to pass. His comment to whomever he wound up trying to throw the ball to was, "Concentrate, MF." He would get up in the air and throw it, then be mad at you because you weren't ready when he passed you the ball.

I made it back to the All-Star Game, as a player in the game itself and also in the dunk contest. I finished third behind Michael and Dominique in the dunk competition. In the All-Star Game, I was three of five from the field, six of six from the line and had 12 points and five rebounds in 15 minutes.

Our 53-29 record that season was the franchise's best since 1977-78, the year after the championship team. I was sixth in the league in scoring at 27.0 points a game and fifth in steals at 2.5 per contest. I was also fifth in voting for the NBA's Most Valuable Player award.

**PATRICK EWING:** Rick Pitino was our coach that season, and we did a lot of trapping. Against the Blazers, every time they knew the trap was coming, Clyde would take it to the basket and I would try to block his shot. He kept telling me, "I'm gonna get you." This one time the Blazers came down and Clyde came in, and I jumped to make a block, and he did a spin and he dunked it on me, and he said, "I told you I was going to get you."

We went into the first round of the playoffs holding the home-court advantage over Utah, which had gone 47-35 and was in the beginning stages of the Karl Malone-John Stockton era. After handling them 108-96 in the opener — I had 26 points, 13 boards, six assists and three steals — we lost three straight and were ousted again in the first round.

Through my first four years in the NBA, I had won one playoff series. But the tide was turning.

In May of 1988, our ownership changed hands, from Larry Weinberg to Paul Allen. Larry was a very good owner who cared about his players and the city of Portland. He always wanted to do the right thing. He and his wife, Barbie, are two of the nicest people in the world.

When I heard Larry was going to sell the team, I was concerned about the kind of owner that would replace him. The tone of a franchise is set at the top.

Paul Allen was one of the world's richest men, parlaying the large fortune he had as co-founder of Microsoft into a variety of businesses and enterprises, most of them linked to digital communications and the wired world. He was also a huge basketball fan who lived in Seattle and had held Sonics season tickets for several years.

I didn't know much about him at first other than he had made a ton of money. The first time I met him, he was really cordial and cool. I liked him right away. You could tell he had a passion for the game. Paul did a very good job of setting the tone and letting everyone know that all he wanted to do was win. He gave us resources, and he never missed a game. He was right there, front and center. I had a lot of respect for him because of that. Paul also saw something in Geoff Petrie, an original Blazers great who was now doing radio analyst work with Bill Schonely in addition to helping out as a shooting coach. Geoff gradually moved into the front office and became an important decision maker for the franchise.

**PAUL ALLEN:** When I was a new owner, I didn't know the ropes with the players, and I was a little slow in getting to know most of them. Clyde and I just hit it off and had a rapport about certain things.

In addition to the changes within the Blazers, it was also a year of change for me personally. I married the love of my life, Gaynell, whom I met on a blind date in New York set up by Andy Thompson, Mychal's brother. Andy used to live in Portland and was now living in New York and working for NBA Entertainment. Andy said, "This friend of mine is from the South like you, from Baton Rouge, Louisiana. When you get to town, I am going to have you go out with her. She is an attorney and all she does is work. She needs a good time."

Andy was going to double-date with us, but had to go away on business. I called her, we talked for awhile and agreed to meet, despite Andy being out of town. We went to a Mexican restaurant in New Jersey after our game against the Nets. It was a cordial, friendly get-together.

Gaynell is the baby of seven children in her family — five girls, two boys. Her father, Eugene Floyd, is deceased. Her mother, Geraldine Floyd, lives in Natches, Mississippi. She is a very sweet lady and a good grandmother. Gaynell graduated from Spelman College in Atlanta with a degree in political science, then got her law degree at Howard University in Washington, D.C. She was practicing corporate law in New York when we met. She was a quality person, smart, fun to be around, and good-looking — that didn't hurt.

We kept in touch, and our relationship became more and more serious. We spent most of the summer together, taking a trip to Europe, visiting Italy, Spain and France before stopping in the Bahamas. You get to know people well in a situation like that. We had a great time and I was convinced we were right for each other.

**GAYNELL DREXLER:** Clyde and I seemed to have a lot in common. He was a very down-to-earth person, easy to get along with. There was a sweetness about him. He didn't seem to be all ego. Because of his southern roots, I could identify with him a lot better than I could with men from the East Coast. He was very generous and liked to have fun.

I proposed in October and we got married on December 30 in New Orleans. I looked at the Blazers' schedule and saw we had a six-day break around New Year's. We picked the date, and I didn't have to miss a game. I missed a couple of practices, but Rick was understanding. Kiki flew down for the wedding.

My third game as a married man, I hung 50 points on Sacramento, a career high and just one short of Geoff Petrie's franchise record of 51.

Two weeks later, I scored 48 points against the Knicks. I guess marriage really does enhance a career. To be honest, though, the week before I got married, I had games of 43, 38 and 35 points. Kiki was hurt and the team really needed my scoring. Plus, I was in a pretty good groove.

Schuler was back for his third season, and he had added John Wetzel as an assistant coach. Wetzel had been the head coach in Phoenix the previous season.

**JOHN WETZEL:** When I first met Clyde, he was very cordial. The thing that struck me about him was that he was always so polite to the wives and girlfriends and those around the team. He was every bit the gentleman. He really impressed me that way. A lot of the players today barely speak to their own wives, much less those of their teammates.

After winning 53 games, I thought we would build on that success during the 1988-89 season, possibly win 60 or more games and challenge the Lakers, who were the toast of the league. With the emergence of Terry, Jerome and Duck and me entering my prime, I figured we were ready to take the next step.

Then the season started. Sam Bowie was injured again and was able to give us only 20 games. Steve Johnson had become a bench guy because of bone spurs in both of his ankles and gave us 15 to 20 minutes of offense behind Duck every night.

I had become tired of Mike nagging at me. At one point early in the season, I told him, "I come to play every night. Why do you keep harping at me?" He would find something. He was a perfectionist. I know he had some valid points, but he just went too far.

The team had a larger concern, though. We still had Kiki, whom I expected to give us more than he had the previous season. But Jerome had taken the starting small forward job, and Kiki had asked for a trade during the summer. His back was still hurting, and Mike didn't insert him into the rotation right away when he was healthy enough to play. There was a major controversy over who should be playing. It was tough on me, because Kiki was one of my closest friends, but Jerome had become a good friend, too. They were both good guys who were nice to each other but were competing for playing time.

**JEROME KERSEY:** I never felt any friction between Clyde and myself. When I came in as a rookie, Clyde took me under his wing. One time we were asked to take part in a fashion show for charity. I didn't have any suits, so he gave me a suit. He had like 20 suits in his closet. And he said, "Just keep it. Don't worry about bringing it back." I think I still have it somewhere.

But Clyde had developed a friendship with Kiki, and they probably thought they were going to play together a long time. There was almost a division — myself and Kevin and Terry against Clyde and Kiki. At least that is the way it was portrayed.

It never really was like that. We were all good friends. It was one of those situations where all you can do is keep playing and let the cards fall as they may. Starting jobs and playing time are up to the coach. Jerome was playing extremely well. He thrived in Schuler's up-tempo game. He played great defense, he hustled, he blocked shots from the weak side, he was a good finisher on the break and he was the hustle guy Schuler liked. Kiki was still an extremely dangerous offensive weapon, though. He could shoot, he had one of the quickest first steps in the game and he was one of the most efficient offensive players I have ever been around.

But Kiki was unhappy and wanted a trade. He felt like Schuler didn't want him there. We flew up to owner Paul Allen's mansion in Bellevue, Washington, to discuss the situation. I was there in support of Kiki. It became a discussion about Schuler. When a team doesn't win, there is always a problem. Our team was hovering around .500, but the biggest problem we had was Mike's relationship with some of his players.

**PAUL ALLEN:** There had been some friction between Clyde and Kiki and Mike, and Clyde and Kiki wanted to talk about it. So they flew up and came to my home and we talked. It was clear the chemistry was not right. Mike was an old-school coach. He had coached at Army. Clyde and Kiki were more like, "Hey, let us freelance a little bit." As things stood, the team wasn't accomplishing what we all hoped they would accomplish.

On their way out of my home they noticed this outdoor hoop I had. They asked, "Do you have a ball?" And we got one and played a game of horse. My shooting was a little better back then, and I made a few threes, and I think they let me win.

Paul won fair and square. In fact, he is undefeated against me. I want a rematch, because I don't think he could do it again.

**PAUL ALLEN:** Yeah, yeah, yeah. At the time I was sure I had won on my own, but now I am not so sure.

Then it got late and it started to rain a little bit, and the court was slippery. Then Clyde said, "I have to dunk." And he told Kiki to lob him a pass at the rim. I had no idea what was going to happen. And Clyde ran in and jumped what seemed like five feet over the basket and dunked it. It was over in a second, and I gasped. He had such incredible hops. And I could just see him breaking a leg on my home court.

**KIKI VANDEWEGHE:** I thought Mike was a good coach. He knew his stuff. Mike had a view of basketball, and it wasn't the exact same view that Clyde had. It wasn't the exact same view that I had either, quite honestly. It made it difficult. All I can say is, regardless of what Clyde thought, he played some pretty darn good basketball for Mike Schuler.

**GEOFF PETRIE:** Mike and Clyde were different guys who saw basketball a different way. But Clyde competed when the ball was thrown up, regardless of who was coaching him.

**MIKE SCHULER:** A lot of the problems I had with Clyde, I brought on myself. He once told me my expectations of him were way too high. I had been an assistant coach in New Jersey when Buck Williams was there, then had been an assistant coach in Milwaukee before I got to Portland. When I left the Bucks, I left as good a group of people as I had ever been around. I assumed every situation was going to be like that. In Milwaukee, we never, ever had a bad practice. Sidney Moncrief refused to let that happen.

**TERRY PORTER:** Mike had a picture in his mind of what a superstar should be like, based on coaching Sid Moncrief in Milwaukee. Clyde was not in that mold. Was Clyde a superstar? Yes. But he was a different type of player than Mike had seen. Mike struggled with that and Clyde struggled with what he should do. Mike had issues at times when Clyde didn't practice. That was a coach/player conflict I stayed away from.

**MIKE SCHULER:** Every situation is different. I think about how Clyde and I didn't get along. The thing I have asked myself many times is what could I have done differently to change the situation? I had expectations of the whole group based upon where I came from. Clyde was a very productive player for me. I don't know if we could have ever won more games than we did if I had done things differently. I had expectations of going further in the playoffs than we did, and that probably led to my downfall as much as anything.

Clyde was such a talented player and athlete. Every night, you could count on him to be very productive. I can't remember a night where he didn't play and compete as hard as he could. He was like a lot of guys. He didn't always double-team when you wanted him to, didn't always switch when you wanted him to, didn't make every shot he took and all of those things, but he had tremendous pride. He never wanted to be embarrassed.

Today you have players to whom being embarrassed is no big deal.

I zero in on the fact that Portland was a great experience for me. I am very proud of the things we accomplished. I wish we had won more games, but I established a lot of great relationships. I have no hard feelings about anyone I worked with in Portland. I see Kiki and it is like he is my long-lost friend. He has always said very nice things about me. When Terry Porter became head coach at Milwaukee, he hired me to be his assistant. Maybe that speaks to the fact I am not as bad a guy as a lot of people thought.

Would I go back and coach Clyde Drexler again? Absolutely, and I would do a much better job.

Mike knew the game and was a real intense guy. I know I wasn't perfect as a player, and I made some mistakes. But I always had good intentions. My goal was always to help the team win games.

**RICK ADELMAN:** It was Mike's first job as an NBA head coach, and he had in his mind the way he wanted the game played, the way he wanted players to practice and to go about doing things. Clyde and Mike didn't see eye to eye. There wasn't a lot of give and take between the two. They were two strong-willed people who got off on the wrong foot. Things went fine when we were playing well, but as soon as we had a problem with the team, there was always that friction in the air. Mike learned a lot during that time with Clyde, and in the long run, maybe Clyde learned, too, that there are other ways to do things.

Mike had done some great things. He opened up the offense, made us a better defensive team, and developed some young players. But his style wore thin on a few of us. We needed a change.

I made the All-Star Game again that year and had 14 points, 12 rebounds and four assists in 25 minutes. I also took part in my final dunk contest, finishing second to New York's Kenny "Sky" Walker. It was time to turn the dunk competition over to younger legs.

At the All-Star break, Kiki was traded to New York for a first-round draft pick. Ironically, the trade came five days after we made a coaching change.

I had been averaging almost 40 minutes a game. I was so tired, my body was shutting down. One day we had a 10 a.m. practice on the road and I overslept. I was about 15 minutes late for the bus. Mike had a conniption fit. We had a private discussion, and he was going on and on about it, saying I had no respect, no this and that. I told him, "Play me 20 to 25 minutes a game, I will feel better, I will make the bus on time every time, and I will practice as hard as anyone you have." He said, "That is not going to happen," and added a few stronger words in response. I said, "Well, shut up, then."

About that time, Bert Kolde — his title was vice chairman, but basically he was Paul's right-hand man — took a road trip with us to get a sense about what was going on with Schuler and the players. At one point he asked me who I thought should take over the team if Schuler was fired. I said, "Rick Adelman is a former player, he has been here for several years, he knows the system, he knows the players, everybody loves him, he would be great." I have no idea if that had anything to do with the decision. For all I knew, Paul figured it out himself.

**PAUL ALLEN:** Bert came back with the feeling that Rick was the right guy, had a good rapport with the players and knew what he was doing.

It was an absolutely great choice. I had good feelings about Rick. He understood the game and he understood people. He was able to take some of the good things about Schuler and eliminate some of the bad. He was more relaxed, and he knew you couldn't wear out your guys who were playing big minutes.

We were 25-22 when Rick took over the team and finished 39-43, meaning we were only 14-21 under Rick. We were real streaky — win four in a row, lose eight of nine, win six of seven, lose four in a row. I finished the regular season with back-to-back 40-point games, against the Lakers and Sacramento. That gave me a regular-season scoring average of 27.2, fourth in the league. It would be my career-high for a season. I also was fifth in the league in steals with a career-best 2.73 a game. Not bad for a guy who never made an All-Defensive Team.

We needed to beat the Kings to make the playoffs, and we got past them at home, 126-120. I played 50 minutes and had 40 points, 10 assists and eight rebounds.

So we kept our playoff streak alive, but as the West's No. 8 seed, that earned us a first-round date with our old nemesis, the Lakers. They swept us in three games. I did all I could, averaging 27.8 points, but they had too many horses for us.

It would be the last time the Blazers would be also-rans in the playoffs for a few years.

# CHAPTER 12

# NBA FINALS, HERE WE COME

The summer after the 1988-89 season, I was mentally drained and disappointed we had lost in the first round again. Being a competitive guy, I wanted to play in the NBA Finals. My main goal during my career was to win a championship. I was thinking about a trade again. I wanted to be traded to a team that had a chance to do something. I told Harry Glickman and Bucky Buckwalter before I went home to Houston that summer, "We have to get some real players in here. We have had to work too hard to lose in the first round every year."

It was frustrating. The last thing I said was, "Whatever you do, get a power forward." We were hurting in that department. We had good players, guys like Mark Bryant and Caldwell Jones, but they were guys who would have helped more coming off the bench. When we played against the better power forwards like Karl Malone, we were in trouble. We needed to have someone who could guard someone like Malone.

Then on June 24, two days after my 27th birthday, word came that we had traded Sam Bowie to New Jersey for Buck Williams. I don't remember where I was when I heard the news, but I was the happiest man on the planet that day. I was saying, "We are going to miss Sam, I hope it goes well in New Jersey, but Buck is a great acquisition. Now we have a complete starting five." He fit our team perfectly. The minute we got him, I knew we were at another level.

**BUCKY BUCKWALTER:** One of the things that helped Clyde's development was Buck Williams. When Buck came to the team, the two of them clearly had a mutual respect. Buck was all business. Practices and game preparation were important. Being teammates elevated both players, and it certainly helped Clyde and the team in focusing on preparation.

**BUCK WILLIAMS:** My introduction to Clyde happened on a ride to Portland from Salem during training camp. He was driving a little sports car that some car dealership had loaned him.

It was a blue Toyota Supra—stick shift. We're two big guys in a little Supra.

**BUCK WILLIAMS:** We were getting to know each other better, talking about the upcoming season, his experiences with the Blazers, and a whole list of other things. Then we started talking about his expectations for the team and how I rounded the team out, how I made the team much better. And he was starting to get into it, looking at me while he was driving. I was getting kind of nervous, because he was driving fast and not looking at the road. And he was not one of the best drivers in the world. He was having a little trouble shifting this car he had only had for about a month.

So we were cruising down Interstate 5, and he said, "Buck, we are going to win the NBA title with you. I have been telling them to get you for a long time. You are going to be the best power forward in the West." I was thinking, "This guy is crazy." His expectations were off the charts. I was coming from New Jersey, where we had won 26 games the previous year and had gotten past the first round of the playoffs once in my eight years there. And here was Clyde going on about winning a championship.

I picked Buck up at his hotel for the 45-minute drive to Salem. We knew each other a little already. I had talked to him at All-Star games. He was a classy guy, young and athletic. I was introducing Buck to the city of Portland and the team. We talked some real estate. And then we got on the subject of basketball. Suddenly, I was like a little kid.

I know the other components we had. Duckworth was a top-rated center. Jerome had worked so hard that he was now a premier young small forward. Terry was nearing All-Star status as a point guard. The final ingredient was Buck, capable of 18 points and 10 rebounds a night. I was telling him he was the final piece to our puzzle. Every position in our starting five was filled by an All-Star-caliber player. As we were talking, it was the most excited I had been in my NBA career.

**BUCK WILLIAMS:** That is the way Clyde has been since I have known him. He expects the most and best out of everyone, but most of all, from himself. Sometimes he gets in trouble, because everyone can't play basketball like Clyde Drexler. But his mentality has always been, "We are going to do what we want to do. We are going to beat you."

Rick came to camp for his first full season as coach with only a year on his contract. The unspoken directive from Paul Allen: Win now. Rick had retained Jack and John as his assistants. Geoff Petrie had moved into a management position and was helping Harry and Bucky make personnel decisions. The previous two seasons, I had averaged 27 points a game and taken a lot of shots. Rick talked to me that summer and said, "Clyde, you don't have to do everything this year. We are going to cut down on your shots, let you do a little less, give you a little more rest so you will be healthier and fresher for the playoffs. You don't have to carry the team like you did the past couple of years. You can just play your game." I was all for it.

**GEOFF PETRIE:** Rick and I talked to him about doing more things. We wanted to put him down at the post some and let him pass out of there. He did that, and his scoring went down some, but it made us a better team. Guys would come and double-team him down there, and the ball was out of there in a flash. Plus, he was an incredible rebounder for a guy at his position, so having him on the block more often made sense.

**RICK ADELMAN:** I saw the way things had developed between Clyde and Mike and, to a lesser degree, Jack Ramsay. I knew Clyde was one who you had to try to reach in a way where he would go out and perform without having to try to dominate him. He didn't respond to public criticism very well. He liked to play the game and not be under a lot of restrictions. When I took over, I just tried to go to the strengths he had on the court. It's like that with a lot of players. If they feel they are being used the right way, they respond in a positive way.

Once Clyde sensed the quality of the players he had around him, he really bought into the fact that he didn't have to score 27 points a game. He realized he could score 23 and get his six or seven assists and rebounds and we were going to be a very good team. Clyde realized he was going to get more credit by winning than if he scored more points. He was the anchor for that team.

**JACK SCHALOW:** When Rick took the job, he told his assistants, "I am going to meet with Clyde whenever we are talking about trades. I am going to go through Clyde and ask him what he thinks, because he is going to win for us. Maybe he will take a few bad shots like a lot of guys, but he is going to win a heck of a lot more games than he will lose." Rick did a fantastic job with Clyde, but he did that with all the players. Terry and Jerome could play for anybody, but they really thrived under Rick.

**JEROME KERSEY:** Under Ramsay and Schuler, Clyde would practice, but his attitude was like, "I'm a baller when the game comes," and he was able to do that and still play at a high level. When we went a notch up as a team, Clyde was consistently at practice and going full hard at it. And we got better. No one can duplicate what Clyde could do at practice. You could build some continuity as a team with him leading you. Rick gave him a lot of rest, but he always stayed sharp. He was able to not practice the day before, then come to the shootaround and score 28 or 30 that night.

**GEOFF PETRIE:** Clyde would always practice if Rick wanted him to, but sometimes he wasn't really into it. We would say, "Clyde, we need you for 30 minutes today." And he was good about that.

**JACK SCHALOW:** Clyde's feeling was, when a guy could produce like he can, why make a big deal out of it?

In preseason practices, he was really good. He busted his tail. All of those guys did. But during the season, Rick let a lot of the starters out of practice. They would have to show up, but they would walk through stuff and sit down. The last six guys, either Wetzel or I would put them through three-on-three drills. Rick believed you couldn't take it out of them in practice.

Normally, I don't like training camp. This year, however, I couldn't wait.

It didn't take me long to figure out Buck had the heart of a champion. He never backed down from anybody in the game. The amazing thing was, our new power forward was only 6'8" and 225. I weighed a couple pounds more than Buck. He was durable, having missed only 20 games in his eight years with the Nets. He was reliable. A tenacious competitor. He wasn't a great outside shooter, but he was effective around the basket and as a trailer on the fast break. His lowest shooting percentage for a season was .523. We never ran a play for him, but he didn't complain. He was one of the best rebounding power forwards in the history of the game. And he knew how to play. Buck worked at his craft. He put on his hard hat, came to work and was an inspiration to play with. And he was an All-Defensive Team player, guarding guys who weighed 30 or 40 pounds more than he did.

**BUCK WILLIAMS:** Clyde and I had a mutual respect. He respected what I did as a player. I had heard some people talk about how difficult Clyde was as a teammate; all I can say is, it was never a problem with me. He just expected everyone to play as hard as he played, to leave everything on the court. He just wanted you to do your job to the best of your ability. We got along very well.

Clyde was a unique player, probably the best player I ever played with. You could dial him in for 20 points and six or seven rebounds and assists ever single night, and he was the ultimate competitor. I played with a lot of great players, but I never played with a player you could count on so consistently. And he made it look so easy.

He had an uncanny knack of finding ways to score. Sometimes I would throw him an outlet pass in the open court, and so as not to alert the defender, he wouldn't look at the ball until the very last minute. And then all of a sudden, he would grab it and have the defender out of position and score. We ran a four-down play, with Clyde on the low box and me out top, and I would throw the ball to him and cut. He gave me three buckets a game that way, I swear. He was an excellent passer who made it look easy, and he played an overall game. He was unstoppable in the open floor. If I got him the ball off a rebound in the open court, no one could stop him. They fouled him or he scored.

Buck's addition keyed our transition game. It all started on the defensive end. We would get a stop, grab a rebound and all of us were going 100 miles an hour to the other end — two guys on the wing, Terry in the middle and Buck trailing.

There was a Nike poster of that era that epitomized what other teams thought about us. It was Buck, Terry and Jerome on a fast break, and the only words were "Uh oh." It was like, "Uh oh, they are going to run you to death."

Terry was in his fifth year with the Blazers and fourth as a starter. He had averaged a career-high 17.7 points, was fourth in the league in assists with 9.5 per game and had become one of the league's top three-point threats during the 1988-89 season. On defense, he made the other guy work. He was such a heads-up player, just like John Stockton and Magic Johnson. If you were open, he would get you the ball. Most teams were double-teaming me, especially if I got the ball in the post area. Rick was smart enough to understand that if he put the ball in my hands and I got doubled, we could spot up Terry and more often than not get three points out of it. When I was in Houston, we did the same thing with Kenny Smith.

Terry was unselfish; he did whatever the team needed. That is what made those Portland teams from 1989-92 so special. No bickering.

**TERRY PORTER:** I learned right away that I had to shoot the ball because Clyde would get the ball off a rebound and go. Our offensive system wasn't a situation like Stockton's, where the Jazz would always get the ball to the point guard. Clyde would rebound and take off and I had to find a way to spot up and make a shot. I was always criticized, "He is not really a point guard," and my assist numbers weren't as big as some guys, but it had to do with our circumstances. If you put Stockton in that situation, he would have had to learn how to shoot, because Clyde was amazing at making plays. He would get the ball in his right hand and he was gone, and he had a great knack of finding the open man.

Clyde was a great teammate. When you think about what a teammate means, he is always trying to do the things that will help the team. That fit Clyde. He had his moments with the coaches, but on the floor, he always tried to encourage his teammates. The only player I played with who approached his greatness was Tim Duncan. Clyde was the best perimeter guy I ever played with, hands down.

**JACK SCHALOW:** Clyde could get to the basket whenever he wanted. He was such a good rebounder. He got us into the fast break. He was really our point guard. Terry was really our two guard. Clyde was one of the best athletes in the league. Rick used to call one of two plays — a two-out or two-down — during the last three minutes of a close game. They were for Clyde, and he passed the ball and found somebody open about 80 percent of the time. That always impressed me about him. He almost always made the right play. He was one of the best passers in the game.

Jerome was one of the hardest-working players in the history of the game. We called him Romeo — he liked the ladies back then — or the "Rundown Man." Somebody would make a steal, and Jerome would sprint back and run the guy down before he could score. Jerome would not only be the first guy to lead the break, he would do it 10 times in a row. He had incredible hustle and stamina. He was the consummate team player. Like me, he wasn't a dead-eye perimeter shooter, but he made his share of jumpers. He could make defenses pay. He improved his jump shot every year, just as I did. He was never an All-Star but should have been three or four times. For a couple of years, he could have been our team MVP.

Duck was a great post-up player who could score with jump hooks using either hand. He also had a nice jump shot from 10 to 18 feet. He was a better shooter than I was. We used to say he was the best midrange shooter on the team. He obviously took up a lot of space inside; if he didn't get a rebound, his man wouldn't, either. And I think he set the best picks in the league. We ran the pick-and-roll a lot. I would run off Duck's pick and often I would be wide open. He also knew if he set a great pick, his man would have to help on me, and he would be the one who would be open. He was reliable, durable and a competitor — a two-time All-Star. If I were picking a Blazers center for one season, I would say a healthy Bill Walton. But for longevity, I would select Duckworth.

Besides Buck, we added two other important weapons that season — rookie forward Cliff Robinson and European guard Drazen Petrovic.

I had seen Cliff play in college when he was at the University of Connecticut, but I didn't think he was that good until I saw him in training camp that fall. He had averaged 20 points and nine rebounds as a senior but for some reason fell to us in the second round as the 36th pick of the 1989 draft.

**PAUL ALLEN:** So many things worked out right in 1989. The trade for Buck Williams, and stealing Cliff Robinson, who was my pick. Before every draft, I watched tape of the players with our coaches and scouts. I saw this 6'10" kid from Connecticut drilling all these outside shots and rebounding; he was very athletic. Our people said, "Well, he is an unusual player but a high-maintenance guy." I said, "If he gets down to us in the second round, let's take a shot at him." Bucky liked him, too, so it resonated. I pushed for that one. Some of the other picks I pushed for didn't turn out so well.

I loved Cliff the first time I saw him play in person. This was the first athletic 6'10" kid I had ever played with. He loved the up-tempo game. He loved the game, period. Before a game, he would come into the locker room, sweating after shooting for 30 minutes. I would be reading a book. I would look up and say, "Cliff, we don't play for an hour and a half." But you loved the enthusiasm. He had an inside-outside game and could play anything from center to small forward and could defend just about every position. We would clear him out on a wing against a big guy, let him take the guy to the rack and dunk on him. I loved that I could throw the alley-oop to him. Before, I had usually been the receiver. You couldn't throw the alley-oop to Richard Anderson or Rolando Ferreira or Maurice Lucas or Steve Johnson, God love them all.

Portland had drafted Petrovic in the third round of the draft in 1986, the same year we took Arvydas Sabonis. Petrovic was a big guard, 6'5", with a great offensive game and a deadly outside shot. He had led Real Madrid to the European Cup championship, scoring 63 points in the title game. The Blazers had bought out his Spanish contract for $1.15 million, and at 25, he was realizing his NBA dream.

I could tell Petrovic was a student of the game. You could see his will to win from day one. He was a competitor. Michael Young had played against him in Europe and told me, "This guy can play." And Petro wasn't soft. In Europe, he used to spit on guys. I liked him. He worked extremely hard on his game. He stayed after practice and we shot a lot together. I could tell he was going to be a very good NBA player.

Two days into training camp, if someone had taken a picture of my face, it would have been one big smile. For the first time, we had the talent to compete with the Lakers. We had a great starting five. Cliff and Drazen were going to help off the bench. We had Wayne Cooper back as our backup center. Coop was a good rebounder and great shot blocker. You couldn't trick Coop. Give him a pump-fake and he would stay on his feet until you really went up for the shot, and he would swat it more often than not. Danny Young was an unsung but dependable reserve point guard, and Mark Bryant was a capable backup to Buck at power forward.

Rick set the tone in that training camp. He wasn't going to accept anything less than hard work. And the players did a good job of policing each other. A player always knows when his teammate is not doing his best. We didn't have to worry too much about that group. Everybody was a professional who came to work every game. I wish every team I played on was that good.

Paul Allen had proved he would spend his money to make our team better, and some of it had nothing to do with personnel. He bought us a private jet, which we called "Blazer One." There was only one other team that had a plane — the Pistons. It is no coincidence those were the two teams in the '90 Finals. It helped so much, I don't know where to begin.

My first few years in the league, once in a while we had a charter flight, but we almost always flew commercial. From Portland, which is not the most conveniently located NBA city, that usually meant a connection or two to where we were going. If I missed a flight or connection, I would be sitting there waiting for the next flight with everyone else. There was a lot of pressure taken off the players when we got our own plane. At the end of West Coast trips, you can leave after the game, get home and get a good night's sleep in your bed that night. Because of the recovery factor, I would say it gave us five or six extra wins a year.

Blazer One was spacious. We had custom recliner swivel chairs that laid flat in case you wanted to sleep. We had couches and something close to a real kitchen. The coaches were up front, where they would talk and watch videotape. Seating in the back went by seniority. The more years a player had in the league, the better his seat. But really, there wasn't a bad seat on the plane.

I usually sat by Duck, Cliff and Jerome. We had a table there and we often played games and cards. I would read — I could zone out on books for hours — or sleep. After games, I was usually exhausted and went to sleep.

The food was great. We had two flight attendants — Flo Newton and Maureen Walker, or Flo and Mo — my entire time with the Blazers, and they really took care of us. You could order pretty much whatever you wanted, from a gourmet meal to KFC or Popeye's. Even Drexler's Barbecue if we were in Houston. It was a life of luxury, and we appreciated it.

We always had group conversations on the flights. On some teams, guys don't even look at their teammates. We talked about current events all the time. We talked about anything — sports, politics, our favorite movie stars, you name it. A lot of times, we would go to a game together on off nights.

**JEROME KERSEY:** Blazer One was the site of some incredible discussions among the players. Clyde and Kevin used to go at it a little. Kevin liked to work on cars. He would always tease Clyde about going bald. On the airplane one time, they got into an argument, and Clyde said, "You don't know what you're talking about, you big hungry mechanic." We all laughed.

Buck and I sparked a lot of debates on the plane. Whatever he came up with, I would take the other side, and we could spend the whole trip arguing the pros and cons of our views.

**WAYNE COOPER:** Clyde was stubborn — very stubborn. I found that out early. Something came up and I thought Clyde was joking about it. Turned out he was dead serious. I used to be the mediator between Clyde and Buck. They argued about everything on the plane, or at dinner. If Buck said something was black, Clyde would say it was white. They would argue the entire night. And they are great friends. But Clyde would never admit he might be wrong.

We were putting Cooper on a little bit. Buck and I would end up laughing so hard, and Cooper would be the guy we ended up talking about. We used to give him the business. He was a young man who thought like a 50-year-old. He used to think old, and we had a bunch of stuff we used to say about him. Truth be told, Coop was a very solid guy and we all enjoyed having him as a teammate.

**KEVIN DUCKWORTH:** I was one of the guys who clicked with Clyde on a personal level. We sat next to each other on the plane. We usually had rooms next to each other on the road. I probably got to know Clyde better as a person than most of his teammates. I am glad I got a chance to hang with him. Clyde is the kind of guy, if he is your friend, he is your friend. If you cross him, you have no chance at ever getting back at Clyde. You burn Clyde, there are no second chances. He would not even deal with you. When people spoke of how they looked up to

Clyde, I can see what they were saying because I looked up to him, too. He is a very smart man. I always admired him for that. He is a very knowledgeable person. But he was always careful to say the right stuff all the time to reporters. I said, "Clyde, you're full of it. You always say what people want to hear. You don't tell the truth." That was true for both him and Buck. I said, "Why do I always have to say what I really feel, instead of the politically correct version?" It got me in trouble lots of times.

The first game we played that counted, I remember Buck gathering rebound after rebound. I was in awe. Now, I thought to myself, I don't even have to help out that much on the boards. I can play better defense on the perimeter and be in position to leak out on the break. Jerome and I were free to get a little bit of an anticipated start, because we knew Buck was going to get the rebound. It was like it had been at the University of Houston with Hakeem.

I was 27 now — almost ready to hit my peak years as an athlete. I have always said a player's peak years are from about 28 to 32 years old. I was almost there. That summer the Blazers had staged an event called "Slam 'n' Jam," which featured a rookie game, some musical and entertainment acts and a unique dunk contest. Jerome, me, and an old Blazers favorite of the past, Billy Ray Bates, were the contestants in the dunk contest. We started at 10 feet and moved the basket upward by increments of a few inches at a time. Billy Ray had been bragging that he was going to go up and dunk at 12 feet. I won at a height measured at 11 feet, one inch.

I wasn't surprised. I grew up dunking on those outside baskets at Sterling High that were close to 10 1/2 feet. I think I could probably have dunked at about 11'7" or 11'8". Maybe even 12 feet at my peak. I used to be able to put my fingerprint on the white line at the top of the backboard at Sterling. Bill Russell once told me he used to touch the top of the backboard. I'd like to have seen that.

I would guess I was one of the greatest leapers in history. I was pretty good jumping off of one leg on the fly or standing still. I could take off a foot beyond the free throw line and dunk; it didn't matter which hand. When I was growing up, I remember older guys had slept with ankle weights on, and they could jump out of the gym. I bought into that. From about 12 years old, I started sleeping with ankle weights on — not every day, just some of the time. I would jump rope with them on, play pickup games with them on. And I wasn't the only one. We had guys in the neighborhood who would never take them off. I think it helped my hops considerably.

Back to the first game of the season, I unfortunately wasn't healthy. I had banged my right elbow during the preseason and had to miss five of the first eight games with what Dr. Cook and our trainer, Mike Shimensky, called a bursa sac inflammation. The skin on that elbow still droops today; that is from hitting the floor so much. We started 5-3, which was okay. We were getting scoring from everybody. In those eight games, all five starters plus Cliff led the team in scoring in at least one game.

When I was finally healthy, we hit the court running. We won six straight. After shooting 55 percent and averaging 23.7 points in four of those games, I was named NBA Player of the Week. In a 125-99 rout of New Jersey, I went 13 for 16 from the floor and had 33 points and eight assists. Four nights later, we blasted the Clippers 116-94, and I had 21 points, eight rebounds and seven assists. Against Detroit, I collected 27 points, 10 boards and nine assists.

I was getting some attention for my defensive work on players such as Derek Harper (10 points), Michael Jordan (16) and Joe Dumars (five). To be honest, I wasn't doing anything different. Maybe the addition of Buck was allowing me to focus a little more on my man and a little less on help defense, but I think I was the most underrated defensive player in the history of the game. I will go on record as saying that. I finished my career fifth in steals. Often, I would turn the other team's offense into fast breaks. That is called defense. A lot of people overlooked that in evaluating my career. Any time a big guy would get in the lane, I would move in to slap the ball out of his hands. He would be making a post-up move, and all of a sudden, the ball would be loose. I did that as well as anyone who ever played the game.

**JACK SCHALOW:** He was such a great athlete. He had such great hands, as good a pair of hands as any player I have been around. When he really had his mind set, he was a heck of a defender.

**JOHN WETZEL:** Clyde had incredible strength from his elbows to his hands. He could get his hands on balls and rip it away from guys driving to the basket.

**GEOFF PETRIE:** Defensively, Clyde was unconventional in the way he guarded somebody, but he was effective. He could steal balls from guys after they beat him. I can't remember how many times I saw him reach out and snatch a ball from a guy who was already by him. "How did he do that?" we would ask. He would play on the outside shoulder of an offensive player coming off pin-downs, which is the total opposite of the way a defender is taught to play it, because the defender would think the offensive player would just go back-door on him. Nobody ever did it to Clyde. He just had these instincts for doing things in a certain way — his own way.

That was one of the great things about Rick coaching Clyde. Rick understood that, and as long as it worked, he was OK with it. Some coaches would have said, "No, that's not the way we do it." Rick gave him some rope, as long as it was working.

**RICK ADELMAN:** I have never seen a guy cover so much ground defensively. We always had ways we wanted to guard people. With Clyde, he did his own thing, but when it mattered, he could get to one spot quicker than anyone I ever saw.

It was anticipation. I would study an opponent on tape and in person. I would watch to see what side he would typically go. I would let him do it once or twice; the next time, I would be there right when he did it and try to take the ball from him.

**PAUL ALLEN:** He had this kind of lying-in-the-weeds defensive approach where he would lie back and not get up on the man he was guarding, but he would study the guy. And then he would steal the ball at some key moment and we would win the game.

People said that I was "just naturally gifted." That let me know they truly had no concept of what it takes. Some physical skills are natural, but others are earned. Strength is not natural. Jumping ability is not natural. You have to practice jumping to become a great jumper. To build up my legs, I would go to the store for my neighbors to pick up groceries, or whatever they needed. I would skip to the store — on one leg down, on the other leg back.

**JOHN WETZEL:** Clyde had amazing quickness with his first one or two steps. The ball would be going out of bounds, and he could get to the ball as quick as anybody I have ever seen. That burst of speed was remarkable.

There was something else about Clyde — a sort of humility that was interesting. There was a gentleness to his soul, something most great athletes won't let you see. They sometimes want to be perceived as macho strong. The gentleness was hidden in Clyde, but it was there. And it was part of that belief in himself.

**WAYNE COOPER:** Clyde had such incredible self-confidence. Once, we were watching game tapes, and he was getting beat over and over by someone. Rick said, "Clyde, what's happening here?" And Clyde said, "I was just setting him up for the next time." Typical Clyde. He was so determined. He would walk out of the locker room, step onto the floor and play. He just believed he could get it done. Always.

**GEOFF PETRIE:** Sometimes we would be watching tape of games collectively as a team. The coaches would go through and point out mistakes. Rick might say, "Clyde, you let this guy cut right to the basket for an easy layup." Clyde would say something like, "No, that's not what happened. I was tricking him." That was Clyde.

Around Thanksgiving, tragedy struck the Blazers. Our rookie forward, Ramon Ramos, was driving on icy Interstate 5 late one night when his car spun out of control and crashed. He was critically injured with massive head injuries, given a 50-50 chance to survive, and remained in a coma for months.

Ramon had been a surprise in training camp. He had gone undrafted after four seasons at Seton Hall, where one of his teammates was Mark Bryant. We signed him to a free agent deal in the summer. He was 6'8 "and 255, only 21, and he had a lot of upside. He was a native Puerto Rican who spoke pretty good English and blended in nicely with the rest of the guys. He was a very tough defender and a good team guy who was destined to eventually be a good player. I think he would have developed into a good backup for Buck. He was on the "injured list" (taxi squad, really) when the accident occurred. He never played a minute of NBA basketball.

Everyone loved Ramon. When it happened, it was surreal. It was like it couldn't have happened to a teammate. Those are the things you read about happening to other people. In the ensuing weeks, Gaynell and I went to the hospital quite often. We would visit with his parents, his sister and his girlfriend. He was on a respirator and was in a coma. Gradually, over a period of months, he came out of it, and he was able to move to Puerto Rico and live with his parents. He regained some of his communication and physical skills, but was never able to play basketball again. For a couple of years, the Blazers kept an empty locker in his name in the locker room at Memorial Coliseum. The accident put things in perspective for all of us. There is always a bigger game going on — the game of life.

Life goes on, and so does basketball. We kept winning. Buck, Cliff and Drazen proved they were impact players. You could see it in practice. Drazen could really play. It allowed me to cut my minutes a little. Before, Mike Schuler or Rick Adelman couldn't afford to keep me on the bench for long. When Drazen came into a game in the second quarter, we usually increased our lead.

We went on a streak where we won 11 of 12 games to improved our record to 31-11, right on the heels of the Lakers for the best mark in the Western Conference. Still, I was our only representative at the All-Star Game. I thought I should have had at least two teammates there with me. Part of the problem was a lack of attention — Portland was a small-market franchise. We were on national television only once that entire regular season. Nobody expected us to blossom the way we did that season.

We were still rolling when I sprained an ankle and had to miss a four-game Eastern road trip. We beat Charlotte, a second-year expansion team, then lost to three tough teams — Cleveland, Chicago and Indiana.

Once I got back, we picked up where we left off. We won 10 in a row to hike our record to 48-18. In early March, we swept a four-game road trip against the top four teams in the East — New York, Boston, Philadelphia and Washington. That hadn't happened with a Portland team since 1978. It was a good indication that we were a genuine title contender. It gave us the confidence that we could beat anybody in the East, if we could just get past the dreaded Lakers.

In the New York game, I was one for 10 shooting and finished with three points, my lowest point total in five years. I had scored in double figures in 183 straight games dating back to 1987. As an NBA player, it was bound to happen sometimes. I had some games where I couldn't throw the ball in the ocean. I felt I was a very good shooter. To be a top-level scorer in the league like I was, I couldn't be a bad shooter if they were going to double-team me every night. In my mind, I was a very good shooter, but my forte was creating for other people, penetrating, and going coast to coast.

If I was in a slump, I never got down on myself. Usually, my thinking was that if I was having a bad shooting night, I should keep shooting. That was my mentality. That doesn't mean to go crazy taking wild shots. There were times when I was playing hurt, didn't have range of motion in an arm. Then you just pass the ball and don't hurt the team by taking shots. But you can't lose confidence in yourself. If you are looked upon as a go-to guy and you don't have confidence, your teammates see that and it takes away from their confidence, too. I probably took it to the point of overconfidence, just to make sure my teammates continued to feel confident. That is an important part of the mental game.

On March 18, we won 120-110 at Houston to set a franchise record for consecutive victories on the road (six) and overall (10). I had a big game with 41 points and 16 boards, hit 18 of 26 shots and had six assists. Afterward, Buck told a reporter, "You talk about gravity force out of a rocket trying to take off. Tonight, this guy redefined the whole gravity thing."

It was probably tied to my pregame meal — a chili dog fetched for me by a locker-room attendant. It was nothing unusual. I had been doing that since I started playing, but only if I didn't eat before we left the hotel for a game. A chili dog or hot dog was the best thing they had to eat at an arena. Besides, I liked them. I would have a dog with ketchup and mustard and relish — got to have that sweet relish. Two of them sometimes, right before the game. I preferred to play with something in my stomach. It never bothered me. It gave me energy, actually. Some of my teammates would laugh. Every now and then I would have a bad game, and someone would crack, "You are what you eat."

I was pretty serious about my nutrition, but once in awhile — maybe four times a season — I would eat a hot dog or popcorn at halftime. I wasn't afraid of doing it. I don't recall any other players doing that. But it never bothered me. If you didn't have time for lunch, you would be starving, and it would be a hot dog day.

It was fun to have a huge game in Houston, before all my friends and family members. That was probably the best I ever played in my hometown during my time as a Blazer. I had some okay games, but not too many great games.

I never felt pressure, though. As a player, I acknowledged pressure. I was aware of what was on the line during a game. It is good to be a little bit on the edge, a little nervous. That means you understand the situation. But it is still just basketball.

I don't remember ever visibly choking throughout my career. If I had two free throws to tie or go ahead late in a game, I don't remember missing very often. That is what truly separates the good players from the great ones — the ability to do it on command. If you need performance, find a way to make it happen.

It is something you don't even think about during the game. I lived for those moments when the heat was on. I would much rather have games like that than games where you beat the other team by 50 points. I was better when the games really counted. When we got up by 20 points, I wasn't as interested in being on the floor, especially later in my career. The NBA season is a marathon. You want to preserve yourself. I didn't play in the fourth period of a lot of one-sided games the second half of my career. I wanted to live to fight another day and still give the fans something for their money.

Our winning streak was snapped on March 22 in a 107-106 loss at San Antonio, when referee Steve Javie whistled me for a foul on Willie Anderson as he tossed up a double-clutch, 25-foot airball with 1.2 seconds left and the Spurs behind by one point. Anderson made both free throws and we lost. Needless to say, I didn't agree with the call. I was livid. I went after Javie afterward and had to be pulled away by teammates. Buck sent a fist through a plastic enclosure to a light fixture, shattering it on the way to the locker room. Our wallets were both a little lighter after the league fines were handed out.

On March 28, we beat the Lakers 130-111 at the Coliseum to move to 50-20 and within two games of the Lakers in the Pacific Division race. In the third quarter, we had one of those streaks that we had every so often with that team. We made 17 of 21 shots to put the game on ice.

Three days later, the Lakers responded with a 135-106 win in L.A., with Magic getting 25 points, 10 rebounds and 14 assists. Coach Pat Riley said Johnson "was as good as I have ever seen him," and I wouldn't quarrel with that. The Lakers exploded for 44 points in the third quarter; they were motivated. It was our fifth game in seven days and we were out of gas. But we finished 14-4 in March, breaking the franchise record for victories in a season.

We ended the regular season at the Coliseum with a 130-88 rout of the Lakers — our biggest margin of victory ever over them, and the most one-sided loss in Lakers' franchise history. There was an extenuating circumstance. The Lakers had already clinched the division title and the best record in the league, and Riley rested Magic, James Worthy and Mychal Thompson, who had joined them in 1986 and was their starting center that season after Kareem Abdul-Jabbar's retirement. Our fans booed the Lakers and enjoyed the win, but we all knew it would be different in the playoffs.

We finished with a franchise-record 59 wins and as the No. 1 rebounding team in the league. We lost three games in a row only once all season. My scoring average was down to 23.3, but I was still contributing 6.9 rebounds and 5.9 assists. I was named as a third-team All-NBA selection and was ready for a long playoff run.

The Lakers were the team to beat as usual in the West, but there were other good teams, including us, Phoenix, San Antonio and Utah. But the Lakers had been "Showtime" through the '80s, and even without Kareem, they were a very good team that was solid defensively, which people don't remember.

Truth be told, we couldn't stand the Lakers. They were so good they were arrogant. We respected them, but the minute we got Buck, we were felt we were the better team, or at least as good. We had won the regular-season series 3-2. For the first time, they had that look of respect in their eyes when they met us. We had a chip on our shoulder and were looking for a showdown. I was hoping we would play them in the conference finals.

But first we had to beat Dallas, whom we had embarrassed 134-92 two weeks before the playoffs began. We felt like we had their number. We had gone 4-0 against them during the regular season and had beaten them on the boards by an average of seven a game. Probably their most talented player was Roy Tarpley, who was a drug- and alcohol-problem guy. Just before the playoffs, their poor coach, Richie Adubato, was moved to note the following about Tarpley: "If you look at the patterns, after a breakdown, there are usually a couple of months before another one. That would take us through the playoffs at least."

Dallas was missing Adrian Dantley, a big scorer who was injured. They still had the backcourt tandem of Derek Harper and Rolando Blackman, who had combined to average 37 points in the regular season. I had great respect for them.

We swept the best-of-five series 3-0. Buck was a man possessed in the opener with 21 points and 16 rebounds as we won 109-102. Now we had somebody who could compete with the big guys who used to kill us in years past.

In Game 2, Terry and I stank. It was one of those can't-throw-it-in-the-ocean situations. We combined to make eight of 36 shots from the field. But Petrovic and Danny Young came to the rescue, coming off the bench to key a second-quarter shooting spree in a 114-107 win. They combined for 22 of our first 24 points in the period. Those guys had done it a lot of times during the regular season, and they came through this time as well. Our depth was paying off.

Our Game 3 win in Dallas came at a cost. Buck scratched a cornea, and Duck broke his right hand. That really hurt, because we would be facing a very tough San Antonio team in the conference semis with a rookie center by the name of David Robinson.

San Antonio had swept Denver in the first round. Under coach Larry Brown, the Spurs had gone 21-61 the year before, which gave them the No. 1 pick in the draft. They used it to get Robinson, who averaged 24 points and 12 rebounds as the Spurs won 56 games for the biggest turnaround in NBA history. He had plenty of talent around him, with Willie Anderson, Terry Cummings, Sean Elliott and Rod Strickland.

As luck would have it, Wayne Cooper's back was acting up, too, and he would miss virtually all of the San Antonio series. So we were forced to go with our own rookie, undersized Cliff Robinson, as our starting center.

Cliff had played significant minutes, but mostly at the two forward spots. Still, he was an outstanding defender and an integral part of the team. We had beaten San Antonio in 14 of our last 15 meetings and had gone 5-1 against them in 1989-90, so we still felt confident. We felt we had the depth to overcome our losses at center if we played well.

Before the series, San Antonio owner Red McCombs told the media, "I don't think Portland is that tough, really. I don't think they have that good a club. If we have more than two guys playing at the same time, we should be able to waltz by them."

Rick made sure that article was up on the bulletin board in our locker room. It's not like we needed extra motivation, but it didn't hurt, either.

We won the opener at home 107-94, as our always sold-out throng of 12,884 roared its approval in the Coliseum. Buck played with a mask to protect his eye. He and Cliff had primary defensive coverage of Robinson, and we swarmed the Admiral, holding him to nine points and nine rebounds in 40 frustrating minutes. Jerome, who always elevated his game in the playoffs, had 25 points and 16 boards.

We missed 16 free throws but did just about everything else right. We won the rebound battle 48-38 and crashed the offensive glass for 23 of them. We created 22 turnovers. And we got to the line 45 times to 15 times for the Spurs. We were the aggressor, taking the game to them. It was a good way to start off the series.

Game 2 was another victory, 122-112. Cooper played 19 minutes and had six boards and four blocks, but he had to sit out the fourth quarter with back spasms. It was our 11th straight home win over the Spurs, but it didn't come easy. We had to work hard to win.

Even though we were going to San Antonio with a 2-0 lead in the best-of-seven series, I was worried. We finally had a chance to go far in the playoffs, but we had a rash of injuries to our big guys. Fortunately, Cliff was stepping up and playing like a veteran.

The Spurs kicked our tails 121-98 in Game 3, and we had more bad news than just the outcome. Cooper played only nine first-half minutes before leaving for good with the bad back. They killed us on the boards 51-35, forced us into 23 turnovers and dominated us inside. David Robinson was superhuman with 28 points, eight boards and eight blocked shots, sinking 11 of 14 from the field.

To say I struggled is putting it mildly. I was five for 15 shooting and scored just 15 points. Plus, I had eight turnovers. I was having a heck of a time getting my perimeter shot to fall. All of my baskets came on layups or dunks. In the series so far, I was 19 of 54 from the floor; in the six playoff games, I was 40 of 111. These shooting woes came after shooting .494 during the regular season.

Truth was, I had little energy. I had been hit by a persistent flu bug, and I had lost some weight and felt really tired. For the first time, I was playing longer into a season, and I wasn't able to shake the tired feeling. I just wasn't at full strength. I didn't really tell anybody, and I wasn't making excuses. I was still responsible for taking shots and making them. I was just hoping I could regain my health before it was too late.

I did feel better for Game 4 and scored 16 of my 27 points in the first quarter, but it didn't make a lot of difference in a 115-105 loss. Duck and Coop were out, and even Mark Bryant, who was giving us important inside minutes, left with a sprained ankle. Terry Cummings went wild with 35 points and 11 rebounds for the Spurs. I hit a few outside shots and finished 11 of 19 from the field, but it was down to a three-game series now. Fortunately, we had home-court advantage in our favor.

I told the media after the game, "If we get Coop back, we should take the series. If we don't, we still have enough confidence in the guys we have. We are not conceding anything."

Game 5 was a classic, one of the greatest games I ever took part in. We earned a 138-132 double-overtime win, and Terry and I finally played to our potential. Terry had a playoff career-high 38 points in 54 minutes and I added 35 in 48 minutes. We had the Spurs on the ropes, but they rallied from a 22-point deficit in the third quarter to force overtime. Coop wasn't able to play, but Cliff gave us some good minutes at center.

When you don't have your full complement of players, everybody who is available has to pick up the slack. In Game 5, Jerome stepped up. Terry stepped up. I mean, it didn't seem like he missed a shot all night. I stepped up. Some of the guys off the bench stepped up. That is the key in having a lot of depth. You can overcome certain injuries to key players.

Back in San Antonio, the Spurs won 112-97 to send the series back to Portland for a seventh game. Cliff had a big game, shooting eight of 13 and getting 20 points and eight boards in 28 minutes. It was a nightmare night for me. I was one for 10 from the field and scored four points before getting tossed after being called for a punching foul on Anderson in the third quarter. All I was doing was using my forearm to get Willie's hands off me. Willie had a huge game, making 13 of 19 shots for 30 points.

Things were really getting heated between the two teams. There were three sets of double-technicals called. Sean Elliott accused Jerome of punching him. Buck and David went face to face in a war of words in the fourth quarter. Bottom line, they played great and we played like crap.

And now we were down to one game for all the marbles — the winner would advance to the Western Conference finals. And surprise! The opponent was not the Lakers but Phoenix, which had upset the Lakers 4-1 in the other conference semifinals. We knew if we won, the Lakers would not be able to block our path to the NBA Finals.

We had won 11 straight over San Antonio at our place, but the Spurs weren't going to just keel over. They were pretty cocky with their comments before Game 7.

Willie Anderson: "Forget the home streak. If we start good against them, they will fold." Sean Elliott: "They have all the weight on their shoulders. All the pressure is on them, without a doubt."

I'm not sure they believed that. But I guarantee you, these teams had no love for each other.

Game 7 was another incredible game, one of the two or three greatest I participated in throughout my career. Final score: Portland 108, San Antonio 105 — again in overtime.

I was still under the weather, but somehow I found the strength to score 12 of my 22 points in the final four minutes of regulation and overtime, including five free throws in the final 26.2 seconds of the extra session. Jerome had one of his greatest performances ever with 21 points, 15 rebounds and six steals. And Terry Porter, as he had done so many times with everything riding on the outcome, was sensational with 36 points and nine assists. It was Terry's steal of the Spurs' in-bounds pass with 5.6 left in overtime that sealed it. We won mostly on effort. We shot only .371 from the field, but out-rebounded the Spurs 60-48.

Duckworth pulled a Willis Reed for Game 7. None of us really expected him to be ready to play, though there were some hints the day before that he might be available. I didn't know he was going to play up until almost game time. We were in the locker room, and I saw Mike Shimensky working on him behind closed doors. We were getting our game face ready, whether we had him available or not.

Then Duck came out for pregame warmups. I have never heard a louder ovation in a basketball arena. Memorial Coliseum shook, and I am not kidding. Wayne Cooper also gutted it out through his back problems and played. Duck and Coop combined to make only four of 17 shots, but they provided an emotional lift and defense on David Robinson. We needed anything Duck and Coop could give that day. Those guys showed a lot of courage. They knew how big that game was. Buck was courageous that whole series, wearing the mask to protect his broken nose. We were beat up. That was the hardest playoff series I experienced in my entire career. We had so many things to overcome.

**KEVIN DUCKWORTH:** That was the highlight of my career. Buck and I had gone to the hospital together after Game 3 of the Dallas series. That could have cost us the San Antonio series. But Buck came right back, and I was able to get back for the last game against the Spurs. When I got that ovation ... I don't know what to say about that. I got tears in my eyes. I felt appreciated by the fans. It was a good feeling.

Cooper came back for Game 7, too. Clyde said, "Duck, Coop went down when you broke your hand, and then when you came back, he came back. What's the deal — is he afraid to start?" We laughed and laughed about that.

We trailed 97-90 with 2:32 left when I bounced in a three-pointer to get us back in the game. The ball touched every part of the rim, bounced four times, almost hit the top of the backboard, and finally went in. I was so weak I didn't think I could get it to the basket. It was the luckiest shot I made in my life, but it put us within striking distance. For most of the game, the Spurs had an answer for everything we did. We were not playing our best ball that day, but the crowd was really loud and pushed us on.

The play everyone remembers, though, came in the final minute of overtime when Rod Strickland tried an over-the-head pass that Jerome intercepted. One of the Spurs was open under the basket, but Rod got a little fancy and Jerome happened to be running to the ball. He made a great play and I just took off on the wing. Jerome knew when I was out there to just throw it ahead of me. I was going to outrun everyone. I got fouled and our postseason was saved.

**GEOFF PETRIE:** That three-pointer Clyde made was a horrible shot, you would say, if it hadn't gone in. But it went in. And that got us back into the game. Every game at home in that series was a close game. Every game on the road was a blowout for them. Lucky we had home-court advantage.

I was still feeling sick, but in the playoffs, you have to play if there is any way you can. We were short-handed, and we couldn't afford to lose anyone else. Jerome was the player of the game for us. We were struggling, and he was keeping us alive with the typical hustle plays he made throughout his career. He is probably the most underrated Blazers player of all time. For the Blazers'

25-year anniversary in 1995, they picked a 10-player all-time team and he was left off. That was an injustice.

Now we were going against the Suns for the right to represent the West in the NBA Finals. To be honest, I was glad we were facing them instead of the Lakers. I had averaged 29.5 points, nine rebounds and 5.5 assists in our five games against the Suns in the regular season. They played the same up-tempo style of game that we did. I loved it when the opposing team tried to run with us. They were still a very good team, though. They had Kevin Johnson and Tom Chambers and Jeff Hornacek. Johnson and Chambers were lethal, but Terry and Buck were two of our best defenders, and they would be on them. I felt good about those matchups and our chances.

We won the first two games in nail-biters, 100-98 and 108-107, running our home-court record to 8-0 in the playoffs. I had 20 points in each of the games — 10 rebounds in Game 1 and nine in Game 2. Jerome was incredible in Game 2 with 29 points and 11 boards. The guy loved it when the stakes were higher.

We had played all season to earn home-court advantage through the playoffs, which we had earned facing anybody in the West except the Lakers. And now they were history. Very few teams in the West won on the road in that year. It was especially true for our opponents in Memorial Coliseum. Our fans were the best in the league. It was one of the smallest arenas in the league, an intimate setting, and it was the all-time loudest arena I ever played in. When we got rolling, the fans got amped, and you could see the look on opponents' faces when we got a lead. It was like the world was crumbling around them. The fans propelled us to so many victories, especially during our championship runs from 1990 to '92.

But when we went on the road, it wasn't quite so easy. In Game 3, Phoenix crushed us 123-89. We shot an embarrassing .360 from the field. I scored 11 points and couldn't make a shot. The Suns led 40-18 after one quarter and were ahead 103-57 late in the third quarter. An 18-0 spurt by our reserves in the fourth quarter made the final score more respectable. Rick called it our "worst game of year," and it was. We were so flat. After winning two hard-fought games in our building, we were tired and just didn't have it. They had played two excellent road games and hadn't come up with a win. They came out with a renewed sense of urgency and put us away quickly.

They won Game 4 119-107 to even the series at 2-2. Jerome put up his second 29-point performance of the series, but I was only average, making six of 13 from the field while collecting 15 points and 11 assists. Phoenix was playing good defense on me, doubling and forcing me to pass.

That made me a little more determined for Game 5 back in Memorial Coliseum. I had averaged only 16.5 points in the first four games, but I exploded for 32 points to go with 10 boards in a 120-114 win. I made 13 of 24 shots from the field, and I was more aggressive in looking for my shot. I wasn't hitting my jumper, so I had to be creative and get closer to the basket and to give myself a chance for post-ups, tip-dunks, steals and transition baskets in order to get my rhythm back. I could always take my defender down on the block, and if the opponent doubled me, someone would be open.

But as a true scorer, my mentality was, "I am not struggling." I never ever admitted to myself that I was struggling. You may work hard to get a better shot, but you have to keep shooting if you are open.

Now we were back to Phoenix for Game 6. We were 0-5 on the road in the playoffs, we had looked awful in our two games at Phoenix in the playoffs. Their coach, Cotton Fitzsimmons, was not one to mince words. He told the media, "They can't put us away. They know that ... and pretty soon they have to quit hiding being that security blanket of the home court, and we will get one. And when we do, we will be fine. It will be the one that hurts the most."

We turned the tide with a stirring 112-109 triumph that made us Western Conference champions, scoring the final six points of the game. Hornacek had 36 points and the Suns led 109-108 inside the final minute with possession of the ball. But Kersey blocked a running shot by Hornacek in the closing seconds. I retrieved the ball and got it to Jerome, who converted a layup to put us in front 110-109 with 27.2 to play.

After a timeout, Chambers drove and Buck stripped him of the ball. He got it to me, I was fouled, and I made both foul shots with 6.9 seconds left to put us up by three. Hornacek's desperation 25-footer went off the rim, Buck grabbed the rebound, the buzzer sounded and he tossed the ball into the rafters. And then we played pile-up on Buck at center court. The Blazers were in the NBA Finals for the first time since 1977, and for all of us, it was the very first time in our careers.

**BUCK WILLIAMS:** I took the ball and I heaved it into the air, and when I lost my balance — I was so tired — I fell to the court. Everybody thought that was a signal to pile on Buck. It was great fun, a great moment, but looking back, we celebrated a little too early. If we had to do it over again, I am sure we would have made more certain that we understood we had another series to play. We kind of lost our focus for a moment.

I continued to struggle to make shots, hitting only six of 20 attempts, but I found a way to contribute in Game 6 with 23 points, 10 rebounds and seven assists. We didn't want to go to another tough Game 7. Before the game, I told the guys, "If we are as good as we think we are, let's step up and prove it." And in the end, our good defense took over.

We didn't know what being in the Finals meant. The Pistons did. They had swept the Lakers to win the championship the previous year and had everybody back. But experts were giving them only a slight edge. They had Isiah Thomas and Joe Dumars, an excellent defensive team and a great bench with Vinnie Johnson, John Salley and Mark Aguirre.

We played completely different styles. We employed the West Coast run-and-gun style, where we would use our defense to spurt on you. They relied on their defense and the offensive talents of their three great guards. Both teams could score in the halfcourt offense and both teams were very good defensively. It was going to be a matter of which team imposed its will on the other team.

They weren't called "The Bad Boys" for nothing. They were very dirty. Bill Laimbeer was probably the dirtiest player in the history of the game. We all hated him. He would try to hurt you and laugh about it. I didn't find anything funny about that.

Some of the "experts" in the East didn't know a lot about us. One of the CBS analysts didn't seem to have done his homework. He called Terry "Kevin Porter" throughout the series and pronounced our coach's name "Aid-el-mun."

The Pistons had home-court advantage and beat us 105-99 in the opener at The Palace at Auburn Hills. We had a 10-point lead with seven minutes left, but Isiah scored 16 of his 33 points in the fourth quarter to bring them back. The Pistons' first lead was 96-94 with 2:24 remaining. They won the rebound battle 54-46, including 30-19 in the second half. I had 21 points, nine boards and six assists, but I felt terrible. We controlled the tempo until the last seven minutes. We should have won that game. It really hurt us the rest of the series. But there wasn't a guy in our locker room who didn't feel we weren't going to win Game 2.

And we did it in very exciting fashion — 106-105 in overtime — to snap Detroit's 14-game home win streak in the playoffs. The Pistons went up 105-104 after Laimbeer sunk a 25-foot 3-pointer with me leaping at him and seven seconds on the clock. They ran a pick-and-roll with Dumars and I had to rotate out on

Laimbeer. I got a hand up, but he had created so much separation, and then he nailed it from a long ways out.

In the huddle, Rick was really calm. He drew up a play for me. He said, "Clyde, we'll put the ball in your hands. We'll have Terry and Duck spot up, and if they double on you, find the open man. If not, do what you do best." Rodman, their best defensive player, was guarding me. I was going to the basket, I saw a lane, and I was going to go up and dunk it when he fouled me with 4.1 seconds left.

There was a lot of pressure. On the other hand, it was a dream come true. I was at the line in the NBA Finals with a chance to win a game. The first one brought the most pressure. You want to nail that to ensure the tie. At that point in the game, I was exhausted, but I had confidence in that situation. I told myself, "I didn't get this far to lose." I just blocked everything out, concentrated and knocked both of them down. That gave the Blazers the critical victory, and I finished with 33 points.

We ran off the floor exhilarated. We were going back home, where we were undefeated in the playoffs that year. We fully intended to sweep the next three games at home and win it right there. But home court didn't mean anything in that series. They won all three in Portland and we should have won both of the games in Detroit.

I had regained my shooting touch by hitting 13 of 20 from the field in Game 2. Terry had 21 points and 10 assists and set a Finals record by making 15 of 15 at the line.

We lost Game 3, 121-106. We were all upset with the referee who would prove to be my nemesis over the years, Jake O'Donnell. Laimbeer drew four charges. Buck had problems during the whole game. Isiah, Dumars and Vinnie combined for 75 points. O'Donnell, Jess Kersey and Joey Crawford whistled 38 fouls on us to 26 for Detroit, and Buck, Jerome and Duck were all in early foul trouble. I had never seen so many bad calls in my life. It was surely not a coincidence that Jake was working the game. Years later, we would get our suspicions confirmed — he was a cheater. I'm not one to come up with excuses after a loss, but this was obvious.

The Pistons won Game 4, 112-109, as Isiah had one of the greatest halves I have ever witnessed, scoring 30 of his 32 points in the second half. Danny Young sank a 35-footer at the end of regulation to send us into overtime, or so we thought. Earl Strom waved it off after a review of the replay. I had a great game, making 14 of 19 shots and scoring 34 points, one shy of my career playoff high, to go with 10 assists and eight rebounds. Jerome was fabulous again with 33 points and eight points. We trailed by 16 points late in the third quarter, then had a furious rally. With Detroit ahead 108-107, Porter drove and collided with Dumars. No call was made, Thomas came up with the loose ball and was fouled with 8.4 seconds left. He sank both free throws and they emerged as winners.

Game 5 was another heartbreaker. We led 90-83 with 2:02 remaining, but they outscored us 9-0 down the stretch to win 92-90. Vinnie Johnson hit an 18-footer with 0.7 left on the clock to win it. Terry had a good look from the baseline at the buzzer, but his shot was off and the Pistons were champions again.

We were devastated. They had won four of five games, but the series was so much closer than that. It was a bad finish to a really good year. Some people say a team has to make it to the Finals and lose once before they can win it. I didn't believe it before the series started. I truly thought we were going to win. But after the '90 Finals, I thought there was some truth to it. Being there before must have helped, because they made all the big shots when they had to. It was just a spectacular shooting exhibition by Detroit. I had never seen a team shoot that well in games of that magnitude.

**BUCK WILLIAMS:**  Really, that was the year we had our best chance of winning. We had a better team than Detroit. I didn't think the three Pistons guards, as great as they were, could beat us. Our 1990-91 team was the best of the three, but our best chance for a title was 1990. But give the Pistons credit. They did what they had to do. They proved they were a better team.

**GEOFF PETRIE:** Getting to the Finals that year was an unexpected breakthrough. What that did was consolidate the confidence of the team and give the players belief in what they could do. We were all sure it was the beginning of something very big.

Two days later, about 7,000 fans jammed Pioneer Courthouse Square to honor the team on a drizzly day. The mayor pronounced it Portland Trail Blazers Appreciation Day. Our fans supported us through thick and thin, and I felt good about our chances to reward them with a title in '91.

# CHAPTER 13

# WHAT COULD HAVE BEEN

**W**e had the same cast of characters back for the 1990-91 season, with one notable exception. On August 1, we traded our No. 1 draft choice in 1989, guard Byron Irvin, along with a pair of draft choices to Sacramento for Danny Ainge. Ainge, who had grown up in Eugene, Oregon, as a Blazers fan, was a 30-year-old veteran who had distinguished himself through seven and a half years of service with the Celtics in the '80s. He was a winner, a clutch performer, a great three-point shooter and a team guy, and we were all excited to have him.

**DANNY AINGE:** I had not heard great things about Clyde. I had even heard comments from referees who didn't like Clyde. When I got to Portland, I was a little skeptical of him. Then I played with him, and it was a great joy. It was beautiful to watch him play. He was unselfish. He played defense. He passed the ball. He was a guy who practiced every day, even after playing 45 minutes the night before. He might only show up one minute before practice started, or one minute after, but he would be there and he would go hard.

I have a picture in my mind. It is of Clyde arriving for 11 a.m. practice at 10:59 or 11:01. He would shed his sweats and be ready to run. It was like, "Wow, the guy is flirting with the clock." Kevin McHale was a lot like that. But I always was amazed how Clyde practiced. Even after back-to-back games, he was ready to go.

**BUCK WILLIAMS:** Clyde was never much of a practice player. One day, he skipped practice to take his kids to a Disney on Ice show. "I need time to spend with my family," he said. Rick let it slide. The rest of us guys just kind of rolled our eyes and said, "That's Clyde." But we didn't resent it. We gave him a little more latitude than anyone else. He deserved it.

We opened training camp in Salem with a measure of uncertainty. Buck and I came close to staying home for our first two exhibition games in Honolulu. I was negotiating with Geoff Petrie, now the Blazers' senior vice president/operations, to extend my contract. I had been paid less than market value, and I wanted to get into the range of a player of my ability. Buck was of the same mindset. We talked about holding out together. And Jerome was looking for an extension, too.

**GEOFF PETRIE:** I had all three of those guys at the same time. They all had a year or two to go on their deals, and Paul agreed to at least talk about it. We got Jerome done and then Clyde and Buck were going to go together and skip our exhibition trip to Hawaii. They told me, "If we don't get this done, we are not going to Hawaii." I said, "That's not good; let's just keep working on it and we can solve it."

We got Clyde's deal done in Honolulu and had to stop at a bank. We were on the team bus on the way to practice, and we stopped at the bank to sign a contract and get it notorized. That one-year extension for $9.75 million — to be paid for the 1995-96 season — was the single largest one-year salary of any pro athlete in any sport up to that point.

We had a great young team and Clyde was still young. He was the captain, our best player and one of the top five or 10 players in the league at that time. We wanted to keep him happy. There was a whole different system back then. Clyde had gone with a series of extensions. As a result, he never became a free agent and landed the huge deal. The reason a team negotiates an extension with a player is because it thinks it is a good deal for both the player and for the team.

Buck also got an extension that paid him about $4 million in 1994-95. Now it was time to go to work.

**BUCK WILLIAMS:** Clyde went to bat for me there. He was very loyal to his teammates, sometimes to a fault. Every time I ever had any kind of issue, he was there for me. I really appreciated that. He would stay in the trenches and battle with you until it was over. When you have not reciprocated such loyalty, he has problems with you. He is a giving kind of person once he invites you into his circle, but he is going to scope you out and make sure you deserve to be in there. He has a big heart. Family is very important to him. I don't know of any other player in the NBA who has done as much with his mother and siblings as he has.

The '90-91 team was my favorite team in Portland. We had the best chance to win a title that year. We had our starting group plus Ainge, and Cliff Robinson was even better. Many preseason magazines were picking us to win the NBA championship, including *Sports Illustrated*, which predicted we would beat Chicago for the title.

My season started rather ominously. In the second game, a 95-93 overtime win over a weak Sacramento team, I was one for 16 from the field. It was the worst shooting game in my career. My only basket was a dunk. But I made two free throws in the closing seconds of regulation, plus I blocked a Lionel Simmons jumper, to get us into overtime. If my shot was off, I always tried to do other things to help my team win.

We had our first meeting with the Lakers in our next game, a stirring 125-123 overtime win at The Forum. I had 27 points, seven rebounds and five assists in 46 minutes. Danny Ainge was off to a terrific start, playing what he called "the best basketball of my life."

**GEOFF PETRIE:** Danny had gotten off to such an amazing start. He hardly missed a shot the first two months of the season.

**DANNY AINGE:** I remember during a scrimmage in training camp, I came downcourt and had a sort of open three but passed it up because one of my teammates was more open. Rick took me aside and said, "Danny, I want you to take that shot. That is why we brought you here." I said, "Yeah, but he was open." He said, "No, listen, take that shot. Because if you miss it, Jerome or Clyde or Buck will get the rebound, and they will put it in."

I thought about that a lot, and as I played more with that team and good things started happening, I learned that Rick was right. Buck and Jerome were going to chase down so many rebounds and score, the chance of me shooting and missing and them getting a putback was greater than me throwing the ball in to them and having them put on a move to score. There was a method to the madness. Rick knew his team. I grew to respect Rick and what he did with the team even more. The perception was that it was just a dumb team. I can understand why outsiders thought that, but there was a method to the way we played. Rick got the most out of that team.

**BUCK WILLIAMS:** Rick was such a great coach — not as much for his Xs and Os, but because he had the pulse of the team. He demanded the same from everyone, but had a way of treating everyone differently, if that makes sense. He knew when he could ease off on guys or when he had to get tough. He was really a fair coach, the ideal coach for the personalities on that team. He got the maximum out of every player.

Drazen Petrovic had slipped behind Danny on the depth chart and received some "Did not play/coach's decision" marks in the box scores of the first four games of the season. Soon thereafter, he went public with a demand to be traded by November 30 or he would return to Yugoslavia. Petrie fined him $500.

We came away smelling awfully pretty in our lone regular-season home matchup with Chicago. We shot .623 from the field in beating up on the Bulls 125-112. It was the fourth straight game we had shot 60 percent or better. I had 30 points, seven rebounds and nine assists while Michael Jordan collected 29 points, five rebounds and seven assists. The "W" was the only thing that mattered to me.

And we were getting plenty of them. We were 9-0, and I was off to a great start, shooting .557 from the field, even with that brutal performance against the Kings. We kept rolling. We beat San Antonio 117-103 in a game that included maybe the best quarter a team of mine ever played. We made 22 of 25 shots in jumping to a 49-18 lead after one quarter. David Robinson and friends looked dazed as they walked back to the bench after the first 12 minutes.

We finally lost, 123-109 to Phoenix at home, and then went on another eight-game win streak, including a 109-101 win over the Bulls on the road (I had 29 points, seven boards and eight assists; Michael scored 35). We were 19-1, the second best start in NBA history behind the 1969-70 Knicks, who started 23-1. Buck was leading the league with a ridiculous shooting percentage of .681. Terry, Duck and Jerome were playing up a storm.

We went into the new year with a 27-4 record and a seven and a half-game lead over the Lakers in the Pacific Division. "Portland is playing the best basketball in the league right now," Magic Johnson told the press before a Lakers-Blazers showdown. "They have impressed everybody with their road record as well as their play at home. They are playing with a lot of confidence, using a lot of people. This is a big game for us, no question. We would like to come in there and win."

The Lakers did, 108-104, with Jerome sitting out due to a calf injury. James Worthy went for 30 points, Magic had 13 points and 17 assists and Sam Perkins collected 19 points and nine boards on seven-of-eight shooting off the bench. We were not going to roll over those guys.

However, we were a team that never quit. Two games later, Seattle had us down by 24 points in the third quarter, but we roared back and Ainge nailed back-to-back threes in the closing minutes for a memorable 114-111 win.

On January 23, a disgruntled Petrovic, who wasn't getting much playing time, was finally traded to New Jersey. We acquired Walter Davis from Denver in the three-way deal. Walter was 36 and on his way down, but he was shooting .474 and averaging 18.7 points a game for the Nuggets. We figured he could be a valuable hired gun off the bench for us.

We beat Milwaukee to reach the midway point in the regular season with a record of 34-7, and Rick told reporters, "It has been a great first half. We have been so consistent with the way we played, no matter who we play. Yeah, we have lost some games that people think we should have won, but every team in the league does that."

We were well represented at All-Star weekend in Charlotte. Terry, Duck and I were named as reserves to the West team. By virtue of our league-best record, Rick and his assistants were the West coaching staff. Mike Shimensky was the trainer, and Terry, Danny and I participated in the three-point contest. I arrived in Charlotte at 3:30 a.m. Friday, got two hours of sleep and then appeared live on NBC's *Today* show. In the game, I scored 12 points, Duck added six and Porter scored four in the West's 116-114 loss on Sunday.

But the Blazers continued to roll. We beat Phoenix 127-106 on February 22 to go 44-9 and in the process set an NBA record with only three turnovers. Even our old doubter, Cotton Fitzsimmons, told the media, "They were sensational. If they continue to play like that, they are going to win the NBA championship. Nobody is going to beat them."

We hit our only road bump of the season in late February with a four-game losing streak. During that time, I took a cortisone shot to relieve pain caused by tendinitis in my right shoulder. Rick told reporters, "The injury has affected Clyde's game, but he hasn't said anything to anybody. He has just gone out and played. That is the kind of guy he is."

In our next game, we got a big win at Boston, 116-107, before a national TV audience. Danny had 17 points off the bench against his ex-mates and my game was on. I amassed 29 points, 13 rebounds, eight assists and three steals. Said Ainge: "You could see the intensity in Clyde's face. He was in that zone — passing, rebounding, shooting, chasing down loose balls. He was all over the place, doing everything."

**JOHN WETZEL:** On the few occasions when Clyde sprained an ankle or had some sort of injury that held him out of the lineup for a couple of games, he could go out that first game back and play 40 minutes, and usually have a great game. He had an incredible stamina and strength about him. He would come out and play and never miss a beat. His body was so strong.

We had a good traveling party that year that included Bill Schonely, our legendary radio play-by-play voice, and his analyst, Mike Rice. On a trip to LA late in the regular season, Rice rented a bike to ride to Venice Beach. He took a spill and was knocked unconscious briefly, sustaining a nasty cut over one eye. Police were summoned to the scene and brought him back to the hotel.

As a squad car arrived at the hotel, I happened to be walking by. "There's someone you can release me to," Rice said, pointing to me. I didn't skip a beat. "Nooo ... he is the Swami," I told the officer. "Take him back to jail."

**MIKE RICE:** We had just done a Blazers TV special in which I predicted San Antonio would beat the Blazers in the upcoming playoffs. All the players had gotten on me about it. So I rode this bike to Venice Beach. The seat was up too high, and I fell off as I hit a curb and took a pretty good spill. The police who arrived shortly after wanted to take me to the hospital. I said no, I'm fine, just take me back to the hotel. We have a team trainer who can look at it. The policeman said, "We are going to have to release you to somebody."

And as we pulled up to the hotel, Clyde was walking by. And I said, "Hey, that's Clyde Drexler, and you can release me to him." Clyde looked at me like he had no idea who I was, and said, "You can take the Swami anywhere you want. Take him back to jail if you want." The cop thought he was serious. I said, "Believe me, the guy knows me." I jumped out of the patrol car door and went up to my room.

**DANNY AINGE:** Clyde was a lot of fun. He loved to talk and joke when we were on Blazer One. He had a good sense of humor. He was just taking up golf and was awful, but he had a pretty good sense of humor about it.

**TERRY PORTER:** Clyde was kind of quiet. If you didn't know him, he wasn't an outgoing guy. But when you got to know him, he was very caring. He would do anything necessary to help you with any situation. We both were married and had young kids, and we used to go to dinner with our families. We went out to dinner on the road together sometimes, too. That really helped those teams. We hung together, me and Clyde and Buck and Jerome and Duck and Coop and Danny Ainge. That was part of what made us special. There might be six or eight or us that would take in a movie together. I don't think you see that very often on an NBA team — then or today. And we had a trust with each other when we stepped on the floor.

**BUCK WILLIAMS:** The chemistry on that team was almost perfect, and everybody had defined roles. Everybody respected each other as a player. That is what made the team go. That was the most memorable team I played with. We were very close, did a lot of things together off the court. Our wives all got along well, which is almost an impossible feat. On the court, we embodied what the Walton-led Trail Blazers had meant to the Portland community. We epitomized what Blazers basketball was all about — selflessness, teamwork, sacrifice.

And off the court, we understood how important the fans were to our success. It was important to try to be good role models for the kids in the community. Nobody is perfect, but we always went in there with that in mind. As professional athletes, kids looked up to us. We had a responsibility that went along with that.

We did have great camaraderie, and it helped that we were together on Blazer One now. A lot of things got done during our flights to games. For a couple of years, we had a little investment club. Buck, Jerome, Terry, Coop and Danny Ainge invested our money from the 1991 playoff pool. We had a pretty good amount invested in a number of stocks. We talked about options, we voted on it and made the decisions collectively. It was a lot of fun.

For a while, we held meetings of our "Kangaroo Court" on the plane. A lot of major league baseball teams had them in those days. I didn't know of another NBA team that had one. It was a way to bust the chops of our teammates. It was Rick Adelman's idea, really. After Duck was elected as the first chief justice, he cracked, "The worst thing they could ever do is elect me."

Players could be fined for just about anything — missing free throws, drawing technicals, passing gas in a concentrated area, such as the airplane or an elevator (on the latter subject, Ainge wondered aloud how Duck planned to prove it).

The original idea was to fine everyone $5 for an offense, or $10 if the player lied about it in court. At our first meeting, forwards Alaa Abdelnaby and Mark Bryant were fined $1 apiece for wearing tiny tennis socks in the games. Terry was fined $2 for calling a cortisone shot a "chromosome shot."

After we had a couple of meetings, Danny said, "I nominated Duck because I thought he would be one of the most just judges. Turns out he is very soft."

**KEVIN DUCKWORTH:** Clyde was the backbone of those teams. We couldn't have accomplished what we did without Clyde. He wasn't a verbal leader. He was a leader by example. He was a leader in the way he played the game and the way he carried himself. He didn't come out and say, "Guys, we got to do this, we got to do that." No. Clyde went out and just played, and nobody played like he did. Nobody I ever played with, anyway.

**PAUL ALLEN:** Clyde was one of the most exciting players the league has ever had. He had some huge games where he would just take over. There aren't many players who can do that. His passion for the game and his competitiveness stood out.

We played some of our best basketball during the final stretch of the regular season, going on a 16-game win streak to wrap up the Pacific Division championship and end the Lakers' run of nine straight titles. We were Cardiac Kids at times, rallying from 24 behind to win 112-107 at Seattle, then coming from 21 down to overtake the Lakers 109-105 in OT.

Meanwhile, Mike Rice was in the news again after he was ejected by Steve Javie in a victory at Washington. Rice had been complaining about the officiating at courtside when Javie, who had also booted two Bullets and their coach, Wes Unseld, gave the Swami the heave-ho. One of our beat writers, Dwight Jaynes, had been kicked out of a game courtside at The Forum, but I think this was the only time in the history of the NBA that an announcer had been ejected.

**MIKE RICE:** Right after the game, I saw Clyde and Terry in the locker room and they said, "Mike, don't worry about it. You were standing up for the team. Whatever you are fined, we will take care of it." The next day, the NBA office called me and asked about the incident, but they didn't say anything about a fine. The next time I saw Clyde and Terry, I said, "Hey, the league is going to fine me $1,500." And they looked at each other and said, "You shouldn't have done what you did, Mike."

We clinched the division with a 118-113 win over the Lakers on April 13. Magic told the media, "They deserve it. They have done a tremendous job. They set the tone at the start of the season and now they have put together 13 in a row at the end of it." I made 14 of 20 shots and scored 31 points, including 13 in the first 5:45 of the game with three straight three-pointers. Laker coach Mike Dunleavy said afterward, "Clyde was terrific. He is a great player. He has been labeled a selfish player in the past, but he is a great passer and a complete player all the way." About the Blazers, Dunleavy added, "They are the best team in the league right now. They play extremely hard. The thing I like most about them is they treat every loose ball like it is the last possession in life. Every game they give a big-time effort, and that is all you can ask from players."

Somebody laid "Pacific Division Champions, 1990-91" T-shirts on each player's stool after the game, but Ainge knew better. "Bonfire. Garage sale," he said, shaking his head. "We don't have any reason to be all that excited. Not yet. We have a long way to go."

We wanted to end the regular season on a 17-game run, but lost our finale 135-118 at Phoenix to finish 63-19. Sixteen and one wasn't bad, though. We were ready.

**JOHN WETZEL:** The best term to describe Clyde is winner. He was a little unorthodox sometimes in the way he played and defended, but he was a winner. He competed every night. When the game was on the line, he thrived. In that run at the end of the 1990-91 regular season, there were games where we would be down seven with two minutes to go. We would call time out, and I would look into the players' faces and see that they believed they could win. Clyde was the biggest part of that. He would make a steal or a block or a big three to get us over the hump. We found a way, based on the kind of players we had, and Clyde was the best example of that. The players really fed off of Clyde. He was the guy who gave them that confidence. He had an incredible self-confidence, and in a cool way. That is why he was able to make big plays like he did. The more pressure, the bigger the game, the more Clyde responded, the better he was.

**GEOFF PETRIE:** The players were working so beautifully together. That was one of the best transition teams I have ever seen. Throughout the regular season, we were the best team in the league. I thought we were going to win a championship. Everybody did.

No eighth seed had ever beaten a top seed in the playoffs. But Seattle gave us a scare, taking us to the fifth game in our best-of-five first-round series. I came up with one of my better efforts to drive us to a 110-102 opening game win. I scored 27 points in the second half and 19 in the fourth quarter. I finished with 39 points, a career playoff high and one shy of the franchise record. I was 14 of 22 from the field, nine of 10 from the line, and had seven rebounds, nine assists and three steals. Jerome, who had 31 points, seven rebounds and five assists of his own, called me "spectacular."

We won Game 2 115-106 and needed just one more victory to wrap up the series. But the Sonics beat us twice in Seattle, 102-99 in Game 3 and 101-89 in Game 4. Benoit Benjamin was playing out of his mind, and we were only 20 of 39 from the line in Game 4, including three of 10 in the fourth quarter.

No way was our playoff journey going to end so quickly. We blew the Sonics away in the deciding Game 5, leading 63-43 at the half and 104-74 on the way to a 119-107 win. I had 22 points, eight rebounds and five assists. And now it was on to Utah, which had dispatched Phoenix in the first round.

We knew what we were getting in Utah. A tooth-and-nail team under the direction of Jerry Sloan, the Jazz were led by Karl Malone and John Stockton. I took a bad spill when Malone fouled me hard on a drive to the basket in the third quarter of the opener, which we won at home 117-97. I managed to stay in the game and was pretty driven the rest of the way, contributing 20 points, a career playoff-high 15 rebounds and eight assists. Rick said: "It scares you. You can't afford to lose Clyde Drexler. It would be like Utah losing Stockton or Malone. After we came out of that timeout, I saw that look in his eyes that something was going to happen."

We squeaked by with a 118-116 victory in Game 2 after nearly blowing a 23-point fourth-quarter lead. Malone scored 40 points in that one, making 19 of 20 foul shots. We were tied at 116-116 with 14 seconds left, but I rubbed Stockton off a Cliff Robinson pick, then passed to Terry, who buried a shot with 3.6 seconds left. Jerome had a playoff career high of 34 points and I had 23 points, five boards, a career playoff-high 15 assists, three steals and four blocks.

Utah got us 107-101 at home in Game 3, but we bounced back to win Game 4 104-101. Duck was at his best with 30 points and 11 rebounds. I notched a triple-double with 15 points, 11 rebounds and 10 assists, but I was hobbled by turf toe and was not really up to par physically.

We wrapped up the series back home with a 103-96 win, breaking it open with a second-half 6-0 run after leading only 52-51 at break.

**JERRY SLOAN:** They were the better team. They had tremendous athletes and were able to take advantage of us. We weren't quite athletic enough to play with them in some cases. We had some great games with them, but sometimes we couldn't put them away.

Clyde was tremendously important to what they were doing. Every team that has won a championship in the last 25 years has had a two-guard who could average five or six rebounds a game. When the Blazers moved him to the guard slot early in his career, that is when they could really take advantage of the opposing defense. Jeff Hornacek and Jeff Malone were both good players, but we never had a guy quite big enough to deal with him. That was a difficult matchup for us. As good as Jeff was, he wasn't as strong or as athletic as Drexler.

Clyde is right at the top among the great two guards in history. There are not that many big guys that athletic. He had a tremendous amount of things he could do that not a lot of guys could do. He could handle the ball, he could beat you off the dribble, he could step out on the floor and shoot, he was great in the open court. That is what great players are capable of.

We went into our Western Conference finals matchup with the Lakers in an unusual position — as the favorite. We had won three of five regular-season meetings and we had home-court advantage, which was important. Over the previous two years, we were 10-0 at home and 11-1 overall in the first two games of play-off series. And we were 15-3 at home in the playoffs, the only blemish being the three losses in the '90 Finals to Detroit.

**ERIC JOHNSON:** I was working as a sportscaster at KGW-TV in Portland during the Western Conference finals that year. During a media session, I needed to interview Clyde. There was an ESPN crew setting up for an interview with him already, so I walked up to the guy doing the interview and asked, "Is this a one-on-one, or can I jump in?" A lot of times in that setting, the interviews were a kind of a group thing, with lots of reporters involved. And the ESPN guy, real snotty-like, said, "This would be a one-on-one."

I was kind of embarrassed and started to back off, but Clyde stopped me. He said, "It's not a one-on-one. In fact, Eric, I will talk to you first, and this guy next." The ESPN reporter stood there, open-mouthed. Clyde took me aside and told me, "You don't have to take that off these national guys. You have been with us all year long." It was Clyde's way of saying to the ESPN reporter, "Don't big-time my home boys."

I have never had an athlete come to bat for me quite like that. It showed me that Clyde had an understanding of the way things worked. He wasn't just a guy answering my questions. He had an awareness of my business, too. I just thought it was the coolest thing.

Eric was there every game that season. I knew Eric. I was hoping we could do the interviews together, so I wouldn't have to answer the same questions twice. The ESPN guy didn't want to do that, so I said, "Eric, let me do yours first."

I practiced before the Western finals with a new pair of shoes designed and modified by Bob Cook to alleviate the turf toe pain. It helped a lot, but I would mostly have to play through the pain.

The mental pain was excruciating after the Lakers rallied from a 14-point deficit late in third quarter to beat us in the opener 111-106. We had shot 57 percent through three quarters, then made only four of 14 shots and committed seven turnovers in the fourth. The Lakers went on a 15-0 run to go from a 92-78 deficit to a 93-92 lead. We came back to lead 104-101 with 3:32 left, then were outscored 10-2 the rest of the way. I had a big game with 28 points, 12 assists and eight rebounds, but it wasn't enough.

We hammered the Lakers on the boards 51-28 — including a hard-to-believe 37-15 in the second half — to win Game 2, 109-98. Then we went to L.A. and lost Games 3 and 4 to fall behind 3-1 in the series. We were in shock. Duck was having trouble staying out of foul trouble. The Lakers were controlling the tempo and we were shooting poorly.

We went back to Portland for Game 5 with our backs to the wall. Buck guaranteed a win, and we backed him up by prevailing 95-84. We failed to score 100 points for the third straight game, the first time that had happened all season. We won that game on effort, setting a team playoff record with 26 offensive boards. But our shooting was awry. After leading the league in three-point shooting during the regular season at .377, we had made only 12 of 45 (.267) in the first five games of the Laker series.

Our hearts were broken in a 91-90 Game 6 loss that eliminated us and sent the Lakers into the NBA Finals. We really felt if we had won that game, we would have gone back to Portland and won Game 7.

We had a great shot at the end, too, though we didn't play that great of a game. We were 11 of 19 from the foul line and couldn't buy an outside shot, but we battled from behind and were right there. We were down 89-88 when the Lakers turned it over. We had a four-on-one fast break inside the final minute. But Jerome's pass to Cliff, who was all alone under the right side of the basket, rolled off his hands and out of bounds.

Even then, we had the ball with 12 seconds to go and a chance to win, trailing 91-90. I drove the lane and fed Terry, who was wide open from the right side of the court. But his 17-footer bounced off the rim, and we were history.

**GEOFF PETRIE:** Losing the opener at home set the tone for the series. But that team never quit. The guys could have cashed it in, but that wasn't their nature. We should have won Game 6. If Cliff hadn't dropped that pass, I think we would have won, and I think we would have won Game 7. Then we ran a perfectly executed play to win the game at the end, and Terry had a wide-open 17-foot shot, and when it went out of his hands I thought it was good. And it just missed, that's all.

**STEVE JONES:** That was a team that collectively had one goal driven by Clyde — to beat Magic and the Lakers and win a championship. They had been chasing the Lakers for several years without much success, but when Rick took over and they picked up Buck, the Blazers came to see that they could beat the Lakers, who were their Holy Grail. They played with that commitment and passion. The most disappointing defeat for that group wasn't losing to Michael Jordan or Isiah Thomas. It came in 1991 when they lost to the Lakers in six games. They lost that first game at home, and it just didn't happen. That really hurt that group more than anything else.

**PAUL ALLEN:** We lost a lot of times at the expense of the Lakers. The toughest was the Game 6 loss in the Western Conference finals in L.A. in '91. After all of those season finales in the playoffs…I went to the locker room and the coaches and players were so upset. It really was heartbreaking. But I feel so fortunate that we made the Finals twice, and there is no doubt Clyde was the key.

**DANNY AINGE:** For me, that season was a failure. It was good up until the Lakers series. We weren't as mentally ready as the Lakers were. One bad weekend in L.A. that we just gave away cost us the whole season. If we had won that game, the championship would have been ours to win. We had a great team. That was the toughest thing. A lot of times when you lose a playoff series, you feel like you lost to a better team. I think we were the better team. That is what hurts.

I was sure 1991 was going to be our year. Of course, I thought the previous year would be, too. The fact is, we didn't get it done. The Lakers won the series. I was just disappointed we didn't go as far as we should have gone. We won 63 games during the regular season. We didn't do too much wrong. We had a bad series against L.A., and yes, it was very disappointing. But I didn't agree with Danny. I didn't consider it a lost season. We did an awful lot of things right. We just didn't win it all.

"Trade Duckworth" was the flavor of the summer on the radio sports talk shows, but that was wrong. He had done some great things for us. We were a young team, yet seasoned. Duck was 27, Terry was 27, Jerome and I were 29, Cliff was 24, Buck was 31, and Ainge was 32. I wanted to give it another try.

I felt the changes to that team should be minimal. The guys all got along. The future was bright. We all felt like we missed an opportunity, but we couldn't wait for the next season to start.

# CHAPTER 14

# CLOSE AGAIN, BUT NO CIGAR

I worked hard every summer to stay in shape. I didn't work out on stationary machines. I ran and lifted weights and went to the gym and shot every day. I spent five, six, seven hours a day working out every summer. That is how I got better.

A typical day's workout would start on a basketball court, with an hour spent working on my shooting, then an hour working on ball-handling drills — up-and-down full-court moves after which I would finish the play at full speed with the ball. Then I would lift weights for 45 minutes to an hour. All this stuff would kill me, but I kept at it. I would finish with either a good session of jump rope, cycling or playing tennis. Or — early in my career — playing a couple hours of pickup basketball. That is how I maintained my body and my talents over the years. People would look at me and say, "Gosh, he is such a natural athlete." Working out seven hours a day for many years, it should be natural.

By now, Gaynell and I had two children, two-year-old Austin and baby Elise. We had purchased a home in the Dunthorpe area of Portland the previous summer and spent most of the summer in Portland for the first time. With the kids, I couldn't run around as much. We traveled a lot, and I always loved doing that, but it was time to settle in a little bit. We loved Portland. I can't emphasize enough how great the city really is. And we wanted to be there in the off season. There is no better weather in the world than Portland in the summertime.

I needed diversions to relax and unwind after a long, hard season. My escapes had always included leisure sports. I had played tennis for years, and in the late '80s, golf became a passion. I first joined Oswego Lake Country Club, but when Oregon Golf Club opened in 1990, they gave all the guys on the team a great deal, so I went over there. Buck Williams, Terry Porter, Rick Adelman, Geoff Petrie — we all became members.

When I started, I could kill the ball, but I didn't know how to control it.

**JOHN WETZEL:** I played golf with Clyde one time at Tualatin Country Club in the early '90s. I remember how far he could hit a golf ball. Distance was a plus, but direction was a minus. With his one-upsmanship manner, he was never going to admit that he couldn't hit it straight. Fact is, he could hit it a ton, but you never knew where it was going to go.

**TERRY PORTER:** Clyde and I started playing golf about the same time, and it wasn't a pretty picture to see us on the golf course back in the early '90s. There were a lot of balls being sprayed all over the place. But that was something we enjoyed doing together.

**GEOFF PETRIE:** Clyde got addicted to golf like a lot of guys. I played with him once or twice during that era. He and Buck were hitting it pretty much left, right, left, right in those days.

At first, you want to break 100. Then you want to shoot in the 80s. Then you want to shoot in the 70s. Now I want to shoot in the 60s. I get there sometimes. I am about a three or four handicap today. I play year-round and have memberships at Lochinvar Country Club in Houston — which has around 200 members, including former President Bush — and Waverley Country Club in Portland. I love golf. When you are on that golf course, it is you against the course. You have to focus so hard on getting the ball into the hole, it takes you away from everything that may be happening in your life.

In Houston, I also spend quite a bit of time at The Houstonian, a posh health and fitness club where I play tennis twice a week and lifts weights maybe three times a week. Fitness will always be a big part of my life.

Back to the summer of 1991, I still shot baskets regularly during the off season, though I didn't play much in pickup games. I didn't need the wear and tear on my body at that point in my career. Of course, sometimes I could get coaxed into a game.

**TIM HANEY:** I can remember going to RiverPlace Athletic Club and playing basketball during the off season. We would just go there to work out, but Jerome Kersey was playing a pickup game, going 400 miles an hour against a bunch of short fat white guys. I asked, "Why is he doing that?" Clyde would say, "That is all he knows. He has one speed, both in practice and games." Then Jerome would bait Clyde into the game, which would get me into the game, and we would get in ahead of a line of people who were waiting for the next game. Clyde would go about 50 percent, Kersey would be going 100 percent, until the end, when Clyde would tomahawk one over the head of Kersey's teammate, and then walk off the court.

Guys would always want to challenge you on the basketball court in pickup games. Some of them are pretty good, but they are not in the same league as NBA players. A lot of times I might go 50 percent on offense, because I could score any time I wanted, really. But defensively, I would go 100 percent. I wanted to shut the other team out, block every shot, make them resort to taking fadeaway hook shots or something.

When guys would get serious, I would say, "It is illegal in 49 states. It is only legal in Nevada, because everything goes there. If I play with you guys, it will be child abuse. I will be in jail." And I would crack up laughing.

In October 1991, they announced 10 members of the "Dream Team" that would be the first professional basketball team to represent the United States in the Olympics at Barcelona in 1992. I wasn't one of them. The team included Michael Jordan, Scottie Pippen, Patrick Ewing, Karl Malone, John Stockton, Magic Johnson, David Robinson, Chris Mullin, Charles Barkley and Larry Bird. The Olympic selection committee said they would add two more players, including a collegian, sometime during the 1991-92 NBA season.

I had no control over the selection process. My main focus was on helping the Blazers get back to the NBA Finals. But after being among the top vote getters in MVP balloting the previous three or four seasons, I certainly thought I was one of the best in the game. To not be put on that team was criminal. It made me question what the criteria was. And I thought Isiah Thomas was slighted, too. I am not sure why he was left off. Years earlier, when Jordan was in the All-Star Game for the first time, there were rumors that Isiah had led a move to keep the ball away from Michael in that game. People were saying that Jordan had told selection committee members if Isiah was included, he wouldn't play. I have no idea if that was true or not. Isiah and Michael were both good friends of mine. I just tried to stay away from it. I hoped someone would not be that petty; I know Michael is a better man than that.

The Blazers had pretty much the same team back from the previous season, a nice blend of big and small, of young guys and old guys, of inside and outside presence. Danny Ainge, who had one year left on his contract, went into training camp considering a holdout because he wanted a two- or three-year extension for about $1.7 million a season. Geoff Petrie was offering a one-year extension of $1.3 million, plus $375,000 in incentives, and a second year at $1.6 million, with a guarantee of $400,000. I could empathize with Danny; I had gone through the same sort of thing before. He didn't hold out, but he did hold it against the Blazers when he became a free agent the following summer.

We wound up waiving Walter Davis and keeping rookie free agent point guard Robert Pack. Walter had been a starter his whole career and was one of the players I grew up watching as "The Greyhound" with the Phoenix Suns. He was not comfortable playing 10 to 12 minutes a game. Robert had impressed everyone with his quickness and energy and deserved his spot.

Terry and Jerome had been captains the previous couple of seasons, but I declared myself the captain before this season for a couple of reasons. I had been ejected a league-high five times the previous year, and I received some technicals primarily because, in those days, only the captain was supposed to talk to the referees. I wanted the power to confer with officials at crucial times. Sometimes it seems we weren't getting the respect we deserved. I talked with Buck and Danny about it, and they agreed it was a good idea. On our team, four or five guys were leaders, so it was no big deal. I just thought I would take a more active role. Since I had been on the team the longest, it was only fitting that I fill that position as captain.

I felt great going into the season, physically and emotionally. We started with an impressive 117-106 win over Cleveland, and I was in a groove, hitting 14 of 20 shots en route to 31 points, seven rebounds and seven assists.

We lost our next three, including a 119-93 pasting at San Antonio. Then we came back to win four in a row, including a 107-102 triumph at Minnesota in which the Wolves led 75-54 late in third. I scored 35 points, including 15 in a row late in third quarter, but Pack was the hero, scoring 13 of his 15 points in fourth quarter. Robert won the game for us, no doubt about it. He defended, he made shots, he penetrated — he did it all. He was a good acquisition for our team, because he gave us so much energy.

On an off day, we had a little fun with Jerome. *Basketball's Funniest Pranks*, a nationally syndicated show, contacted our PR man, John Lashway, and asked him to suggest a player who would enjoy helping them stage a prank. He chose Alaa Abdelnaby, who asked Ainge to help put one over on Mr. Kersey.

Jerome had mentioned he was interested in buying a stable of horses in Oregon someday, so the scenario was arranged: Abdelnaby and Ainge were supposed to be going in on the purchase of a prize racehorse who was unbeaten in three races and a young up-and-comer. Each had chipped in $50,000 and were looking for a third partner. Alaa said he knew Jerome would be a total sucker for it.

They met in the Coliseum parking lot to view the horse, which in truth was a nag with one eye and swayback who looked about 15 years old. As Alaa put it, "we are talking about an ugly, ugly horse." They were unbending in their support of the venture. Ainge told Jerome, "The one eye might be an advantage, because he could concentrate on the rail."

Kersey admitted they had him going for a while. He said he had reservations about the horse, "but I was trying to be nice. I was thinking, 'Are they sure they want to invest $50,000 apiece in this?'" Jerome recalled.

After Alaa left to discuss terms with the trainer — an actor hired by the show — Ainge changed his story to Jerome, pointing out the horse's obvious shortcomings and saying he was going to ask for his money back. Then the trainer returned and said he had the money from Alaa and Ainge and needed Jerome's check. Kersey said he needed more time to think about it, but the trainer told him he already had Kersey's signature on the contract. Alaa sheepishly admitted he had forged his teammate's signature, and Kersey exploded. "You did what?"

Alaa said, "Jerome would have hit me in the mouth if the other people hadn't been around."

Kersey was stalking off when Alaa led him back to the cameras to let him in on the stunt. Jerome took it well, relieved it was just a gag.

Every day was a new adventure with that group. Danny hadn't received his contract extension, supposedly because management had run out of money on the rest of our deals. At Christmas, Danny bought boxes of chocolates for everybody and gave them out on the plane. He handed Petrie a box; when Geoff opened it, it was empty. "Sorry, I just ran out of chocolates," Ainge told him. Everybody just roared. Petrie was good-natured about it. He had to admit it was funny.

We played the Clippers, coached by my old friend Mike Schuler. Somehow I mustered up the motivation to score 39 points. Afterward, Mike told reporters, "I don't know too many people who have had success defending Clyde when he is hitting the jumper the way he was. You just have to try to control the best you can the number of really easy baskets he gets — the dunks, the layups, the offensive boards. He is such a great athlete, such a great runner, and they ran extremely well on us."

I was playing some of the best ball of my career. In a 116-111 win over San Antonio, I went for 48 points, hitting 17 of 28 shots from the field. Even Willie Anderson was impressed: "It is something only a few guys in this league — David Robinson, Michael Jordan, Larry Bird — are capable of doing. It is rare when a guy can get 40 or 50 points, but Clyde's one of those guys."

**RICK ADELMAN:** Clyde always felt he could do whatever it took. Sometimes that hindered him when he was first starting out, but that is a trait many of the great ones share. During that 1991-92 season, he was doing the impossible nearly every night. I don't know a lot of guys in our league who could do the things he could do. You just don't come across players like that. Everything on the team revolved around him.

The Bulls were the team to beat in the East, and they came to Portland with an 11-2 record. We were 9-5. They came away with a 116-114 win in double overtime. Jordan and I had another classic duel, but it wasn't enough to get us a "W." Michael scored 40 points but was only 16 of 39 from the field. Scottie Pippen had a big game with 28 points, 11 rebounds and eight assists. I had 38 points — on 15-of-27 shooting — and 12 boards before fouling out late in the second overtime. Asked by the media afterward, Jordan said I was "really making a run at an Olympic team spot. He is building a very strong case with the way he has been playing." Lord knows I was not thinking about an Olympic spot; I was trying to win the game.

A day after being named NBA Player of Month for November, I went for 34 points, 10 rebounds and seven assists in a 124-115 win over Orlando. It was my seventh 30-point game in the last 11. Rick told reporters, "Clyde was unbelievable. He has been on such a roll. When he is shooting the ball as well as he has been, he is impossible to guard."

Still, despite all of my big games, we weren't playing as well as we had hoped. After losing to Detroit at home, we were only 13-9 overall and 8-5 at home.

But things turned around, and we started winning big — 12 of the next 15 and 19 of 24 to go into the All-Star break 32-14.

There are always moments of levity in a season. In a 115-102 win over Philadelphia in January, Manute Bol didn't like a call and tossed the ball toward Alaa Abdelnaby. Alaa tossed it back at Bol and caught him on the back of the neck. Manute had a few choice words, but it ended there. Alaa, who was a funny guy, quipped, "He called me a damn Egyptian. We almost needed a Middle East/African summit there."

There were also some internal matters that caused some hard feelings within the organization. In January, the Blazers waived Danny Young to keep rookie guard Lamont Strothers. The coaches all wanted to keep Danny, a cool veteran who had been an important backup to Terry the previous season. But Brad Greenberg, director of player personnel, had traded a pair of second-round draft picks to Golden State for the rights to Strothers, who had played at a place called Christopher Newport College. Rick was really upset with Brad, who apparently won the power struggle — this time, that is. Danny wound up playing for the Clippers. Strothers, who could really defend and possessed some NBA skills, played four games for us that season, nine for Dallas the next season and then was out of the league for good.

Rumors were flying that we were going to acquire Charles Barkley, who was in his eighth season with Philadelphia and was on the "could-be-had" list. Supposedly, we were going to send Duck, Kersey and Ainge to the 76ers for Charles.

It bothered the three Blazers mentioned, but you had to take it with a grain of salt. "At least I will still be with Jerome,"

Duckworth told reporters. "Maybe we can get an apartment together in Philadelphia."

No trades happened, however, and we continued to win, hiking our home streak to 15 games. I made my sixth All-Star team, but my first as a starter, meaning the fans had voted me in for the first time. It was nice to be voted in, but to be honest, I thought I should have been voted in years before. I felt I had been slighted three or four times.

People used to say, "You are from a small-market city, and not a lot of people get to see you play." Well, that's not my fault, and I wasn't buying that, anyway. That was just an excuse.

I don't mean to sound ungrateful. All-Star games were a nice honor, and I appreciated playing in them. But I had mixed emotions, too. After two or three All-Star games, it went through my mind that it would be nice to have a few days off, too.

During All-Star weekend in Orlando, I did a lot of interviews. Among the questions and answers:

How much better are you now than when you started your career? "I thought I was pretty good then. I could be wrong. I tried to do the things the team needed. That's still my basic approach."

Are you a smarter player now? "I thought I was pretty smart back then. You grow smarter with time, but in terms of the game of basketball, there are rookies who come in and play smart. I thought I was one of those guys."

Is your confidence greater than ever? "If you don't believe in yourself, who else is going to believe in you? Sure, there's a fine line. You don't want to be arrogant or cocky, but you have to have a quiet belief in yourself."

How did you improve your perimeter shot? "My fourth year in Portland, I raised my scoring average to 21 points, and that was the year I really improved my jumper. The biggest change is I exert less energy and have better results. I used to put too much energy into jumping too high. Now I barely jump and use strictly wrist action. Geoff Petrie worked with me one summer, and I worked a lot with Kiki. That's when my jumper really improved, became more consistent. Defenders won't even give me the three-pointer any more."

Would your career be unfulfilled without a title? "I would think it would be lacking. Every player who ever played pro sports will tell you that."

And I was asked about not being among the original 10 selected to the Dream Team. "I thought I was slighted, to be perfectly honest. There's nothing you can do but move on."

The coach for the West team was Golden State's Don Nelson, a man I had little patience for. Two years earlier, before the seventh game of the Western Conference semifinals against San Antonio, he had popped off on a subject he knew very little about. Asked by a writer who the league's most overrated player was, Nelson said, "Clyde Drexler. He chips away at what an organization is trying to do. He is the worst of all kinds, because he comes off as polite. He is religious, devoted to family. Yet in the context of a team, he is destructive."

Nelson was getting his information from Mike Schuler, an assistant on his Golden State staff, where he made the remarks about me. Nelson was making his remarks to support Schuler, who was named head coach of the Clippers the following week. I guess Schuler couldn't stand to see the Blazers doing great things. I don't know what it was. I had only met Nelson once in my life.

That summer, Nelson had written a letter of apology to me. Still, it was hard for me to let it go. He had made a very public comment and then a very private apology.

When I found out Nelson was going to be the West coach, I told a reporter, "I have never understood how somebody can make comments like that without even knowing you. What he said was wrong, any way you look at it. It took every piece of restraint in my body not to go after him when I first saw him. I think he should have been fined by the league for making that statement. You can talk about my performance until you're blue in the face and we can argue about it. But when you attack my character, I will come back at you. When you do that, you are insulting my whole family. That is something he has to account for. He was trying to use me as a scapegoat to cover up for Schuler's failings as a coach. I have to admit, there is a lot of uneasiness on my part playing for him."

In Orlando, Nelson was asked about his comments and said, "I made a foolish mistake a couple of years ago when I said those things. I have apologized publicly many times about it. If that's what he wants, let me say, 'I'm sorry, Clyde, I was foolish.' It will have no effect on our relationship. He has been the bigger man by accepting my apology. Is that groveling enough?"

The truth of it was, I loved Nelson's brand of basketball. He would tweak his lineup to make the game more up and down at different stages and just try to outrun the opposition. I love that style. But I was still ticked about his statement.

This was the All-Star Game in which Magic Johnson came out of retirement to play. He had quit the previous year after it was announced that he had tested positive for HIV. But he was doing well, and public opinion wanted him included in the festivities. So Tim Hardaway graciously stepped aside as a starter, Magic started and was outstanding as we routed an East team that included Jordan, Ewing and Barkley by the score 153-113. Magic's line: 25 points and nine assists in 29 minutes. He hit three three-pointers in the final three minutes, including an off-balance heave that swished as if by magic on the game's final shot.

I had the best All-Star performance of my career, making 10 of 15 shots and finishing with 22 points, nine rebounds and six assists in 28 minutes. In the second half, I was on the bench sitting next to Hakeem Olajuwon. Hakeem kept telling me, "You are going to be the [game] MVP. You've got it." I told him, "I don't want it." Emotions were running high for Magic, and that was fine. He drew nine of 11 votes — I got the other two — and he won the MVP trophy.

**TIM HANEY:** I was at that game, repping for Avia. Clyde was all set to be the MVP, and I remember Hakeem leaning over on the bench to tell him, "You are gonna be the MVP." But Magic was such an emotional story, and he played well. At the end of the game, Magic hit those three unbelievable threes. Three straight times down the stretch, Clyde had an open 15-foot jumper, but he was looking to pass the ball to Magic. I was in the locker room after the game when Magic came over to Clyde, out of earshot of everyone, and said, "Thank you." Clyde just nodded back. He didn't seem to mind Magic taking the limelight.

Magic told reporters, "A lot of guys could have won the MVP. Clyde, for one, really put on a show." He came over to me in the locker room, hugged me and said, "You were wonderful." I told him, "For you, babe."

It didn't bother me at all not to win the MVP. My sentiments were with Magic. I just enjoyed being on the same court with him. I was glad he won. There is no better way to honor a guy who has been a legend in our league. It was truly a Magic-al moment.

Don Nelson said afterward, "I wanted to have them both on the floor at the end. I thought it was between those two for MVP, and I didn't want to influence that Clyde had an amazing game. Not just his offense, but he was very good defensively and our leading rebounder. I told him in several huddles today, I was definitely wrong about the guy. He is a terrific talent."

When Magic came down with HIV, everyone thought within a year or two he would be dead. For him to go out there and play like that, people were touched emotionally. I must say, if I had known Magic would stay so healthy — he will probably outlive us all — I wouldn't have been passing him the ball! I'm kidding, of course. We have been and will always remain friends.

A couple of years ago, I went out to eat with Nelson and Kiki and we had the best time. Everybody has said things we wish we hadn't said. Nelson had taken a lot of heat for his comments — from his wife, his friends. That he wrote a handwritten apology showed me that he is a decent human being. It takes character to write a letter like that. I have forgiven him and we have a good relationship now.

At the All-Star Game, Chicago's Phil Jackson, who coached the East, told the media, "If there is anybody in this game who comes close to Michael in terms of talent, it is Clyde Drexler. Basketball aficionados think his game is absolutely terrific, and he was terrific today. There are two spots left on the Olympic team, and I am definitely lobbying for this guy."

There was actually only one spot, since one was reserved for a collegiate player who turned out to be Duke's Christian Laettner. But the way I felt about that last spot was this: People see me play every night. I am not a guy who is trying to convince anybody of anything. I never sent out a resume or tried to impress someone. My statistics indicated I was worthy of selection on the Dream Team. I didn't need any validation. It was kind of an insult to even talk about it. If they picked me, fine; if they didn't, fine. My focus was on playing as well as I could and helping the Blazers win.

We were playing really well now as a team and moving toward our second straight division title. Phoenix coach Cotton Fitzsimmons, who always liked to damn us with faint praise, said, "We aren't like Portland, who can just go out and overwhelm you with athletic ability. We're a bunch of Hornaceks. We have to overachieve to win." Cotton would always talk; that didn't detract from the fact that he was an awesome coach.

Cotton's words didn't sit well with Rick Adelman. "He is just blowing smoke. That is a way of saying if they win, it is because of hard work; if we win, it is because we have so much talent. That is not true. They have so many skilled players — Kevin Johnson, Tom Chambers, Andrew Lang, Dan Majerle — and great shooters like Hornacek and Chambers. Cotton is always saying things like that, and I don't know why, because we work as hard as any team in the league."

The Clippers had fired Mike Schuler and hired Larry Brown as coach, and he improved his record to 3-0 by upsetting us 107-106 at the Coliseum on February 16. I had to sit out the game with a sprained big toe. We weren't used to losing to the other L.A. team. The Clippers had lost 27 of 29 overall against us and 30 of their last 31 visits to Portland.

I returned to help us beat Phoenix 129-116, contributing 28 points, eight rebounds and five assists in 33 minutes. Rick said, "Clyde never ceases to amaze me. He can be out three or four days and just pick up where he left off. Just having him on the floor was a steadying influence to our team. Having him out there makes me a much better coach."

Duck was struggling, shooting .433 from the field and .707 from the line and moping about playing time. The previous three seasons, the big fella had shot a combined 48 percent from the field and 76 percent from the line, averaged 16.7 points and 6.9 rebounds and twice made the All-Star Game. His minutes were down to 27.3 a game, with Cliff Robinson getting time at center in the fourth quarter of games.

Duck told the media, "I hate to say I am frustrated, because when I get frustrated, it affects my game big-time. I don't want to take my jumper; that's the bad part about it. I'm not really looking to take it. I'm head-faking and looking to throw the ball to someone else."

Duck was struggling after his subpar performance in the Lakers series the previous year. Our fans had made him a target for criticism, and Duck was sensitive to it: "That is the bad part about my personality. I could never take criticism, even as a kid." A lot of the criticism was focused on his weight, which had increased some from the previous season. Duck was hearing a lot of fat jokes and was sensitive to that. He just wanted to blend in with his teammates.

Duck could play. The weight wasn't that much of a factor. He was still productive on the court. When a team loses some games, everyone has to put them under the microscope. He was one of the top five centers in the league, overweight or not. He was the one guy who had some weight on the team. Everybody else was quick and fast. We needed some meat in there.  He set the best picks, and he would always make the jumper. I loved playing with Duckworth.

**GEOFF PETRIE:** Kevin never recovered from the series against the Lakers when Vlade Divac outplayed him so badly. It was such a psychological thing; he was so sensitive to anything that was said about him, and his weight. He was so upset emotionally, he hadn't worked out at all that summer, and he had gained so much weight.

We went back to New Jersey, where the Nets, who came into the game with a 24-31 record, beat us 98-96 on the scoreboard and by an unbelievable 64-38 count on the boards. Our old teammate, Drazen Petrovic, led the Nets with 17 points. I made 13 of 21 shots and scored 31 points in the game, but I was pissed afterward: "You have to be ready to play regardless of who is on the floor for the other team. To say we were out of sync is an understatement."

The next game, we buried Washington 117-96. I had a pretty good third quarter — 18 points on five of six from the field and seven of seven from the line — and finished with 36 points to go with six boards and seven assists.

**DANNY AINGE:** Clyde better have had a great game, after all the trash he was talking on the plane [following the New Jersey game]. He just picked over all the things we did wrong against New Jersey. It made everybody a little more aware of what we had to do. Nobody wanted to take abuse for two more hours after that one.

Our next game was at Chicago. There was an incredible amount of anticipation nationally for the game, and to be honest, I couldn't wait until it was over. A lot of people had been talking about the game for a long time, giving it such a big buildup. The talk was it was going to be the championship matchup. I just thought the hype was premature, and it was kind of irritating.

We didn't look like a title contender in that game; we were totally out of sync. The Bulls blew us out 111-91. I had 26 points and 12 rebounds, but we turned the ball over 23 times in what I termed "poor thought-processing."

**STEVE JONES:** Clyde's leg was bothering him, but at one point he got the ball in the open court and Bill Cartwright was between him and the basket. And Clyde just cocked the hammer and threw that thing down and woke everybody up in Chicago Stadium. That was Clyde's "I take what I want" stance.

That is the one thing that always sticks out to me. He was always going to make it his way, and it wasn't going to be the normal way. He was so strong, he could overpower most two guards. He used the strength of his body and his ability to get in the air. He would either jump over you or take it around you, and if he missed it, more often than not he would chase the rebound down very quickly.

The loss to the Bulls dropped us to 39-18 for the season, but then we ran off nine wins in the next 10 games. On March 3, we beat the Lakers, who were falling out of the race. Magic was gone, and now James Worthy was out for the year with a knee injury. But we had plenty of competition for the best record in the West. Golden State was right there chasing us, and Utah and Phoenix were not far behind.

On March 31, we lost to the Suns 128-111 in Phoenix as Jeff Hornacek scored 34 points and Kevin Johnson added 27 points and 20 assists. I was only four of 17 from the field for 14 points and 12 assists, and I missed a fourth-quarter dunk.

I was concerned with my health. My toe was still bothering me, and so was my right knee. I was trying to play through the pain. Our next game was against Utah, and I didn't know if I could play until I participated in the shootaround. I decided to play, and I was pretty good, hitting 13 of 16 shots — including 13 of my last 14 — and scoring 33 points in 29 minutes in a 118-86 drubbing of the Jazz. We beat the Warriors back to back to wrap up the division title with two weeks left in the season. But, I was hurting. The knee was inflamed and accumulating fluid, and Dr. Cook had to drain it.

I got the knee drained five or six times that year. Surgery was out because I couldn't afford to miss any time. It affected my play tremendously. The knee had to have constant maintenance. When it has fluid in it, it takes away quickness and mobility. When I woke up in the morning and there was a game that night, and I knew I would have to get that thing drained, it was not a good feeling. I was concerned about doing more damage to it. It took away from my aggressiveness at times.

But I am one of those guys who believe in fate. I wasn't going to quit until the leg fell off. We were too close to our goal of a championship. Every now and then, I had to sit out a practice or take a day or two off. Rick was very good in those situations. He said, "Clyde, let me know how you feel. We want you as healthy as you can be for the games." We were on our third straight season going late into the playoffs, and those games take a lot out of all the players. That is why it is so hard for a team to make it to the Finals year after year. It makes what the Bulls of the '90s and the Lakers of the '00s accomplished more amazing.

I sat out five of the last six regular-season games to give the knee as much rest as I could going into the playoffs. Terry and Jerome were nursing leg injuries, too. Health seemed like it was going to be a major issue for us this time. One good sign: Duck had gotten his game together in the last month, shooting .522 over the last 20 games.

I finished the regular season with averages of 25.0 points, 6.6 rebounds and 6.7 assists. I finished second behind Jordan in balloting for the MVP award and I was named first-team All-NBA for the first time.

Our first-round matchup was with the Lakers, who were not as scary as in the past because they didn't have their big guns. We beat them easily at home in the first two games of the best-of-five, but in Game 2 my right hamstring started to bother me.

*Sports Illustrated* sent a writer to Portland to profile me, but they canceled the assignment when we couldn't hook up. He wanted to come to my house and claimed that I had cancelled three interview appointments. Truth was, I was undergoing treatment for my knee and hamstring. That was the most important thing for me at that time. I told the reporter everything I had to do. And coming to my house was not part of the package. I was willing to talk to him any place, but not at my home. You have to keep some part of your life for yourself. That is imperative.

**TIM HANEY:** Clyde was always big, but that year, he became huge. I remember getting hounded by people around the country wanting to know why he was not a national spokesperson for somebody. Their feeling was, it was a wasted opportunity. I actually kind of agreed. Hey, Avia was just a little shoe company. No one picked up on Clyde as a national guy, but Avia ran our ads national in '92 for the first time ever. He gave up an opportunity to do other things. He said, "I don't need it."

After John Stockton switched to Nike, he said, "They are making me go to New York to be in a commercial." He was so mad. Most athletes are dying for those opportunities. Clyde was kind of the same way as John. He did do a local Smith's Home Furnishing TV commercial. He was pretty savvy. He knew people wouldn't mess with him in Portland. When you do a commercial shoot, typically it lasts an entire day with maybe 25 takes, so you can get it just right. Clyde would do it once, maybe twice, then insist he was done. He would tell me, "They just want to keep you around."

We went to L.A. for a photo shoot for an Avia TV commercial, titled "Dr. Drexler and Mr. Clyde," that took us four days to complete. We wanted to show the two sides of Clyde — on the court, and off the court. We released it in New York, L.A. and Chicago. We didn't play it in Portland; everyone knew him there already.

Clyde had a fan club at GI Joe's that was huge. It was a pretty major investment. We had about 50 interactive video kiosks where you could sign up, get a newsletter and other stuff. It was funny. Clyde appealed to the 40-

year-old women. The kids liked the Iverson kind of player. Clyde was so clean-cut and said all the right things; he had no street cred because he was such a solid guy. His demo was business guys and moms and dads. With his national reach, he appealed to the older, more affluent crowd as well.

We flew to Los Angeles for Game 3 and wound up on the losing side in overtime, 121-119. Unheralded Terry Teagle went for 26 points, and Byron Scott and Sedale Threatt combined for 72 more. I did everything I could to wrap up the series. I scored a career playoff-high 42 points in 46 minutes, sinking 14 of 23 from the field and 12 of 13 from the line to go with nine boards and 12 assists. I really wanted to finish them off so we could get a little extra rest for our assorted wounds. But the Lakers were really tough and made a ton of free throws (39 of 48), and we just couldn't overcome that.

I was afraid we had given them room to breathe in the series.

After the game, we walked out of the Forum and into a war zone — the fallout of the Rodney King trial verdict. Blacks rioted in protest through many parts of Los Angeles, including the area surrounding the Forum. We strode onto our bus, viewing smoke and hearing sirens in the distance. We bused to our Marina del Rey hotel mostly in silence as businesses in nearby Watts were looted, burned and destroyed. That night, a curfew was enacted, and streets were emptied as if martial law had prevailed.

The next day, we practiced at the Forum as the city of Inglewood declared a state of emergency, requesting that National Guard troops be deployed in the area. Later that day, Game 4 was moved to Las Vegas, which was fine with us. We all felt strange being in L.A., and besides that, it took away a little of the Lakers' home-court advantage.

I had been glued to the TV set as much as I could the next day after the King verdict. I will never forget the fire, the smoke, the sirens — just a feeling of being uncomfortable and a little scared. It was like being in a third-world country. During the game, we had not been aware of the things that were happening around us, which was good.

We went down to Vegas and took care of the Lakers 102-76. I had 26 points and 12 rebounds, and my legs felt better that day. I remember before the game at Thomas & Mack Center, we all went out and had kind of an impromptu dunk contest. I usually didn't do that sort of thing, but it was a good way to loosen up and the fans were calling for it. They didn't get to see many NBA games in that city, so we wanted to give them something to cheer about.

**JACK SCHALOW:** The greatest play I ever saw Clyde make was in the clincher of the playoff series in Vegas. I will never forget it. It was in the second half, and our basket was at our end. We came down on a fast break, with Clyde on the right wing, and Terry threw a lob pass to Clyde for the layup. But it was too high, and it looked like it was going to go into the 10th row, way up over the top of the basket. Clyde jumped up near the top of the backboard, grabbed the ball and threw it down as he went by in the air. I remember Wetz and Rick and I looked at each other, and we couldn't believe he went that high to get it. I asked him later, and he said, "I just jumped as high as I could." His hand was probably four feet above the basket.

We moved on to another matchup with Phoenix. The Suns had won the regular-season series 3-2 and had a great offensive team with Johnson, Hornacek, Chambers and Dan Majerle. We won the first two games at home in thrilling fashion, 113-111 and 126-119. In Game 1, we hit 19 of 24 foul shots in fourth quarter, including Porter shooting 10 of 10. Terry scored 31 points total, and I added 26 points and 10 rebounds, but we shot only .387 from the field. Good thing we were 38 of 47 from the line.

We went to Phoenix for Game 3, and the Suns won 124-117 as Hornacek went for 30 points. I scored 37, including our final 13 points of the game, but it wasn't enough.

Then came Game 4 on May 11, which proved to be one of the greatest nights of my life. First, we won the game 153-151 in double overtime, the highest-scoring playoff game in NBA history and one that took three hours, 32 minutes to complete.

We knocked down 14 of our first 16 shots and led 42-29 after the first quarter and 74-65 at the half. The Suns came back, and we missed a whole bunch of free throws that could have clinched it for us in regulation. Duck was our hero, scoring eight points in the second overtime, including four free throws in the final 43 seconds.

I finished with 35 points, eight rebounds, 11 assists and three blocked shots in 51 minutes, and Danny Ainge came up big as he did so many times, scoring 25 points off the bench, hitting nine of 14 from the field and four of six from behind the arc.

Ainge said he had been involved in only two games of the same magnitude: the 1988 finals in which Bird stole Isiah Thomas's inbounds pass to win the title for Boston, and in 1984, when Gerald Henderson's steal and layup sealed the Celtics' win in the finals against the Lakers. Adelman said it ranked with Portland's seventh-game playoff win over San Antonio as the two most exciting games he participated in through 17 years as a coach or NBA player. Phoenix owner Jerry Colangelo compared it to Boston's triple-overtime win over the Suns in the '76 Finals — the shot heard round the world — as the greatest game in franchise history.

**KEVIN DUCKWORTH:** That was a great game — one of the best I have ever participated in. I couldn't believe the guys who always made free throws — especially Terry and Clyde — were missing them. I didn't play much during the second half. Rick used Cliff a lot in that game. He put me in during the overtime and I won the game. Phoenix was a rivalry to us like we became to the Lakers. They were such competitive games. Some people never get to see a game like that. They don't score anything close to that total anymore.

After the game, I got official word that I was the final NBA player added to the Dream Team. Rod Thorn, a member of the selection committee, said I had been slighted when I wasn't originally included, "but we rectified it. We got another shot. Although Clyde has always been a terrific player, he really jumped out at us this year. He is at the peak of his game. If it weren't for the Magic Johnson show, he would have been the MVP at the All-Star Game. It's been like that the whole year. He stepped up into another category within the league as to how people think of him. Everybody always thought he was a great player, but now it's beyond that."

**HARRY GLICKMAN:** I will never forget that night. Russ Granik, the NBA's deputy commissioner, had called the night before, and I had given him my word that I wouldn't say anything until after the game. We got on the plane to head home, and finally I told Clyde and his teammates that he had been selected for that Dream Team. It was a thrilling moment for me, for Clyde and everyone involved with the franchise.

Clyde and I had a special relationship. I don't consider myself a friend of a lot of players I had over the years. I consider Clyde a damn good friend. He once said something about me that made me feel proud. Something like, "As long as Glickman is with the Blazers, it is going to be an honest operation."

I had the honor to be named First Citizen of Portland in 1992. A whole bunch of ex-hockey players, guys who had played for the Buckaroos when I ran the Western Hockey League club, showed up. The only basketball player who came — and I never even told him about it — was Clyde.

Harry had always been a rock for the franchise. I got to know him as a person, liked him very much and came to admire his leadership qualities. He gave his blood, sweat and tears for the franchise for many years, and he was a big reason why it was such a successful organization over the years.

We returned to Portland and wrapped up the Phoenix series with a 118-106 win. The fans gave me an unbelievable ovation before the game, and I responded with 34 points, eight rebounds and eight assists. Life was good.

Our Western Conference finals opponent was Utah, which provided for a classic matchup between teams that had split their four regular-season meetings. It was the Blazers' racehorse ball against the Jazz's rugged slow pace. Buck against the Mailman, Porter vs. Stockton, Jeff Malone challenging me.

**BUCK WILLIAMS:** I never had so much fun playing with anyone as I did with Clyde. Part of it was his confidence that spilled over to the rest of the guys on the team. We would be playing a good team like the Lakers or Utah, and he would say before the game, "Buck, let's get a 20-point lead so we can sit down and let other guys play." Well, that wasn't easy. But Clyde would say, "We are a much better team than these guys," and he meant it. Against those teams, we always had a spurt in the game where we just went on a tear. If a team could hang in there, they would have a chance to beat us. If not, we would be on the bench, having fun and watching the reserves in the fourth quarter.

We routed the Jazz 113-88 in the opener in Portland, jumping to a 37-19 lead after one quarter and making 24 of our first 30 shots from the field. Terry was sensational, making five of his club-record six three-pointers in the first half. He finished six of eight on threes and eight of 12 overall for 26 points and eight assists in 28 minutes. That made him an unbelievable 22 of 40 from three-point range in the playoffs thus far. He was so underrated as a player. He was a terrific shooter, but he could penetrate and get to the line as good as anyone I have ever played with. That was Terry's real skill. When we needed a bucket, quite often he would drive and get to the line. And a lot of times, he would make a left-handed shot — he was great with the off hand — and convert a three-point play. Young point guards would do well to learn to use the off hand the way Terry did.

In Game 2, Porter bombed in 41 points — his career high in either a regular-season or playoff game — to lead us to a 119-102 win. I had 36 points, 12 assists, six rebounds and three steals, but it was Terry's game. He was 12 of 14 from the field, four of five from three, and 13 of 14 from the line. He also had seven assists, six rebounds, three steals and just one turnover in 38 minutes. Toward the end of the game, the fans were serenading him by chanting, "Ter-ree! Ter-ree!" Afterward, Terry admitted, "If I got any hotter than tonight, it would be a scary thought. I don't think it is humanly possible."

When somebody asked me if we were the best backcourt in the league, I answered, "They should have been saying that years ago."

**TERRY PORTER:** Clyde and I just bonded over the years. We started in the backcourt together for eight years in Portland. We never talked about ourselves and trying to outdo other guard tandems. There were some good ones in the league — Isiah and Dumars in Detroit, Magic and Byron Scott in L.A., Harper and Blackman in Dallas. I think maybe the Utah series was the best playoff series Clyde and I played together. I think a lot about that series.

We went to Salt Lake City knowing our plate was full. The Jazz won Game 3, 97-89, with the Mailman going for 39 points and Porter making only three of 13 shots after sinking 20 of 26 shots in the first two games. And they also took Game 4, 121-112. We were whistled for 34 personal fouls and six technicals, and the Jazz make a club playoff-record 48 of 55 at the line.

I had a little trouble with official Joey Crawford, who gave me my second technical and ejected me with 1:30 to go. I had just hit a three-pointer to get us within 116-110, and I thought I was fouled by Jeff Malone. I complained to Joey, and boom! I was gone. Joey's explanation afterward: "He kept trying to disrupt things. He was aggravated and had been that way for some time. [The three referees] talked about it. We knew from the second quarter that if they were behind in the fourth quarter, he was going to go. He looked liked like he was going to take everything out on us. [On the second T], he wanted to talk, and I felt it was better off if he went to the dressing room."

I got both technicals for asking a question. On the last one, I said, "I was tripped." That's it. I wasn't even talking to him. It wasn't like I was in his face. Joey had a short fuse that night. The national media was all over us for lack of composure, but we didn't feel like we deserved it. All we did was play extremely hard.

Back in Portland, Game 5 was one for the ages. We scored on all 10 possessions in overtime to win 127-121, going seven of seven from the field and six of seven from the line. Utah got a bad break when I inadvertently poked Stockton in the eye just before the halftime buzzer, and he couldn't play the second half. I felt really bad, as he has always been one of my favorites. All he did was produce. But those are the breaks of the game. Jerome had 29 points, 10 rebounds and five assists, and Terry, Duck and I all had 24 points. Duck was really good, hitting 11 of 15 shots. Big Sexy, which was his nickname, had a monster game.

We went back to Salt Lake City for Game 6 determined to end the series, and we did with a 105-97 win. The Jazz went into the game 45-4 at home that season, including 8-0 in playoffs, and we had to rally from an early 13-point deficit. I scored 12 of my 18 points in the third quarter as we came back to take the lead. Danny Ainge hit back-to-back threes to ignite a 15-4 fourth-quarter surge, and we played great defense in the second half as the Jazz could make only nine of 40 shots in the final two periods.

It had been a war, and when it was over, Malone cupped Buck's head in his hands and whispered, "Great job. Now go to the Finals and win it all." It was a show of class from the Mailman, who is one of the all-time greats.

**KARL MALONE:** Those Portland-Utah battles over the years were epic. I had Stock and Clyde had Terry Porter. The Portland fans were very knowledgeable about basketball, just like our fans were. It was an intense rivalry, on the court and in the stands. We knew if we played those guys, regular season or playoffs, it was always a test for us.

They couldn't beat us at our place; we couldn't beat them at theirs. I miss those guys. I am the only one still standing in the NBA.

In the week leading up to the Finals and the matchup with Chicago that everyone had hoped for, I was interviewed by just about every news outlet in the country, including *Sports Illustrated, The Sporting News* and *Courtside.* I was profiled on TV by *Inside Stuff* and *SportsCenter.* NBC interviewed Gaynell.

The following are some of the questions I was asked, and my responses:

What do you think about the head-to-head matchup with Michael Jordan? "I don't think you play for being in the spotlight. You play to do the best you can to help your team. His team is in the Finals, and so are the Blazers, and I'm just happy to be a part of it. ... I'm just doing my job. It's a team game. You have to do everything within the context of the team. That's the way I feel. That's the way I think."

What do you think about all the acclaim you have received this year? "It has been great. I have been very happy to have received those honors. But I see those things as bonuses. I would rather see the team do well than to have the awards."

Does it bother you that Jordan gets more attention than you? "He is a good friend. I have received some national attention since college. It has been very light compared to Jordan, who has constantly been in the spotlight. But that's something that, if it comes, fine; if it doesn't, well, you still have a job to do. Sometimes, I think the less said, the better. That's always been my attitude."

I didn't want to get into critiquing Jordan as a player because "it may give him an edge." But I said, "Jordan is a good guy. I have a lot of respect for him. He is an immensely talented player with very few weaknesses, if any. That sums it up."

**GEOFF PETRIE:** Michael and Clyde were so far above the other two guards in the league, it wasn't even debatable. They hurt you in so many ways — on the fast break, on the glass, driving to the basket. And as Clyde's long-range shooting improved, it got to the point where you couldn't just not guard him out there on the perimeter. Like all the great players do, they start out pretty good and then they just keep getting better. I worked a little with him on his shooting, but I don't know that I had any impact. He was a guy who liked to do things on his own.

**JACK SCHALOW:** Before the Finals, everybody was asking the same thing: Who is the MVP, Clyde or Michael? Clyde was really that good. You had to compare the two that year. Clyde made big steals, grabbed big rebounds, made big plays at the end of games. Rick had tremendous confidence in Clyde at the end of a game, because Clyde was going to make the right play — either a pass, a post-up or a drive to the basket.

We had a little extra incentive against the Bulls. After they had drilled us 111-91 in Chicago in March, they had made some comments. Jordan seemed to question the intelligence of our team when he said, "They run the open court so well, we try to get then in a halfcourt game and make them utilize their minds as much as possible. Look at their team. They have more athletic ability than we do. But to win, you have to play together, and you have to play smart."

When he was asked if he meant we were a dumb team, he responded, "I am not saying they're not smart. With our experience of playing together, it gives us a very big advantage over them. They have played well together for a period of time, too, so I can't take that away from them or their coach. But I give the edge to us because we have been together for so long."

That made no sense. Our core group had been together just as long. When that was pointed out to Michael, he mumbled, "Well, that's just their problem." Obviously, our basketball IQ was pretty impressive. We were in the same spot as they were — the NBA Finals.

Buck put it pretty well when he said, "Let's see. They questioned our decision-making ability. That sounds better than saying we're dumb. Any time the defending champions make derogatory statements about your team, it has a tendency to give you a great deal more motivation. I thought it was unsportsmanlike for the coaches and players to make the remarks they did."

In the days leading up the finals, Phil Jackson started the woe-is-us stuff. He said, "We are undermatched the whole way around. Physically, Portland overmatches us at every single position. Maybe Michael and Clyde are the two guys who can compete physically. Other than that, they really have physical dominance."

Adelman's response was precise: "It's amazing to me how we do that when they are the defending world champions."

My knee was still bothering me. It was maybe at 85 percent strength, and I was still getting it drained occasionally. All I could do was grit my teeth and play through it. It had been bothering me for some time, but leading into the Finals, I was averaging 26.9 points, 7.2 rebounds, 7.7 assists and 40.6 minutes in 15 playoff games.

The Bulls crushed us in the opener at Chicago Stadium, 122-89. That was the famous game where Jordan nailed six threes, hit 14 of 21 shots and scored 35 of his 39 points in the first half. After his sixth one, Michael looked into the stands and shrugged as he ran downcourt as if to say, "I can't believe it either." Afterward, Rick laughed weakly and said, "We held Michael to four points in the second half. That's the only good news I can think of tonight."

What people don't remember about that game is that we started really well. We hit our first seven shots from the field and were 13 of 19 in the first quarter. We were ahead 25-17 late in the period and were still shooting 60 percent at halftime, but Michael was just too much. Afterward, Ainge had one of the better quotes of the year when he said, "It's not the Tour de France. We don't start out 33 points behind. We start out with the score 0-0. I have been involved in this situation twice, and both times the team losing big came back to win the series. It doesn't mean anything more than they won a game."

And Danny was right. We won Game 2 115-104 in overtime, and Ainge was the hero after tying an NBA Finals record with nine points in the extra session. I fouled out with 4:36 remaining and Chicago in front 92-82, and my teammates got the job done. Afterward, Rick, laughing, told reporters, "Well, we got Clyde out of there and finally started to play a little bit." And Buck chimed in: "That is why we started playing better. It is hard carrying around that kind of excess baggage for 48 minutes, you know?"

We scored on seven of our last eight possessions in the fourth period and nine of 10 possessions in overtime. Buck really came up big, hitting seven of nine from the floor and five of five from the line for 19 points and 14 boards.

Heading back to Portland for Games 3 through 5, we felt good about our chances. We also remembered what had happened two years earlier, when the Pistons swept three games at our place. We were determined not to let that happen, but the Bulls got Game 3 94-84. I had a big game, making 9 of 17 from the field and 12 of 12 from the line, for 32 points and nine boards. But as a team, we were outplayed, shooting .359 and committing 20 turnovers. I told the media afterward, "I don't think we have played well yet in the series. We haven't played our game like we are capable of. But Chicago has played a big part in that."

We won Game 4 by a 93-88 count to even the series at 2-2. The Bulls led 80-74 with 7:42 left, but we outscored them 19-8 down the stretch. Jerome had 21 points, we won the rebound battle 45-33 and we held Michael scoreess over the final 10:27 after he had scored 32 to that point.

With the Bulls ahead 82-81, I stripped Michael at midcourt and scored on a layup to give us our first lead of the game. "The biggest play of the game," Rick said afterward. I finished with 21 points and eight boards.

**PAUL ALLEN:** Clyde, who was playing with a sore knee, made that great play at the end. Afterward, I went into the locker room and he was covered with icepacks, exhausted from guarding Michael Jordan. I started to say, "Wow, Clyde, you knew all Jordan's moves, and at the last minute you tipped the ball away ..." And he started shaking his head and cut me off, saying, "Paul, you don't understand. Most really good players have two or three go-to moves. Jordan has like nine. I just guessed right, that's all. There is an old saying: sometimes you get the bear, but usually the bear gets you. I got lucky."

That stuck in my mind. He put it into perfect perspective. Trying to guard Jordan at his peak playing on a bad knee, you aren't going to win that battle every time.

Phil Jackson was angry. He felt the Bulls should have swept the first four games. "By all rights and purposes, this series should be over," he told reporters. Rick took offense to that: "Unless they have changed the rules, I believe each game is 48 minutes long. If it's a 42-minute game, they have a 3-1 lead, but it's 48 minutes. I looked at the paper this morning, and yeah, I was right, it's 2-2."

The Bulls handled us 119-106 in Game 5, sending us back to Chicago for Game 6 down 3-2 in the series. I had 30 points, but we never really had a chance in that game. Jordan scored 46 points, more than anyone had ever scored against Portland in a playoff game, and Scottie contributed 24 points, 11 rebounds and nine assists. And our old antagonist, referee Jake O'Donnell, was there to torment us as usual. He particularly enjoyed stuffing it up the shirt of Buck, and he nailed me with a sixth personal on a charge taken by Scottie Pippen. Replays confirmed that it was a totally bogus call.

"Obviously, we gave them that one," Adelman deadpanned to the press afterward, playing off Jackson's comments of the previous game. Then he gave credit to the Bulls, saying it was their best game of the Finals, even better than the opener.

We told ourselves to just look at the last two games one at a time. Win the first one, then it would go to a Game 7 and anything could happen then. We had already won in Chicago, so we knew we could do it.

And it looked like we had it under control, leading 79-62 late in the third quarter. By that time, Jackson had four starters on the bench, with only Pippen on the floor. We were dominating the action and had the Chicago Stadium fans sitting on their hands.

Then it unraveled. Bobby Hansen hit a three-pointer, and after a Hansen steal, Jerome was called for a flagrant foul. Stacy King made one free throw, and the Bulls got the ball and Pippen scored on a layup. Suddenly, we couldn't get a call. Five straight calls went against us, and before we knew it, they had gone on an 18-4 run to pull to 83-82 with 5:57 left.

We had lost momentum, and we never got it back. Jackson inserted his starters, and they took over in a 97-93 win that secured the championship for Chicago for the second straight season.

I dressed pretty quickly, did my media duties, then walked to the other side of the arena and into the Bulls' locker room to shake hands with their players. Michael and Scottie weren't around, but I found John Paxson, Bill Cartwright, Bobby Hansen, Horace Grant and Scott Williams. Williams told me, "True to your pattern, man. You're class."

Over three years, we had averaged nearly 60 regular-season wins, had taken home two West titles and made at least the conference finals three straight years. The only thing missing was what we so desperately wanted — an NBA championship.

A few days later, Rick looked back at what happened and said, "I am very proud of our team. I don't think the guys quit. We flat-out ran out of gas in the fourth quarter [of Game 6]. It is devastating to lose a game like that when we felt we should have won it, but that's life. We are still the team that came out of the West two of three years. Our goal is to get back here. And maybe it will be our time to win it all next year."

**KARL MALONE:** If you were starting a team and looking for a two guard, you would choose Michael. The second one would be Clyde. There is no shame in that. That is just the way it was. Clyde was a remarkable player in all ways. I have a great deal of respect for him. His ability to get to the basket was his greatest strength. He always wanted to get to the basket, and he usually did. Later in his career he improved his jump shot and he got better every year.

**KEVIN DUCKWORTH:** Clyde was on a level with Mike. We didn't get a ring in Portland, but we had a lot of success. Clyde was the foundation of what we achieved. He might not be as flashy or as creative as Mike, but so many times with the game on the line, he would come in and say, "We are not going to lose this game." And Clyde would go in and do something spectacular. I would think, "I couldn't have done that." Not too many players could do what he could do.

**TERRY PORTER:** Clyde carried our team on his shoulders that season. He had an unbelievable year. He was the MVP of the league outside of Jordan. There was no doubt. That is why there was the big debate, Michael or Clyde? That is why everyone was drooling over the Finals that year, to see those two go at it against each other. That season, Clyde was tremendous every night. Whenever we needed a basket or a steal, he would come up with it.

I am sure he thinks those years in Portland were great, but also disappointing in that we didn't win a championship with that group of guys. Another time, maybe that team could have won a couple of championships. I played on a championship team in San Antonio, and those Portland teams should have had at least one, too. We just weren't able to win those final four games.

**GEOFF PETRIE:** That was a great series against Chicago, but in all fairness to Clyde, his knee was not right. We were all beat up. Buck and Terry had injuries, too. Not that we would have won, but ... Clyde was a real warrior that year.

**DANNY AINGE:** My two years in Portland were so much fun. I was always campaigning with Rick to play me and Clyde and Terry together more. It didn't happen until late in the second year. I wish there could have been another year or two with all of us together.

We figured we would reload and get after it again next year. Little did we know our run at a championship was over. Our three-year window had closed, and pretty soon, upper management would break up our team.

# CHAPTER 15

# END OF AN ERA

I didn't have as much vacation as I really needed during the summer of '92. My knee wasn't really right, but there were obligations to honor with the Olympic team. I had four days off after the NBA Finals — the same as Michael Jordan and Scottie Pippen — and then it was on to San Diego, where the 12 members and four coaches of the original Dream Team met up with each other.

I knew most of the guys fairly well, especially the guys I played against from Western Conference teams. Our head coach was Detroit's Chuck Daly and his assistants were Lenny Wilkens and a pair of college coaches, Duke's Mike Krzyzewski and Seton Hall's P.J. Carlesimo. Ironically, P.J. would succeed Rick Adelman as coach of the Trail Blazers just two years down the road and be my coach for a half-season.

It was a good group of guys. Everyone came ready to work. And we did work hard in practice. Chuck and his staff did a wonderful job keeping that team motivated and well prepared.

The six weeks I spent with that group were a riot. There was never a dull moment. We spent about 10 days in San Diego preparing for the Tournament of the Americas, which was the Olympic qualifying event for our region of the world and was going to be held in — ta da! — Portland. Pretty amazing coincidence.

We practiced at the University of San Diego. All our workouts were closed to the media, and security was tight. Chuck wanted to minimize the distractions and have us stick to basketball. We practiced hard, harder than most of us expected. It was less like summer vacation and more like fall training camp.

He did what he could to mix things up. Some days we scrimmaged Eastern Conference vs. Western Conference. The USAB also brought in a developmental squad that comprised college All-Americans such as Chris Webber, Grant Hill, Penny Hardaway, Jamal Mashburn, Rodney Rogers, Eric Montross and Bobby Hurley. Those guys were tough. In one scrimmage, they beat us. They definitely helped prepare us, and it was an unforgettable experience for them as well.

All the players brought their families wherever we were during the time we were together — San Diego, Portland, Monte Carlo, Barcelona. Gaynell and I had Austin and Elise with us. Our third child, Adam, was not yet born.

After the 10 days in San Diego, we made the two and a half-hour flight to Portland. It was great to have the Tournament of the Americas in my city. It was fun to play in front of the home crowd — having a Blazers player on the team made it extra special for the local fans who attended. And it was fun for me, having all the Dream Teamers in my city. I got to host. We held a dinner at my house for my teammates and their wives one night, and quite a few of them showed up. Nike also had a party for team and media at its Beaverton world headquarters, which was great. The weather was perfect, as it always was during the summer in Portland, and I think a few of the guys were surprised by that. They had only been in Portland during the winter, when it was usually rainy.

The Dream Team didn't have any competition in Portland. We opened with a 136-57 victory over Cuba that could have been just about any score that we wanted. Somebody asked Charles Barkley if he felt guilty about drilling an opponent that bad. "I was found not guilty last week," Charles deadpanned. Then he shrugged. "You don't want to kill teams, but what do you do?"

Being a member of the Dream Team was like being on a team you would consider unbeatable. After many years competing against the likes of Michael and Magic and Bird and all the other players, it was nice to be on their team for a change. You could just see how truly great they were.

People wondered if we might have too much talent, that there wouldn't be enough shots for everybody. There is no such thing as too much talent. It so happened that a lot of the guys were hurt. Patrick broke a thumb in San Diego and missed three of our games during Tournament of the Americas. Bird's back was about shot, limiting his participation, and Stockton hurt his knee in the second game of the Tournament of the Americas and had it scoped, missing part of the Olympics. Magic injured a knee in Barcelona and missed some time. My knee would flare up and I had to get it drained a couple more times. I sat out some practices, but I missed only one Tournament of the Americas game and none at the Olympics. Michael, Scottie and I were supposed to get some rest after a long playoff run, but we never really did.

No complaints, of course. This was a once-in-a-lifetime opportunity, the chance to play for your country on the greatest team ever assembled. Any guy in his right mind would cherish the chance.

I have been asked many times since the '92 Olympics — Did you worry about losing? The answer is no. I always respected my opponent, but I never worried about losing. Most of the time the guys we had were pretty overconfident by nature, anyway, because of their immense accomplishments. But honestly, not once did losing ever pop into anyone's mind. We had way more talent than any other team, but we were not going to let them outwork us, either. We came out and hustled, and it was going to be hard for us to lose.

We were trying to beat teams by 50 points or more. Not because that is what people said we should do; we just thought we were supposed to. We set goals that would help motivate ourselves. We would say, "Let's not let them get within 30 or 40 or 50 points of us." Chuck Daly was a good motivator. He would always have lofty goals for us. But really, Chuck didn't need to preach to us about playing hard. There was a lot of pride amongst those guys.

No team got within 30 points of us in Portland. We beat Canada 105-61, Panama 112-52 and Argentina 128-87 in pool play. In the semifinals, we beat Puerto Rico 119-81, then took out Venezuela 127-80 in the finals. We had done our job. Canada's Bill Wennington, the journeyman center with the Bulls, was asked what our chances were of losing at Barcelona. "The world will end before that happens," Wennington cracked.

It was funny how our opponents treated us. They were as interested in shaking our hands, getting autographs and having their pictures taken with us as they were in playing basketball. I had played well during the week, shooting .692 from the field and averaging 13.8 points and 6.2 assists while playing only 20 minutes a game. But stats didn't matter a lick on this team. We were in it to win it, that's all.

We took a few days off, and it was on to Monte Carlo, where we spent about a week. I had been there before, but it was fun to have Gaynell there with me. Everything the U.S. Olympic Committee and the NBA did for us there was first-class. Our hotel was overlooking the Mediterranean. There were a lot of social events planned. We had a reception dinner with Prince Rainier. We got to tour the city and check out the sights. It was a great time.

We practiced daily and played the French national team in an exhibition, winning 111-71. I even got to play a little golf with Charles Barkley and David Robinson. I remember it was an escalating course. We had to walk it, and it was like climbing a mountain. We had a great day, playing golf, cracking jokes and laughing.

We went to Barcelona a few days before our first game. The best thing about our time there was that the USOC rented out the entire hotel for the players and their families. There was a video game room and a coaches' lounge. We ate our meals in a central cafeteria, and the food was wonderful. All the details were well taken care of.

I had been to Madrid but never to Barcelona before. It was outstanding. We had time for sightseeing, and we really enjoyed that. There was a lot of great culture and history to take in. We went on a couple of tours of the city. I love architecture, and you see a lot of the Marco Degrassi structures in Barcelona — they really stand out.

Wherever we went in Barcelona, we were supposed to go with armed guards to make sure we had protection. Gaynell and I snuck off with friends a lot of times, went out to eat and did a little shopping. I got to play tennis a couple of times. One day I played with my old friend from Houston, Zina Garrison, who was representing the U.S. in the Olympics. Another time we took a little bus to some clay courts and played with Lenny Wilkens, commissioner David Stern and Coach K. It was pretty hot, so we had to play in the mornings.

Whenever the team went to practice, we had a chopper overhead and armed militia in front of and behind our bus. There

was great concern about terrorism. It was almost scary.
Fortunately, we got through the Olympics incident-free. We continued to work hard in practice. It was a good way of staying in
shape and keeping our game together. My knee was holding up
okay. If we had a hard practice one day, I would take the next
practice off.

Some of the guys were playing card games at night. I went
to one or two. It was guys sitting around laughing, drinking beer,
smoking cigars, talking and being typical jocks. Michael and
Magic were always the ringleaders and head comedians. And, of
course, Charles.

**CHARLES BARKLEY:** Michael, Magic, Scottie and I were
playing cards every night, pretty much all night long. We
probably drank a little beer along the way. One night
after we had been out pretty late, we got to practice the
next day, and I called a timeout. I looked at Chuck Daly
and I nodded toward Clyde and said, "Hey, Coach, I
can't practice today. I got to be drunk. Something's
wrong with my eyesight. It looks like that guy has two
left shoes on."

Then somebody said, "He does have two left shoes on."

The thing that made it funny, Clyde said it happened
because he got dressed in the dark and picked up two left
shoes. Everybody started laughing. I mean, you can't
deflect that one very easily. You put on two left shoes and
go through part of practice that way, you got to expect to
be the butt of the joke.

I woke up that morning in the hotel room and the family
was all still asleep, so I didn't turn on the lights. The basketball

shoes were all stacked up in the corner. I picked up a pair, put them in my bag and wore flip flops out of the room. It was a game-day shootaround, so it wasn't like we were going to do much. When I got on the bus, I realized I had two of the same shoe. I was sitting next to David and I said, "Guess what I did?" He said, "Ahh, it won't be any big deal. We won't be running around much."

Rather than just sit there and not do anything at the shootaround, I put the shoes on and figured I would do the stretching, go through the layup line and just blend in. Then Charles looked at me and said, "Hey, he has on two of the same shoe." He made a big spectacle of it. Charles would never let anything get by him. I couldn't do anything but laugh.

**KARL MALONE:** I had played against Clyde through the years and had played with him in All-Star Games, but I really got to know him as a person during the 1992 Olympic run. I learned about all the stuff he does away from the basketball court, things that I had heard about but he never talked about that he did in the Portland community. A lot of guys toot their own horn. That wasn't Clyde's way. I try to pick up one or two things about people and apply it to my life. With Clyde, it was the way he carried himself on the court. He never started talking to an opponent. He just played. I liked that. He never had an excuse, and he never tried to cut an opponent down. He had character. We never really hung out or anything, but you don't have to be around a guy long to know what he is about.

**PATRICK EWING:** Clyde was definitely a great player and a great person, also. I have the utmost respect for him, on and off the court. He handles himself very professionally, and he showed what a great player he was whenever he stepped onto the court. While with the Dream Team, we sat and talked some when we had our free time. I got an opportunity to know Clyde Drexler the person, and I thought he was a great guy. I enjoyed our time together, talking back and forth on the bus and in the locker rooms. He is the type of guy I like spending time with.

There was so much anticipation for our games, and everybody wondered if we would win as easily as most observers expected. "Some of these teams — Lithuania, Croatia, Germany, Spain — might give us a good game," Charles told a reporter. He paused, and added, "For a half."

We were treated like royalty by everyone during our time in Barcelona. "Even the people giving us accreditation were asking for autographs," Chuck Daly said. "Being with this team is like traveling with 12 rock stars."

We blasted Angola 116-48 in our opener. That was the game where Charles shoved an Angola player who had fouled him in the second half, drawing a technical foul and raising charges of "ugly Americans." It was just Charles being Charles. It wasn't that big a deal, really. For the most part, our guys were very sportsmanlike. We helped opponents up off the floor. But Charles was an easy target in this case.

In succession, we beat Croatia — with Toni Kukoc and Drazen Petrovic — 105-70, Germany 111-68, Brazil 127-83 and Spain 122-81 in pool play. In the quarterfinals, we blasted Puerto Rico 115-77. Our semifinal victory came over Lithuania, which was led by Arvydas Sabonis, 127-76. And in the finals we blew out Croatia 117-85.

No way in the world were we going to lose. The opponents reacted to us much the way they had in the Tournament of the

Americas, getting our autographs and basically looking starstruck. They were competitive, but the looks on their faces said, "We will have fun today, but we know we can't beat you guys."

After the championship game, we lined up to receive our gold medals. It was a great moment for all of us. I had a feeling of pride. We had accomplished our mission. I felt good representing my country and my cities — both Houston and Portland — in grand fashion.

We had been a family for six weeks. Now we were splitting up to head home. When we came back to play against each other the next season, it was hard to look at each other the same way again. You had a different view of your opponent, because he had also been your teammate.

The biggest change in Blazerland for the 1992-93 season was that Danny Ainge was gone. On July 1, the first day free agents could sign contracts, Ainge put his John Henry on a three-year, $5.2 million deal with Phoenix. Geoff Petrie was willing to offer only two years for Ainge, who was 33 years old at the time. But Petrie said the Blazers "probably" would have matched any offer. "I am disappointed we didn't have a chance to match," Geoff said.

During the Tournament of the Americas, Barkley had told me, "Now we are the team that is going to come out of the West." I responded, "We came out of the West when we didn't have Danny. We will do it again."

Danny had been an integral part of the team. If it were up to me, I would have kept him and given him more playing time. But those are things I had no control over. I had to play with the guys who lined up alongside me.

Paul Allen had signed Rick to a two-year contract extension, which was a very good thing. We had a late first-round draft pick, No. 26, and took Dave Johnson, a 6'5" swing man from

Syracuse. Dave was a good guy, an excellent post-up shooting guard, but not much of a factor for us. He played 42 games for us and was waived just before the start of the following season.

We did get some important help, though. In July, we signed point guard Rod Strickland to a six-year, $12.6-million free agent deal. We also traded Alaa Abdelnaby to Milwaukee for the draft rights to UCLA small forward Tracy Murray. And we signed free agent swing man Mario Elie, who became a very important piece for us off the bench.

I had an arthroscopic procedure performed on my knee on September 18. After the Olympics, I met with Dr. Cook. We wanted to give it a month of rest to see if it would heal on its own, so that maybe we wouldn't have to do the surgery. But my knee didn't respond, so we went ahead with the procedure, figuring it would give us time to get ready for the season opener in November.

That fall, they put me on a Wheaties box, with a story about my accomplishments. It was only a regional edition that was sent to the Northwest, but it was indicative of the fanfare the Blazers had created. And it sold out very quickly. Today, it is a collector's item in the Portland area.

Duck reported to camp in great shape. Buck kidded him by saying, "People are going to get us mixed up. He looks almost anorexic." Duck was still one of the better centers in the league, and I was hoping he would be able to show it.

**JIM PAXSON:** I returned to Portland in 1992-93 as a workout coach and advance scout. At that training camp, I noticed Clyde working harder than anybody in camp. With all the things he relied on early in his career, the great athleticism and physical gifts, the knock on him was that he didn't work hard enough. It definitely wasn't true at that point in his career. Later in his career, the rea-

son he was as great a player as he was is because he figured out how hard he had to work. I gained a great deal
of respect for him. He was one smart player, and he kept
figuring out what he needed to do to be better. He was-
n't as physically dominating, but he was a more efficient
player later in his career.

I was able to play in the first game of the season, but I was
pushing it a little bit — for a reason. With what was still an excellent array of talent, bolstered by the addition of Rod and Mario,
we figured we had a good chance to be on our way to the Finals
again. I wanted to be out there for the team.

We kept winning, and we improved our record to 8-0 with
a 95-91 win over San Antonio in a game in which I scored my
15,000th career point. Play was stopped and Geoff presented me
with the game ball. I had read it in the game notes before the
game that I was at that milestone, but those things are going to
come. I was more interested in winning the game. I scored 24
points on 11 of 21 shooting from the field. I had been struggling
with my shot since getting the scope on my knee and came into
the game shooting only .398 from the field and averaging 17.7
points.

I felt like my knee was about 85 percent healthy. Some
nights, it felt good; other nights it didn't feel as good. There was
no pain, but sometimes I felt like I could explode and other times
I felt like I couldn't move. I was also bothered by soreness on the
ball of my left foot. I played the first 13 games, sat out two to rest
the knee, then played the next eight. I had a big game against the
Lakers, going for 30 points, 11 assists and six boards in a 124-111
defeat, but the knee wasn't right. I went on the injured list and sat
out seven games in late December and early January. After a
scope, a leg atrophies. I lost all of my muscle tone, which I now
had to rebuild.

I wasn't alone. Injuries were slowing the Blazers. Duck had sore knees. Kersey missed seven games with tendinitis in a knee.

We struggled for a spell, losing six of 10 games to fall to 12-6. Then we got rolling again, winning 16 of 21 to improve to 28-11.

I came back and played pretty well, making my seventh All-Star Game appearance and my second in a row as a starter. I was joined on the West squad by Terry Porter, which was nice. But when we got back from the break, my knee injury was too much. I had to shut it down for 13 games in March to see if I could nurse the knee back to health.

I returned on March 26 and felt pretty good, playing five more games before pulling a hamstring on April 3 against Washington. The injury came from overcompensating for the knee injury, I think. That put me back on the injured list, where I stayed for the final 12 games of the regular season.

**MIKE RICE:** Just to show you how competitive Clyde is, when he was out with that pulled hamstring, we were in Seattle to play a game the following night. We practiced at the court on Paul Allen's estate. Paul also had an indoor tennis court. Clyde and I had kind of an ongoing tennis game at the time, so he said, "Why don't we hit a few?" And we hit for about five minutes, basically just standing in place. Then I said, "Clyde, you know I have won two points in a row." Now he was hitting the ball harder. And I hit a beautiful drop shot and he was behind the baseline, and there was no way he could get to it. And he swooped in — zoom! — and hit a winner. And just as he did it, Paul walked in and saw it. I said, "Clyde, I don't think I want to play any more." I didn't want to lose my job. He had that hamstring injury, but he was just competitive. He couldn't let me win three points in a row.

I finished the regular season with a 19.9-point scoring average, leading the team for the sixth straight season. I also averaged 6.3 rebounds and 5.7 assists. But I missed more games — 33 — than I had combined through my entire nine-year career, and served three stints on the injured list.

We managed to win 51 games, our fourth straight 50-plus-victory season. That gave us third place in the Pacific Division behind Phoenix and Seattle and fourth in the West. It meant we had home-court advantage against first-round opponent San Antonio.

I wasn't ready to go for the opener. The hamstring was still bothering me. Before the series, Geoff Petrie told me, "We think we can win the first round without you. We want to give your hamstring as much rest as possible. We want you ready for the second round." I said OK. Then, despite 24 points and nine rebounds from Jerome, we lost 87-86 when Sean Elliott hit a pair of free throws with five seconds left, leaving us in a huge hole in the best-of-five series.

I wasn't quite ready to play, but I knew the situation was dire. I went to Petrie's office and said, "If you guys need me, I am ready. I would rather take a chance on playing than to have us go three and out. I will come off the bench if you want. I feel like I still can do a lot to help the team. I just don't know how the hamstring is going to hold up."

I came back for Game 2 and had 21 points, five rebounds and five assists as we won 105-96 to even the series after the Spurs had led by eight points late in the third quarter. I didn't have the explosiveness I normally had, but I could still play. I just couldn't move as quickly as I would have liked.

In the fourth quarter, with the Blazers clinging to a 99-94 lead, the Spurs isolated Sean Elliott on me, figuring I wasn't healthy enough to defend him. I picked his pocket and fed the ball to Rod for the game-clinching basket. When you're hurt, you do what you can to compensate. I had to laugh when Houston coach John Lucas, a longtime friend, cracked, "Clyde ain't that hurt." I was, but I appreciated Luke's sentiments.

**RICK ADELMAN**: Clyde was amazing in that game. He hadn't played in almost a month, and then he walked out in a critical playoff game and played the way he did. He stayed within himself and didn't try to force anything that wasn't there. Even at less than 100 percent, he was the best player on the floor.

**TERRY PORTER:** An opponent was wise never to under-estimate Clyde's ability to come back from an injury. He had an ability to raise himself up in tough situations.

We went to San Antonio for Games 3 and 4, and I wasn't able to do what I needed to do to get us a win. The Spurs beat us in a pair of to-the-wire games, 107-101 and then 100-97 in over-time. We led in the final three minutes of both games, but we weren't able to get things accomplished down the stretch. With all the injuries, we never had any continuity all season, and it final-ly caught up with us. For the first time since 1989, we were look-ing at an early vacation.

I took more time off than usual that summer, and the short-er playoff run helped my injuries heal. I felt good.

Reebok had purchased Avia, and I started wearing Reebok shoes. It was like being in the same family. I was with Avia and Reebok for 10 years. They always made good, quality shoes. In comparison to the way Nike promoted their athletes, they didn't match up. I could have earned more money elsewhere, but I did-n't want to be the kind of guy who switched around for the high-est dollar. I had to have some loyalty and integrity in my business.

We made a major move in June, when we sent Kevin Duckworth to Washington for veteran small forward Harvey

Grant. Duck had averaged only 9.9 points and 5.2 rebounds and shot just .438 from the field. He was also getting fewer minutes and seemed chronically unhappy, but I still didn't like the trade at all.

Geoff Petrie was usually good about consulting the starters about potential trades or player movement. He didn't consult me about Danny Ainge when we lost him to free agency, or about the Duckworth trade. If he had, I would have told him to keep both of them. Surely Petrie was only doing what he thought would improve our team.

A center is the most important part of your team. Every guard knows that. If you lose a center, your middle becomes hollow. Duck was coming off a subpar year. The fans and radio talk shows were getting on him. He didn't have the same teammates setting him up, because I was hurt a lot and Terry was on the bench a lot, and he was playing with a different group. Duck didn't produce like he normally did, he had gained a little weight, and the losing was frustrating him. Somebody was going to take the blame. But we reacted prematurely in letting him go. I would never have gotten rid of him. Good centers are very hard to find.

We signed Chris Dudley as a free agent to replace Duck. Dudley was 6'11", very active on the boards and as a shot blocker. He had been been effective for New Jersey the previous season and is one of the nicest guys I ever met. But Geoff signed him to a one-year deal with the intention of re-signing him for the following year under the Larry Bird Exception. After that season, Chris was set to get a six-year contract worth $24 million — more than anybody else on the team. That caused some problems with the rest of us who had been the players who had taken Portland to a lot of success the previous three seasons.

**CHRIS DUDLEY:** Clyde was a tremendous athlete and a tremendous competitor. I really enjoyed playing with him. He was great to me. He made me feel right at home right away when I joined the team. We hung out a bit, caught dinner and a movie sometimes when we were on the road. He was a very good teammate.

Clyde ranks up there with anybody I ever played with, including Patrick Ewing and Jason Kidd. If Jordan hadn't been around, Clyde would have been more recognized for his abilities. He was right there behind Jordan. I remember how he was such an asset to the team, because he could punish two-guards down on the block. Nobody could match his strength. When I was playing for other teams, our guys did not like guarding him.

We all liked Chris, and he was a good player. He was the best center on the free-agent market that year, but I didn't think he was that good a fit on our team. Chris would have been great if we still had Duck, who was an excellent offensive player. Chris was a good defensive player, but when you put him with Buck — who was not going to shoot or score much — it gave you almost no scoring at the four and five spots. I was more of a slasher, and when I drove, I dished to open teammates. Now there weren't enough teammates who could hit the open jumper on a regular basis. They picked up Arvydas Sabonis two seasons later, and he was the perfect complement to Dudley.

**BUCK WILLIAMS:** Clyde was unhappy with his contract. He could not handle the fact that Chris Dudley was making more money than he was making.

I asked Geoff Petrie to either give me a contract extension or trade me. I was making $1.2 million per year. There were rookies coming into the league making more than that. Even with the balloon payment for the 1995-96 season, I had three years and

$12 million left on my deal, well below market value. Most owners at that time would do something to make it right. It was disappointing, but nothing ever got done.

Whether or not Dudley was worth the impending contract was academic that season, because Chris wound up breaking an ankle the second game of the season and played in six games total for us all year. That left us a pretty good void in the middle.

We had the rest of the team intact for the 1993-94 campaign, but it was the beginning of the changing of the guard. Rod Strickland had supplanted Terry as the starter at point guard, and Harvey took over for Jerome at small forward. Terry had been a starter since the 1986-87 season, Jerome since 1987-88. That was tough on both of them.

When it happened, I was sitting there thinking, "Are you kidding me?" It wasn't that Rod and Harvey weren't decent players. They were. But to disregard everything that had happened the previous three years was mind-boggling to me. I thought we changed the lineup way too quickly. My feeling was, let's take it as far as we can with the proven players. It was also a panic move, a move for the sake of a move, and some chemistry was lost. It takes time to develop new chemistry.

We started the season off slowly with a 9-8 record. Then we got going, winning 16 of the next 24 games to hit the midway point at 25-16.

I didn't make it quite that far. On December 19, I sprained an ankle and had to go on the injured list, missing the next 13 games. I came down on someone's foot and never felt so much pain. I was always completely disappointed when I couldn't play. There is nothing worse than showing up for a game and being in street clothes and not being able to participate. That is real pain.

I didn't return to action until January 21. Cliff was playing the best basketball of his career, fortunately, at one point leading the team in scoring eight straight games while hitting the 30-

point mark four times. He moved into the starting lineup early in the season, replacing Jerome. Cliff made his first All-Star Game; I was named for the eighth time. Cliff became the primary offensive threat, playing with Rod and Harvey.

We were pretty much up and down the rest of the regular season, losing 13 of our last 22 to finish 47-35. That put us only fourth in the Pacific Division and seventh in the West, giving us a first-round playoff matchup with Midwest Division champion Houston.

I still felt like we could beat the Rockets in the best-of-five series. I had a big game in the opener with 26 points and 13 rebounds, but we lost that one, 114-104, and then the second one, 115-104. We knocked them off 118-115 in Game 3 back in Portland, with Buck making nine of 10 shots and scoring 22 points. But we were eliminated when the Rockets jumped in front by 21 points in the first half of Game 4 and held on for a 92-89 triumph.

I averaged 19.2 points during the regular season, my lowest scoring output since 1985-86, my third year in the league. And I wasn't quite sure how I felt about remaining a Trail Blazer.

During the summer a wave of change swept over the coaching staff and the front office. Rick was fired after five and a half seasons as coach. P.J. Carlesimo replaced him. And Geoff Petrie resigned as the team's senior vice president. In his place came Bob Whitsitt, whose titles were now president and general manager. Whitsitt had been in charge of the Seattle SuperSonics for the previous six seasons.

I never would have let Rick go. We had a great relationship. It hurt when he was fired. I mean, first you take away my center, then you take away my coach? Then Petrie was gone. And they also removed the team doctor, Bob Cook. I really enjoyed those people. I had some problems with that. I was extremely unhappy with those moves.

Change is inevitable, but it was clear now that everything was going to be torn apart. I never talked to Whitsitt until training camp that fall. I wasn't sure what to think. Later, I found out for certain.

P.J. was a very nice guy. I liked him a lot. Nothing against him, but Rick was an All-Star-caliber coach. P.J. was coming straight out of college. He had an excellent staff. I have great respect for Dick Harter, and Rick Carlisle proved himself as a fine head coach at both Detroit and Indiana. I enjoyed playing for P.J., but he was not on the same level as Rick. It kind of set us back. Time was running out for this team to win a championship, and I felt it was in the best interest of everyone to trade me and continue the rebuilding process.

During camp, I went to Bob and told him I wanted a trade. He said, "Clyde, let's wait and see what we have, see how this team is playing. Let's give P.J. a chance. If you really want to be traded, play well so I can get someone good in return for you."

I just wanted to get out at that point. My role on the team had changed. I was no longer the do-everything guy. I had fewer opportunities to do things. It was probably for the best. They weren't sure how healthy I was going to be. P.J. tried to work with me. He was trying to get Rod more of a chance to create and penetrate, trying to get Cliff a few more scoring opportunities, and trying to bring along some of the younger players. The team worked well together. We played hard. P.J. demanded that. I liked that about him.

We knew Whitsitt was brought in by Paul to be a hatchet man. Paul wasn't tricking anybody with that move. We were all going to be gone pretty soon. It was time for them to rebuild, and I needed a change of scenery.

It didn't happen for a few months. With Cliff, Rod, Buck and a healthy Chris Dudley, we still figured to be pretty tough. I started the season feeling good. We played our first two games against the Clippers in Japan, and I was hot in the second game, hitting 16 of 21 from the field and five of five from the line, collecting 41 points, seven rebounds, six assists and five steals in a 112-95 victory.

But things weren't clicking for us as a team. We hovered around the .500 mark through the first half of the season.

**JACK SCHALOW:** This will tell you a little about Clyde as a person. I was out of work after we were let go as a staff the previous May. My wife threw me a Christmas party that happened to be on a Blazers game night. She still invited some of the players — I was pretty close to Clyde, Terry, Buck and Jerome. Buck and Jerome called and said, "Jack, we would love to come but we can't make it. We have a game that night." I told them I understood and appreciated the call.

Terry and Clyde came by the party a couple of hours before the game. Terry stayed a short time and left for the Coliseum. I started looking at the clock, and game time was getting closer. I told Clyde he better leave, and Clyde said, "Jack, you are a friend of mine. It is important to be here. I will get to the game in time." And I swear, at that moment it was only an hour before the game that he left my house, and it was 15 minutes to the arena.

The next day I picked up the paper, because I wondered what kind of a game Clyde had. They had played the Knicks, and he scored 33 points, hit 14 of 19 shots, with five rebounds and five assists. That was the kind of thing Clyde could do.

I was healthy again, and I was doing what I could to help the team. I was averaging 22 points, still rebounding and playing hard, but I wasn't shooting very well. I wasn't sure what was going to happen with the future of the team, other than I knew I still wanted to be traded. On February 14, two days after the All-Star Game, I got my wish and more.

# CHAPTER 16

# HAPPY VALENTINE'S DAY

February 14, 1995, was a big day in my life. Not because it was Valentine's Day, but because I was given a fresh start with a new team.

I was tipped off a few days ahead of time that the Blazers were working on a trade with Houston. I spoke to Paul Allen about it. He didn't really want to do it. He said there really wasn't anybody other than Hakeem Olajuwon they wanted back for me, and to trade me for anybody else wouldn't be smart on his part. "I am only going to do this because I want you to be happy," Paul told me.

**PAUL ALLEN:** Clyde had asked for the trade, and Bob Whitsitt asked me if it was okay to explore options. I just said try to find him a place where he has a chance to compete for a championship. Do right by Clyde. When Bob told me we had a chance to trade Clyde to Houston, well, that was a godsend for Clyde. What better outcome than to try to win a title with Olajuwon? A player of Clyde's caliber deserves to end his career with a chance to win a title.

We were in a rebuilding mode at that time and felt like the group we were with had peaked. When we made the deal, I called Clyde and wished him well and thanked him for everything he had done for the franchise. He said he appreciated everything, and he wasn't upset about it. He wasn't joyous at the time. Later, he became joyous.

For me it was a very sad time. Any time you trade a guy who had made such a significant contribution to your franchise, and you have watched him play hundreds of games for you... to trade him was a very emotional moment.

**CHRIS DUDLEY:** Clyde had wanted to extend his contract. He probably got himself in trouble sometimes because he did the negotiations himself without an agent. Bob wanted to wait a little bit. It came to a head pretty quickly. Before we knew it, at midseason, he was gone.

**JIM PAXSON:** When Bob came in, the feeling was that group had done everything it could together, and he needed to start breaking it up and retooling. Clyde had done so much, carried that '92 team, and if the opponent in the Finals had been against anybody else but Chicago, Portland would have won that year. But very few players finish a career where they start. Bob was trying to get younger and more athletic and versatile players and felt that group had run its course.

I hated to leave Portland. The fans were so awesome to my teammates and me. Honestly, Portland has some of the best fans in the game. They really love their Blazers. I enjoyed my teammates. P.J. was working hard as coach. But I knew that it was not going to be a championship-caliber team. They were trying to start over, trying to get rid of all the veterans. That is the nature of sports, but I was only 32 years old. I knew what I could still do. The front office was intent on breaking us up because they thought we had run out of gas, and that hurt. Maybe Paul had been spoiled a little bit by our early successes. We had some great teams that weren't quite good enough to win it all, and now it was over.

**BUCK WILLIAMS:** I never understood why we traded Clyde to Houston. That was a huge mistake. The demand for a contract extension or a trade before the 1994-95 season was a good excuse for Whitsitt to get rid of Clyde. I think the Trail Blazers took his loyalty for granted. The franchise has never been the same since he left.

I have always appreciated the trade to Houston. Paul did that one for me. And I appreciated Bob taking care of it like he did. When he told me he was in negotiations with Houston, I strongly suggested that he make it happen. I was gung-ho for that trade. The coach, Rudy Tomjanovich, and his assistant coach, Carroll Dawson, both called me. And finally, Bob and Houston's vice president of basketball operations, Bob Weinhauer, announced the trade. The Rockets were getting me. The Blazers were getting Houston's starting power forward, Otis Thorpe, and a first-round draft choice. The Blazers also agreed to pay about $7 million of the $9.75 million balloon payment on the final year of my contract for 1995-96. Now I was going to the team I had grown up watching, the team that had won the NBA championship the previous season.

**RUDY TOMJANOVICH:** There was a very important thing we had to consider when we were contemplating the trade — whether we wanted to break up a team that won a championship the year before to bring in another player.

When we looked at everything and thought about all the different factors, we thought there was only one guy in the whole league we could do that with — Clyde Drexler. First of all, there was his relationship with Hakeem. Then there was Clyde's relationship with the city of Houston. And thirdly, there was his hunger to win a championship. He had come so close, been to the Finals twice with the Trail Blazers. We knew he would make sure nothing could stand in the way of the ring if he came to us. What was really interesting about that situation was there were people around the league who came out publicly and criticized that trade. I am talking about basketball people saying how foolish we were trading a power forward for a shooting guard.

**CARROLL DAWSON:** We had won the title the year before, but we had suffered a bunch of injuries, and it was evident to us midway through the season that we weren't going to be able to get back to where we wanted to. We were looking at things we could do. It was unusual to break up a championship team, but we did it. We felt if we had a chance to land a player like Clyde, we had to do it.

Otis had been an important player for us and had helped us win a championship. There were some things said about the trade, about how the guys hated to lose Otis. But once Clyde got here and people saw the difference he made, there were no complaints. It strengthened us in an area we needed to be strengthened.

A week before the trade, Houston guard Vernon Maxwell was involved in an altercation with a fan during a Rockets-Blazers game in Portland and was suspended for 10 games. That night, Hakeem and I went to dinner after the game and talked again about someday playing together. As it turned out, Max's suspension made the Rockets even more eager to get something done with the Blazers.

I really wanted to go somewhere I had a chance to win a championship. When that turned out to be Houston, I felt euphoric — as if I were dreaming. I called my mother and she was going crazy. We couldn't believe it was happening.

I flew into Houston, and they gave me a nice little party the first day at The Summit. The Rockets were playing the Clippers that night. I came in during the fourth quarter, and the fans gave me a standing ovation as I went over to sit down at courtside next to Rockets owner Les Alexander. Les was telling me how happy he was to have me, that he felt I was one of the best guards in the league. He said, "With you here now, you guys are going to win the title again." I said, "We are going to try, but I don't want to let anybody down."

You could feel the electricity in the building. I had chills down my spine. The crowd let me know that I was really wanted.

**LES ALEXANDER:** On the night of his first game, Clyde came over and gave me a big hug, and it cemented our relationship. I have a picture of Clyde hanging on the wall in my office that he signed, "Thanks for bringing me back to Houston. No. 22." Of all the players I have had over the years, Clyde is the guy I am most friendly with. I like him a lot.

I care about winning more than anything else, so sentiment didn't enter into the trade, but it was a great added bonus that he was a hometown kid. We didn't have to debate too much over taking on Clyde. When we got the chance to obtain a player of such quality, a top 50 player of all time who could still do everything on the court for us, it was an easy decision. It worked out exactly as we wanted. I don't think there was any chance that we would have won a championship that year without Clyde being there.

**TIM HANEY:** Right after Clyde was traded, Avia did an autograph-signing party at a sportings goods store in the Galleria in Houston. It was like the Messiah had returned home. There was a line two miles long. It was a Who's Who in line to get an autograph. People were using that as a venue to get to see him. It wasn't just kids and parents. It was city councilmen, actors, Oilers football players. Warren Moon came by, because he said he couldn't figure out another way to get ahold of Clyde. It was like he was The Beatles or something. We had to stop the signing after a couple of hours, and the lines were still wrapped around the building.

I was so eager to get started. The next day, we went out on an East Coast road trip. I had one day of practice. Our first game was at Charlotte, but I couldn't play until the trade was approved. At halftime, news of approval came in from the league office. Rudy put me into the game in the third quarter, and I was a little nervous.

The first time I got the ball, we were in our set offense, and all of a sudden, my guy left me to double-team Hakeem. I was thinking, "I'm not used to this. Defenders just don't leave me like this." I had an open shot inside the key, looked around, and didn't know what to do. Hakeem had the biggest smile on his face. He said, "Shoot, Drex, shoot!" I traveled, and then I threw up an airball. I'll never forget that. At our next timeout, we went back to the huddle, and Rudy was laughing. Hakeem said, "Drex, you are going to kill people playing on this team." It was a great feeling. We won that game and scored 41 points in the third quarter — my first with the team. And really, we never looked back.

**HAKEEM OLAJUWON:** Over the years, every time I played against Portland and when we saw each other at All-Star games, Clyde and I would talk about playing together. We would catch up with each other for dinner and talk about what it would be like to play together. It was a shared dream, but it didn't look like it was ever going to happen. Clyde was a longtime All-Star, one of the important members of the Trail Blazers, and they were never going to let him go. In early February, after a game in Portland where the Blazers had blasted us by 38 points, we got together in the hotel lounge and dreamed about being teammates.

"You would take care of the inside," Clyde said. "I would take care of the outside."

Just thinking about all the things Clyde could do — steal passes, run the floor, rebound, shoot — made me excited. "Wow," I said, "that would be wonderful." He would make my job so much easier!

Portland had its chances to be champions. The Blazers had been to the NBA Finals twice in the last five years, but that winter they knew they weren't heading toward the title, and management was looking toward the future. Clyde's contract was almost up, and it would cost the Trail Blazers a lot to re-sign him; perhaps he wasn't the ideal player to have on a rebuilding team. Clyde wanted to play in Houston, where he grew up and his family still lived and the fans loved him.

A few days later, Rudy came to me and asked, "How would you feel about playing with Clyde again?" He didn't go into details about who might be traded; he just asked me my feelings. "There is no way you can pull that deal off. If you can, I dare you to do it," I told him.

I liked the makeup of my new team a lot. It started with Hakeem, the greatest center in the game and one of the greatest of all time — just as I had predicted when we were in college. Robert Horry moved into Thorpe's slot as the power forward. Robert was an excellent player, a very underrated player. He was super defensively, a good rebounder, could run the break and finish. He could really shoot the three, and he came through time after time in clutch moments. Robert, Kenny Smith, Sam Cassell and Mario Elie — all those guys were clutch shooters. The other forward spot was shared by Carl Herrera, Chucky Brown and Mario, who had played with me a year in Portland. We were usually undersized at that position. We were really stocked at guard. Kenny was the point guard, and I moved into the shooting guard slot. Sam was the first guard off the bench, and Vernon Maxwell, who had started before I got there, got his minutes at the two. We were a deep team. At the end of a game, we often went with a small lineup that included Hakeem, Robert, myself, Mario and Kenny.

**ROBERT HORRY**: I remember looking at the trade as both good and bad. The good thing was we were getting a great player. The bad thing was, we traded Otis, so we really didn't have a power forward left. I remember thinking, "I hope they don't try to make me the power forward." And it wound up being me some of the time, but that was cool. Clyde was an extremely gifted player, and he came in with that extra drive. He hadn't won a championship. We wanted to do it again, and he gave us that extra kick. Sometimes when we were down that season, he came out and gave us the will to win.

**KENNY SMITH:** Clyde brought us a spark, brought the energy back into our team. After winning the year before, we had fat-cat-itis. We were resting on our laurels. That trade woke us up. It was like, "We might not be that good, and everyone might not be here forever." He came in with a hunger to win one, and that made us go. It was like we were back in business. Then it became kind of, "Let's play hard for Clyde and see if we can't get him a ring, too."

**SAM CASSELL:** I first got to know Clyde when I started to go in to eat at his family restaurant while he was still with Portland. We spoke. I was a young player, and he was Clyde Drexler, and of course I was going to acknowledge him, first and foremost. And he was such a good person — no big shot in him at all.

Once he came to the Rockets, my locker was right next to his. He told me, "Play your game, cude. Do what you can do, because I am going to do what I have to do." As a result, I felt better about my role. If I had to come in and score, I scored. If I knew I had to get Clyde a shot, I would give it to him and get out of the way. He wanted to take all the pressure off of me and put it on him. He wanted to make sure other guys would produce, because he knew he was going to. If he had to, he would always step up.

Clyde gave us that dominant second scorer we had never had. He was the ultimate guy we needed. Vernon Maxwell did tremendous things for our ball club, but he wasn't a guy who could get you 20 points every night. Clyde was that guy. On a bad night, Clyde would get us 20 points, even if he had to go 18 of 18 from the free throw line to do it.

**HAKEEM OLAJUWON:** We had been playing against Clyde for many years, so we all knew him. Clyde was a natural player, a very flexible player who could bring the ball up, could play shooting guard or small forward. And whatever he did, he did it to win. He had only one style of playing: All out. It was one of the things I admired about him all those years.

When Clyde came back to the team, Maxwell felt very insecure. He had been suspended, then he was sick, then he had to come back to the team and see a future Hall of Famer in his starting spot. I asked Clyde to talk to him, to make him feel comfortable. Clyde told me, "You know I would do that, anyway."

I just told Max I was here to try to help the team win. Whether that was playing with him or coming off the bench, I didn't care what my role was — that was up to the coach. I wanted him to know I liked him, that we were friends, we would continue to be friends, and now that we were teammates, I would be rooting for him every step of the way. He said he felt the same way. "All I want to do is win," he said. I considered him a good teammate for the short time we played together.

**HAKEEM OLAJUWON:** When Vernon returned from his suspension, I went to him again and said, "Clyde is an eight-time All-Star. You are not in competition with him. When you are on the floor he will play forward. There is going to be a rotation. Now you can come off the bench and use your speed to create instant offense and give us the spark we need."

Mario knew Clyde from having played together in Portland. He knew now, with himself and Maxwell and Clyde at the off guard, his playing time would be cut down. Clyde would be on the floor at times when it otherwise would have been Mario. But Mario is a role player and probably felt he wasn't getting enough minutes as it was, so why complain? He handled it well.

Mario was a consummate professional. When I came in, he welcomed me with open arms. There were some other guys who had reservations, because we didn't have a power forward. A couple of guys had that question, including Max, who obviously realized my arrival would cut into his playing time.

But I was healthy, I was happy, and I could see we had the makings of something special, even though we went only 17-18 the rest of the regular season. We went through a little rut in early March when we lost five in a row, including a 107-96 loss at home to Orlando, whom we would see again down the road.

**RUDY TOMJANOVICH:** What was trying about that season was that we had a lot of injuries, and what we envisioned our team being, we never had a chance to have until the playoffs started. Through it all, Clyde was so fantastic. He came to a team that had one of the best records in the league, and because of the injuries, we were having a little bit of a down year, and a lot of things could have been internalized. He was so positive, the way he handled himself as a professional, the leadership he showed ... he did it in a very quiet, dignified fashion. Hakeem and Maxwell both missed some time with iron-deficiency anemia, and Horry was hurt a lot of the time. Clyde led us with class. His presence alone brought something to us.

**CARROLL DAWSON:** Within three or three and a half weeks, we started playing really well. We were growing as we hit the playoffs. The chemistry was a big reason. It wasn't just Clyde's talent, which was immense. Getting him and Olajuwon back together was electrifying.

We were up and down through the regular season, but everything was geared toward peaking as we headed into the playoffs. I felt better than I had in years. In a wild 156-147 double-overtime loss to Dallas on April 11, I had my 18th career triple-double with 29 points, 11 rebounds and 11 assists, but it wasn't enough. In our 12 games in April, I averaged 22.8 points, 6.7 rebounds and 4.3 assists, mostly as a secondary scorer behind Hakeem. I was ready.

**SAM CASSELL:** When Hakeem went down for nine games during the regular season, Clyde was our go-to guy and averaged 30 points and 9.3 rebounds over that period. He scored 40 twice and never had fewer than 20 during that span. He showed me that he really had it. He just took us on his back. It was like, "I can get it done; y'all just follow my lead." Kenny, Mario, Robert, we all just followed. We would run him off of screens and let him create something. He was such a great passer.

**RUDY TOMJANOVICH:** During the stretch when Hakeem was out, Clyde made a 33-foot bank shot from straight on at the buzzer to beat Denver 123-120. And I was sprinting out there when the ball went through the net, hugging him. I don't know if he was used to having a coach as emotional as I was. He was pretty cool. He looked at me like, "What the heck, this game is over. Stay calm, man."

**LES ALEXANDER:** One of the fun things to me was bringing Hakeem and Clyde back together. How they coalesced was fabulous. There were times when you watched them play and it was like men against boys, they were so superior to the guys they were going against. There wasn't anybody who was a tougher competitor than those two.

**CARROLL DAWSON:** From the first day, you could see not only how happy Clyde was to be back in Houston, but also how happy the team was to have him. Rudy eventually moved Robert from the small forward to power forward, which worked out well because Robert could shoot the ball. A lot of times, defenders wouldn't go out to guard him. That put Mario back in the starting lineup with Clyde at the 2-3 spots. It was great, because they were very good offensively and okay there defensively. We were able to start Kenny Smith at the point and come off the bench with Sam Cassell.

**RUDY TOMJANOVICH:** The thing a lot of people over-looked about Clyde was how great a passer he was. Then you noticed his physical strength. He was stronger than most players at his position. His hands were strong. He had numerous times where he would just go in and phys-ically take the ball out of somebody else's hands. It was amazing. He gave us that strong post-up two guard and also a slasher. He was a very impressive athlete, even at that point in his career.

**CARROLL DAWSON:** By the time we got him, Clyde was complete — leadership, clutch free throws, clutch shots, steals. And you know Olajuwon did the same things. Before we acquired Clyde, we relied a lot on Olajuwon to win a game for us at the end. Now we had another guy capable of doing that.

Of all the things Clyde did, what I remember most is that he had the strongest hands I have ever seen in 40 years of coaching. He had the ability to play defense alongside a dribbler and when the guy went up to shoot a layup, Clyde would reach in and pull the ball out and go the other way with it. It was unique. I don't think he ever got enough credit for the strength of his game. For him to get in there and fight the big guys for rebounds and loose balls, to complete a play when he had been hammered, to reach in and steal the ball ... and the guy never got tired. He had to be in the best shape. He was a machine. He was blessed with a great body for basketball. Everybody talks about his scoring and his speed, but from a coach-ing standpoint, the strength in this guy really blew me away.

Every year he seemed to lead the league's two guards in rebounding. He was always up there in steals. And he was such a professional. He followed the game plan. It is so hard to win in this league. You get a guy who knows how to win, you can't place a value on that. Everything fell into place for us after that.

Carroll was one of the best coaches I ever had. He really knew the game, especially from a defensive standpoint. At a time-out, he could usually give me one or two pointers to help shut down the guy I was defending, which usually resulted in a steal or a turnover. He was always a step ahead. He was an innovator.

**LES ALEXANDER:** I consider Clyde the greatest NBA player of all time in going for a loose ball. I mean, you have to be tough, because you are going to bang heads or bodies and you are going to get skinned up. But if there was a loose ball, I always figured Clyde was going to get it. He had great timing and the strongest, surest hands I have ever seen.

**SAM CASSELL:** We went into the playoffs as the sixth seed, but that was not discouraging for him, or for us, either. We understood once we got everybody on the same page, we had a great package as a team. Clyde was always the second dominant scorer, and we all understood it. We let Clyde shoot 12 balls in a row; we didn't complain, because we knew if he shot 12 he was probably going to make six of them. And when he got the ball in the open court, the other team wasn't going to stop him. He was one of the best finishers in the game. He had those huge hands. I would throw the ball out to him early on the fast break, and if he took two or three dribbles, he was gone.

**RUDY TOMJANOVICH:** I wanted to put the ball in somebody's hands who could make something happen. Clyde could make things happen. But it wasn't always about him. What I really loved — and this is what I love about basketball — Clyde had a chemistry with certain players who weren't stars. What he and Chucky Brown had was something special. Chucky was not a big-name player, but we had a couple of pick-and-roll plays from different angles on the court. Clyde would look over the defense, and the defensive guy would jump up, and Clyde found a way of getting Chucky a couple of layups every game. He made us look like a smart team. We were getting layups when you put the ball in his hands.

Chucky was an undersized power forward, but he made up for it with energy. He just wanted to play and accepted any role he was given. When you have that attitude, it makes it easy to have team chemistry. He had a good midrange jump shot, and he could finish going to the basket. Rudy used to run the pick-and-roll with Chucky and me. If his man committed to me a little bit, Chucky would be there for a little five-footer or a dunk, and he would always put it away. It was much like the way we used to run the pick-and-roll with me and Duckworth and Buck Williams in Portland.

**ROBERT HORRY:** Clyde and I ran a three-drop for me on the block. He would be at the foul line, drop a pass to me and then cut to the basket. On the two-drop, I would pass in to him at the post, and he would drop it to me as a cutter. Certain players have a good rhythm with one or two teammates. Clyde had it with just about everybody.

He was doing some things for us nobody else could do. He could grab offensive and defensive rebounds as the two guard. His post-up game was great. He could do so many things physically that almost nobody as his position could do. He was a very intelligent guy. He tried to keep the locker room light, to keep his teammates at ease. He wasn't a veteran who was stern and stone-faced. He would always talk to guys.

Clyde is right up there among the great players I played with. I have been very lucky. Look at the team you could put together of my teammates — Hakeem, Shaquille O'Neal and Tim Duncan on the front line, Clyde and Kobe Bryant in the backcourt. That's a pretty miraculous team, a team I would take any time.

**SAM CASSELL:** I used to tease him a lot. Everybody prepared differently for a game. He prepared strangely; it was crazy to see. He was a guy who used his athleticism so much, but he didn't stretch, and he didn't shoot before the game. He sat there and read his books. I would come in after shooting and running around and I would be sweating. I would look at Clyde, and he had still had his jacket and suit pants on, his shirt buttoned down with his legs crossed, reading some kind of novel. I was like, "Ain't your body going to be tight?" He would laugh at me. He would walk onto the court, and his first layup would be a tremendous slam dunk. I would think, "Damn." I never saw a guy prepare like Clyde did. But he was always ready.

Before a game, I had to relax. The best way for me to do that was to read. I was always reading something. I could get hyper quickly, especially when it came to competition. I don't need a lot of time to prepare, especially in a hot climate. If it was winter or if it was a cold day, I would be more inclined to go out and do some early loosening up. Normally I didn't, though. In a team's regular warmups, a player has 12 to 15 minutes, and that is a lot of time to get loose. I would run up and down the court four or five times, take 30 or 40 jump shots, and that is really all I needed. I stretched a little bit while I was warming up. Not a lot. I was never big on stretching.

**KENNY SMITH:** Even though we had struggled all through the regular season, we felt our playoff experience made us the best team. We all understood where everyone should go at both ends of the court. We had leaders in different aspects of the game, but we always knew that Clyde and Dream were our 1-2 options at the offensive end.

I hadn't played very long with Clyde by the time we got to the playoffs, and a big responsibility of the point guard is getting teammates the ball at the right time. The passes I was able to throw him, I couldn't throw to anyone else. He had a knack for getting to the right spot. It could be a terrible pass for everyone else, but it was a perfect pass for Clyde. That was one of the things he brought to our team — someone I could throw the ball to in a certain position that normally would be considered a bad play.

I averaged 21.4 points and 7.0 rebounds and shot .506 from the field in my 35 games with the Rockets, but they had gotten me to help them in the second season. After finishing the regular season 47-35, we opened the playoffs as the sixth seed against the third seed in the West, the Utah Jazz, who had won 60 games during the regular season. From my days in Portland, I knew how tough it was going against Karl Malone and John Stockton in the postseason.

We lost the opener 102-100 despite a brilliant 45-point performance by Hakeem. I was disappointed with my game — seven points, four rebounds and four assists in 37 minutes. I guarded Jeff Hornacek and held him to five points or two-of-10 shooting, but I had to do better at the offensive end.

After that game, Vernon Maxwell left the team and never played again. Max had been simmering, and apparently he had a beef with Rudy about minutes. It ended what had been a very testy relationship between the two. That had probably never happened before — a key player leaving a team in the middle of a playoff series.

I had no beef with Max. It was the coaches who got the pressure from him. We got along fine. Max had been the starter on a championship team the year before. I could understand his frustration. It never affected our relationship.

Some teams handle adversity in a positive way, as we did with this situation. And it started with the coaches. Before Game 2, they told the players, "Max is gone. We can't control that. It is something we don't have to deal with any more." It was unfortunate, but we just had to move on.

We won Game 2 140-126, and I was back in stride, sinking 12 of 17 shots for 30 points to go with seven assists. Kenny Smith led us with 32 points, and he was unconscious from three-point range, hitting an NBA playoff-record seven treys. As a team, we were 19 of 28 from beyond the arc, also a league playoff record. And we had four players score 20 points or more.

The Jazz put our backs to the wall with a 95-82 win at our place in Game 3. Malone was huge with 32 points and 19 rebounds. Hakeem had 30 points and 10 boards, but we needed to give him more help.

We were tremendous in Game 4, shooting .574 in a historic 123-106 victory. I scored 41 points and Hakeem added 40, and we became only the third pair of teammates in playoff history to score 40 apiece in the same game.

**HAKEEM OLAJUWON:** I am sure you can imagine what it was like to have two players combine to score 81 points — in a playoff game at that! It speaks for itself.

Eighty-one points — that is more than a lot of teams score in a playoff game today. I remember talking to Hakeem before the game; we didn't want to go out like this. We felt that if we could somehow win that game, we could win the series. We took control early, and I remember feeling on top of my game. They used both Hornacek and David Benoit on me, but I made a lot of shots both from the outside and close to the basket. And Hakeem was awesome at both ends of the court. We ran a lot of pick-and-roll plays between the two of us, and they just couldn't stop us. Had we not won that game, all the great things that followed wouldn't have happened.

We still had to go back to Salt Lake City and win the deciding Game 5 on Utah's home court. They got the jump on us and had a big third quarter. But we got it together down the stretch, scored 31 points in the fourth quarter and won 95-91. Hakeem was sensational, making 10 of 16 shots while collecting 33 points and 10 rebounds. I was eight for 15 from the field and had 31 points and 10 boards. We had cleared the first hurdle.

**HAKEEM OLAJUWON:** When we were down in the fourth quarter, Clyde did a great job of keeping everybody in the game. He talked to me. He talked to Sam, telling us not to be discouraged. At the time, we were down only seven points. He was very astute.

**RUDY TOMJANOVICH:** The Jazz were up by 12 at one point in the fourth quarter, and their fans were dancing in the aisles. The PA was playing the theme to *Rocky*. Ever since then, I have hated when that song was played during a game. It was deafening in that arena. I had to draw things on the clipboard because we couldn't hear each other. We pecked away and pecked away at Utah's lead and found a way to win.

That game was the springboard for us really believing that we were going to be as good or better than the year before.

The Western Conference semifinals were against the Phoenix Suns, who had won 59 games behind Charles Barkley, Kevin Johnson, A.C. Green and a great bench led by Wayman Tisdale, Dan Majerle and Danny Ainge. Johnson pointed out before the series that we were the team they wanted, because the Suns had held a 2-0 lead in their playoff series with the Rockets the year before being eliminated.

The Suns drilled us in the first two games in Phoenix, 130-108 and 118-94. It was embarrassing and unacceptable. But the most embarrassing thing was what happened in the opener between me and my old nemesis, referee Jake O'Donnell.

Early in the second quarter, Jake called me for a clear-path foul against Majerle on the fast break, meaning that I had interfered with what was going to be a sure basket. I had stepped into the passing lane, cleanly picked the ball from Majerle and was heading for a dunk when the whistle blew. As soon as I heard it, I thought, "I can't believe he is going to stop the play." With Jake, I always assumed the worst. I just kept walking toward our basket. I had my back to him. I never turned around or said a word. And he kept blowing the whistle, like, "Hurry up and bring the ball back." I guess he didn't like my body action.

Finally I turned around, and he said, "You are out of the game." He had already given me two technical fouls and ejected me, and I hadn't said anything to him. That is when I got real hot. This guy was flat-out cheating, which is something he had done against the Blazers for a long time. But let's give Jake all the credit. The guys in Houston thought he had been killing them the last couple of years, too. He had given me two technicals for nothing, not to mention taking away a sure two points. He had gone too far. That was beyond cheating. He was trying to alter the outcome of the game, and I had reached my limit with him. If it wasn't for Rudy and a couple of guys stopping me, I probably would have done something I would have regretted. I don't think I have ever been angrier during a game. I never had a fight in 15 years. That wasn't going to be a fight; it was going to be a ripping-apart.

**DANNY AINGE:** I wanted to win that game really bad. But when that whole incident happened with Jake and Clyde was kicked out of the game, I was physically sickened by what I saw. It was a situation I am sure Jake regrets. I liked Jake. I thought he was a good referee. But that was one thing I didn't agree with. That just made me feel, "Oh man, that's just not right." Clyde did nothing to warrant what he was getting from Jake on that night.

**LES ALEXANDER:** I was at America West Arena that night when Jake O'Donnell booted Clyde and ended Jake's career. Gaynell Drexler was sitting next to me. I remember some fans around us started to get on Clyde, calling him a hothead, and I turned around and said, "This is his wife right here." I am not a guy who calls the league and says the refs are bad. I just don't do that. I think it's foolish. But this time, I felt it was necessary. The next day, I spoke to the NBA's deputy commissioner, Russ Granik. The league did an investigation, and O'Donnell wound up paying a very stiff penalty.

Normally after a player is ejected, he is contacted by the league so that he can share with them his side of the story. After the incident with Jake, I never heard from anyone with the league. I was ready and eager to talk, believe me, but they already had conclusive evidence that Jake was incredibly wrong. He had done that kind of thing 100 times before, of course, but he had gotten away with it. This time, he got carried away in a playoff setting, and he was exposed. My $1,000 fine was rescinded, and Jake never worked another game.

The next year, *Houston Chronicle* sports columnist Fran Blinebury caught up with O'Donnell, and here was Jake's version of what happened:

"Nothing happened that was different than 1,000 other calls I have made. I thought the Phoenix player got pushed and I called the foul. Clyde told me to f— myself, so I hit him with a technical."

That was a lie. How could I tell him that from 60 feet away?

"As I was walking toward the scorer's table to signal the fouls," Jake continued, "I heard a commotion behind me. I turned and saw players holding him back from charging at me. That is automatic. Another technical and he's gone. Then I heard after the game that Houston was all upset because I didn't shake Drexler's hand in the pregame captains' meeting, and that was supposed to mean something.

"Let me tell you, I hadn't shaken his hand since the 1992-93 season, and it was his doing. It was after his team had lost in the Finals to Chicago, and most officials will tell you they hated games with Portland. That was the [whiniest] bunch of players and coaches I have ever been around. They whined at every call from every official.

"So it was early the next season, and I was in Portland for a game against Detroit. I was standing at midcourt for the captain's meeting and Drexler walked up and told me, 'If you say anything, I'll knock the s— out of you.' I had no idea what that was about, still don't to this day.

"After the game, I faxed my report to the league office and told Rod Thorn and David Stern that I wanted to have a conference call with Drexler on the matter and get it resolved. I didn't shake his hand after that. For most of his career, Darell Garretson wouldn't shake Larry Bird's hand. Jack Madden didn't shake Kevin Johnson's hand. It doesn't affect how you call the game. If personalities got to you that much, you would never rise to the pro level in the first place."

O'Donnell also told Blinebury that we never had a conference call, but that I was fined $10,000 for what I said before the Detroit game, and that I later sent a letter of apology to him.

Jake is full of it. During the '92 Finals, he cheated us like never before. I was pissed off at him the whole summer. During the Olympics, I told both Rod Thorn and Russ Granik about it. They laughed and said, "Let it go, Clyde. You lost. The guy is doing the best he can. Accept it."

But Jake wasn't doing the best he could. Believe me, I would rather not have had a conversation with any ref other than to say hello before a game. But this was beyond that. Before that Detroit game, the refs were meeting with me and the Pistons captains, Isiah Thomas and Joe Dumars, and I did give Jake a piece of my mind. If I was fined for what I said, I don't remember paying it. And I never sent him a letter of apology.

In an ESPN interview a couple of months before the Blinebury article, O'Donnell provided a little more information

when he said, "I wouldn't give Drexler much leeway because of
the way he reacted with me all the time. I thought at times he
would give cheap shots to people, and I just would not allow it."
Jake had also told another interviewer, "I cheated on him at every
chance. Didn't give him a break, because I didn't like him." That
Jake admitted that he cheated let me know how crazy the guy
really was. And I wasn't the only one having problems with him.
There were a lot of players, including Buck Williams.

> **BUCK WILLIAMS:** My troubles with Jake went back a
> long way. I don't know if I brought Clyde into it, or if he
> had his own issues with Jake before I arrived. I do know
> we didn't like Jake, and Jake didn't like us. We felt he was
> unfair, he was unreasonable, and in the end, it cost him
> his job.
>
> There are very few people who were in or around the
> game during my career whom I didn't care very much for.
> But Jake was one of those guys. I certainly never had an
> official have as much of an impact on my game as Jake
> did. I kind of walked on eggshells when he officiated. I
> knew if I got close to someone I was guarding, he would
> call a foul. He even told some of his colleagues that he
> didn't like me. I can't to this day understand why the man
> in charge of the league's officials, Rod Thorn, didn't get
> us together to talk it out. I know I complained to Rod
> about it several times. I guess they didn't want to add fuel
> to the fire. We got caught up in a very bitter relationship,
> and Jake took it very personally with Clyde, too.

I got into it with Jake initially because I was protecting Buck
the first season he came to the Blazers. I had no history with Jake
to that point. I didn't really even know who he was. I saw Jake
looking for minute things to call against Buck. In one game, he

made a bad call on Buck, and Buck stared at him, and Jake said, "Don't you eyeball me." Buck would never say anything back. I didn't have that kind of discipline. When a referee is cheating, he is definitely going to hear about it from me. I got along with 99 percent of the officials. But when you see a guy going out of his way to cheat on your team, it is hard to just take it.

Jake had worked our Game 3 in the Utah series, and during the game, Hakeem asked him, "How do you sleep at night?"

"Very well," Jake responded.

"You must not have a conscience," Hakeem told him.

Hakeem told me, "This guy is the worst." And he was surprised to hear I had a history with him, too. Hakeem is a mild-mannered guy, but he was disgusted with Jake. We thought he was scum, to be honest. People said he was a great official. I never saw it. I think he did know the game, but he would make calls on you just for the hell of it. He refused to do the right thing, and that is to make unbiased decisions. When you fail to do that, you fail to do your job.

After losing Game 2 to Phoenix, we were down 2-0 again, and some people were counting us out.

**RUDY TOMJANOVICH:** The year before, after pulling out so many games at the end on the way to our first title, the headlines in the Houston newspapers read "Clutch City." After going down 0-2 to Phoenix this year, however, the headlines read, "Choke City."

We came back to rout the Suns in Game 3 by a 118-85 count. We jumped to a 22-point halftime lead and were never really challenged. Hakeem had 36 points and Charles Barkley missed all 10 of his shots and finished with only five points.

But they pushed us to the brink of elimination with a 114-110 win in Game 4. We led by 15 points midway through the third quarter, but they chipped away and beat us with a 15-4 run over the final 4:30. Kevin Johnson was unstoppable with 43 points and Charles added 26. Hakeem scored 38 points and I added 22, but we were in big trouble, down 3-1 and going back to Phoenix for Game 5.

Charles was popping off. He told a couple of Houston writers, "Bring your golf clubs to Phoenix, because the next round of the playoffs will start there next week."

And suddenly, I was sick. Real sick. I had caught some sort of flu and was really out of it. I was hooked up to an IV during most of the day. I wasn't supposed to play, but a couple of hours before the game, I got out of bed and went to the arena and somehow staggered through that game. I was 0 for six from the field and scored only four points in 32 minutes. But I was out there, and we won 103-97 to stay alive.

**RUDY TOMJANOVICH:** Clyde was walking dead. No way in the world was he going to play. I didn't expect him to even come to the game. But he showed up, suited up and went out there and inspired our guys.

After Game 5, Kevin Johnson said our team had the "heart of a champion," meaning that we just wouldn't die. Charles Barkley wasn't that flattering. He said we were like Texas roaches. Once you step on them, you think you got them, and they keep scurrying away.

We were back at home for Game 6. We took charge of the game in the second half on our way to a 116-103 victory to even the series at 3-3. Hakeem was sensational as usual, nearly getting a triple-double with 30 points, eight rebounds and 10 assists. I was still under the weather but I was feeling a little better, and I contributed 20 points and eight boards.

Game 7 turned out to be an unforgettable game for both franchises. After Game 6, Charles had told the media that he was going home to America West Arena where he was going to "have a party with 19,000 of my closest friends. And Hakeem had what I thought was a great comeback: "I like parties, too."

Kevin Johnson was up to the task, scoring 46 points, including an NBA-record 21 straight free throws. But it wasn't enough to beat the Rockets. We were down 15 points in the first half, but we kept plugging away. And Johnson finally missed a free throw with the game tied at 110-110 in the closing seconds. We got the rebound and Robert Horry passed the ball to Mario Elie, who swished a three-pointer with 7.1 seconds left. What a shot by Mario. That one was known in Houston as the "Kiss of Death" for the Suns that year. Quite often, Mario used to blow teams a kiss after hitting threes. When he made that shot, we referred to it as the Kiss of Death for the Suns. I made a pair of free throws with 3.5 seconds remaining to ice it, and Houston became the fifth team in NBA history to come back from a 3-1 deficit to win a playoff series.

I still didn't feel right, but I was able to score 29 points, the same as Hakeem. All of our other guys — Kenny, Sam, Robert, Mario, Chucky Brown, Pete Chilcutt, Charles Jones — they were pumped up and did a great job. In my mind, they were the heroes.

Afterward, Hakeem wondered aloud, "What happened to Charles's party? Oh well. Tell him he can come to ours."

**RUDY TOMJANOVICH:** I was on cloud nine after that game. And I kept thinking about how we had taken so much criticism concerning the trade for Clyde. Some people had said, "You are going to be the only championship team not to make the playoffs the next year." This was just sort of our way of saying, "You underestimated what we had here." Our guys were champions. We weren't just going to hand over the crown to somebody. Yeah, we really did have the heart of champions.

Our opponent in the Western Conference finals was San Antonio, which had won 62 games during the regular season and had swept Denver and dispatched the Lakers in six games. David Robinson was in his prime, and he had plenty of help, with Sean Elliott, Vinny Del Negro and Avery Johnson. And they had added a power forward named Dennis Rodman. In between act-outs that season, Rodman had provided them with great rebounding and interior defense.

**CARROLL DAWSON:** Rodman could be dominant on the boards, but he refused to go out with Robert on the perimeter. Rodman would just stay in the basket area, and Robert hurt them from outside several games in the series.

The Olajuwon-Robinson matchup had the best two centers in the game going against each other. David had won the MVP trophy for his play during the regular season, and Hakeem had won it the year before.

It turned out to be a strange series. Neither team won on its home court until the final game.

We won the opener 94-93 when Robert nailed a 17-footer with 6.4 seconds left. Another big shot by Horry. A winning team needs superstars, but the other players have to make shots as well. With us, those other guys were not role players; they were players who knew their roles. There is a difference. Hakeem collected 27 points, eight rebounds and five assists; I had 25 points and 12 boards. The Dream was unstoppable in Game 2 with 41 points and 16 rebounds as we won 106-96 to stake a 2-0 lead in the series.

Then we went back to The Summit and gave up our home-court advantage, losing the third game 107-102 despite Hakeem's 43 points, then getting crushed 103-81 in Game 4. We blistered them in Game 5 at the Alamodome 111-90, with Hakeem scoring 42. "Sam I Am" Cassell came off the bench to dish out 12 assists and score 30 points — hitting a lot of clutch shots along the way.

**RUDY TOMJANOVICH:** It was the strangest playoff series I was ever involved in. The Spurs felt as if they would break the cycle in Game 5. Now we felt we were going to find a way to break the cycle in Game 6.

Finally, we broke through by winning Game 6 by a score of 100-95 to claim the series. Hakeem had another monster performance with 39 points and 17 rebounds. I had 16 points, 10 rebounds and seven assists. But Robert was the man of the hour, scoring 22 points and sinking six three-pointers, including one with 1:58 remaining, to bring us home.

Hakeem was incredible in the series, averaging 35.3 points and 13.2 rebounds. Robinson was outstanding, too, averaging 23.8 points and 11.3 boards, but the Dream clearly had the advantage, and we had a ticket to the Finals.

**CARROLL DAWSON:** The San Antonio series was one of the best I have been a part of. Nobody could win a game on their home court until the finale. That was the heyday of those two centers; what a battle between those two gladiators. That was a lot of good basketball, and we won out.

**RUDY TOMJANOVICH:** After we had beaten the Spurs, somebody said, "We are going back to the Finals, but we have to stay hungry." Then somebody else said, "And we have to stay humble, too. Our slogan became, "Stay hungry and humble." That became sort of our battle cry.

I knew we had to be on the top of our game to beat Orlando. That was a really good team. I mean, look at their lineup — Shaquille O'Neal, Penny Hardaway, Nick Anderson, Horace Grant, Dennis Scott. That was great collection of young talent. And remember, they had beaten the Bulls in the Eastern Conference finals. Even so, I went into that series confident. I had been in a championship series twice before, so it wasn't like it was a strange situation for me. Both times in Portland, we had finished second. I figured the third time had to be a charm.

**KENNY SMITH:** With Shaq and Penny, Orlando was the young up-and-coming team. They were going to be the next dynasty of the NBA. Even though we had won the year before, people had kind of forgotten about us because it had been such a struggle for us to get to the Finals. And in the same sense, people didn't realize how tough the Western Conference was that year. So we went into that series as underdogs.

The opener in Orlando is a game people will always remember. For most of the first half, Shaq and Penny were having their way with us and the Magic were blowing us out. Four minutes before halftime, we were down 20 points, and it was, "What is happening here?" Hakeem was in foul trouble and was out of the game. It looked bad.

We took a timeout and I said, "Look, let's get this thing down to 10 or 12 points by halftime, and we will be in it."

**HAKEEM OLAJUWON:** That is when Clyde began making his move. He was brilliant in the open court, rebounding, stealing the ball, running the floor, converting circus layups. He scored 15 points in the second quarter, including the last seven, and we cut the lead to 11 at the half.

**SAM CASSELL:** Orlando was kicking our butts, Hakeem was on the bench with three fouls, and basically, we were ready to pack it in. During the timeout, Clyde said, "Hey, let's chip away at that lead. We ain't done yet." And he played phenomenally the next few minutes. I will never forget one play. Clyde stole the ball from Nick Anderson and passed the ball to Kenny in the corner, then sprinted downcourt and got the return pass and slammed down a two-handed dunk. That was the turning point in the game.

**KENNY SMITH:** We were shell-shocked those first 16 minutes. During the timeout, I remember Hakeem saying, "We need to make a run." And Clyde said his piece, and then he went off and kind of single-handedly kept us within striking distance. And suddenly, there was a little doubt in Orlando's minds. We went in at halftime feeling we were still in the game.

We trailed only 61-50 at the half, and Orlando went into the locker room looking kind of stunned. We felt like we had momentum. And then Kenny Smith went into a zone like I have never seen before. He started hitting three after three — we were applying some pressure.

**HAKEEM OLAJUWON:** We ran a play for Clyde three times in a row, and each time before Clyde could come around the pick and get the ball, Kenny Smith had a clear look at the basket and bombed from the outside. Kenny couldn't miss.

Clyde couldn't believe it! Kenny was hitting from five feet beyond the three-point line. Clyde had never seen anybody shooting like that when it was most needed. He went "Whooa!"

**SAM CASSELL:** Kenny came out in the third quarter and hit back-to-back threes, and suddenly we were down five points, and we were in business. I remember Clyde saying, "They don't want it; let's take it."

**KENNY SMITH:** Clyde and Sam always used to say, "Kenny, if you make two in a row from the outside, you have the license to shoot as many times as you want." I hit two in a row, and they were saying, "Don't stop shooting" the whole second half.

Kenny set an NBA Finals record by sinking five three-pointers in the third quarter, and we took an 89-80 lead early in the fourth period. But the Magic didn't die. And it looked like we were dead when Nick Anderson went to the foul line for two shots with 10.5 seconds left and Orlando ahead 110-107. If he made even one free throw we were probably done. But he missed both. Amazingly, he rebounded the second miss, and we had to foul him again.

Same situation. And again, he missed both. And we rebounded and called a timeout. We inbounded and got the ball to Kenny, who faked Hardaway into the air, ducked under his arm and buried a three to force overtime. Again, the shot-making ability of my teammates in the clutch had done wonders for the team. Robert, Mario, Sam and Kenny did it time after time. That one was the biggest shot of Kenny's career. I almost wanted to go over and kiss him. The key word is almost.

**KENNY SMITH:** Everyone thought I was going to be the one to get the ball, but I wasn't the first option. Rudy drew up a pick-and-roll with me and Dream. We thought they would double-team me and Robert would probably be open. I started to come off the screen and saw Horace and Penny cheating over, and I decided to come back around the screen. I faked Penny up and shot it. I thought, "No way in the world I am not taking this shot."

But that shot, it was like divine intervention. Penny is 6'7", and if had he jumped straight up, I couldn't have gotten the shot off over him. But it seemed like someone picked him up and moved him over, because he jumped sideways.

In overtime, with the score tied 118-118, we had the last possession and Rudy called a play to run a pick-and-roll at the three-point line. When the pick was set, I ran off it really hard. Shaq had to move over to pick me up; otherwise I had a clear path to the hoop. I went to the hole very strong. I was going to go up and dunk it, but Shaq came over strong. I was in stride and knew I had to get it up real high or he would block it. Usually when I jump at full stride, I look down at people. When I got up there this time, I thought, "Who is that up here with me?" I tried the finger-roll. It felt like I threw it as high as the backboard just to get it over him. The ball rolled in and out, but Hakeem was there to tip it in as time expired.

**CARROLL DAWSON:** Clyde was smart enough to miss it where it would go over the rim and Olajuwon could get it.

It was more luck than anything. I really thought my shot was going to go, but Shaq was there just when I didn't want him there. The play was designed just the way it was executed, except that I was supposed to make the shot.

**KENNY SMITH:** It worked out beautifully. Hakeem's man went to Clyde, and Hakeem followed, and he didn't even know he had hit the shot. I ran and jumped on him, and he said, "Did it go in?" And I yelled, "Yeah!"

**HAKEEM OLAJUWON:** Clyde did a fantastic job of penetrating, and he shot the ball so high. I had inside position. When I tipped the ball in, it was so quiet in the arena, I didn't realize the basket was good for a minute.

**KENNY SMITH:** Clyde had a hell of a second half. That was the difference in that game, and it set the tone for the whole series. When you debate about the game's great scorers or shooters, I always cast my vote for the guys who can do it with the game on the line. Can he hit a shot with the score tied, or if his team is down one, and the clock is running down, and everyone knows you are going to have the ball? That was Clyde, even if he didn't make the last one in that game.

We had a lot of heroes. Hakeem had 31 points. I contributed 23 points, 11 rebounds and seven assists. Kenny added 23 points and seven assists. When it was over, we couldn't believe we had won the game. The Magic couldn't believe it, either. They were demoralized. I really think they never recovered from that game. After that one, we had a good feeling that the series was going to be ours.

We waxed Orlando 117-106 in the second game, building a 22-point halftime lead. Hakeem finished with 34 points and 13 rebounds and I had 10 of my 23 points in the fourth quarter. Sam was incredible off the bench, going for 31 points in 30 minutes. And we were up 2-0, going back home for the next three games, if necessary.

Game 3 was the scariest game I ever played in my life. We knew we had to take care of business. It was my best chance to win a championship ring and I didn't want to blow it. It was the most important game of my career. There was a lot of pressure there. We didn't want to let Orlando off the hook by blowing Game 3 and giving them new life. I had butterflies in my stomach the whole day just thinking about it.

We didn't play that well at the start of the game, but we kept it close.

**RUDY TOMJANOVICH:** We were ahead 96-94 with less than two minutes to go when Clyde snared a rebound, went coast to coast with it, put a move on an over-matched Dennis Scott and threw down a dunk that shook the Summit.

I saw a guy I thought I had a great chance to beat, and I went for it. And Robert — how many big shots has that guy hit through his career? — sank a three-pointer with 14.1 seconds left to lift us to a 106-103 win. I finished with 25 points, 13 rebounds and seven assists to support Hakeem, who in his usual brilliance rang up 31 points, 14 boards and seven assists.

**HAKEEM OLAJUWON:** Game 3 belonged to Clyde. He pushed the ball up the floor the whole game. It seemed like every time I looked he was stealing the ball and finishing on the other end of the court with a slam.

When a team is down 3-0, the series is pretty much over. The Magic played hard in Game 4, but we weren't going to be denied. I had 15 points, nine boards and eight assists, but numbers are irrelevant in a situation like that. For the second time in my life — the first time being my wedding day — my ring size, 15 1/2, mattered. Eight days before my 33rd birthday, I was a champion at last.

**KENNY SMITH:** Clyde had that All-Star presence and the Olympic team experience and everything, but until that moment, he didn't have a ring. Before the Finals, he had told us, "I am planning on it this time, guys. Winning it means everything." Then when he got it, he was whole as a player.

**RUDY TOMJANOVICH:** That whole scenario was like a fairy tale. What are the odds of a guy coming back to his hometown, reuniting with a close friend and ex-teammate, having already been so close to winning a championship, getting a chance to do it, and then seeing it through? Man oh man, that's movie stuff, I'm telling you.

**KARL MALONE:** When Clyde won the championship in Houston, I was happy for him. He got a ring, and that was good. There are three guys I played against that I wished could have gotten a ring — Patrick, Charles and Clyde. Clyde was the only one of the three who got one.

**MYCHAL THOMPSON:** I am glad Clyde won a title in Houston. That validates every great player's career. Barkley, Stockton, Dave Bing, Dan Marino — with all of them, you say, "Yeah, but they didn't win a ring." That's the last crowning achievement on a great player's resume. And Clyde got one.

**JACK RAMSAY:** I never saw Clyde play better than he did that season. He was playing more within himself. When I coached him and throughout his years in Portland, he thought he had to carry the load. He wanted to be involved in every play. He wanted to be the guy who handled the ball. In Houston, he was on a team where there was a player he really respected, Hakeem, and he was willing to defer his status to him. He asserted himself when Hakeem was on the bench. And when he was on the court with Hakeem, he knew if he got the ball in to Hakeem — and nobody did that better than Clyde — he was either going to score or find someone else for a good shot.

**CARROLL DAWSON:** I am a Texan. I grew up in the state. It was never thought of as much of a basketball state. To coach with the first two basketball championship teams in the state — I am very proud of that. The second year was Clyde's first, so for him, nothing will compare to that. It was so big because Clyde came home and was able to get a ring. That is how great players look at capping their career.

Our run to the championship that year was one of the most incredible in NBA playoff history. So many times we were down, but we never quit fighting. We came back to beat Utah in five tough games, including the last game at their place. We beat Phoenix in seven games in the conference semifinals, and they had Charles Barkley and had gone to the Finals in 1993. Beating David Robinson and the Spurs was a huge hurdle, and we got by it. And finishing it off by sweeping a great Orlando team with Shaq and Penny — how sweet it was.

I will never forget the feeling after Game 4 of the Finals. Finally, after so many years getting so close to a title in college and the NBA, there was an unbelievable amount of personal satisfaction for me. Not a lot of teams are good enough to win it all. You can have the most talent in the world, but if one or two guys go down, if the breaks don't go your way, you might not win it. That year, we were good, and we were also very lucky.

A couple days later, there was a championship celebration party at the Astrodome that was televised live in Houston and hosted by Jim McInvale, affectionately known as "Mattress Mac." About 52,000 fans, paying $5 to get into the Dome and $20 for a seat on the floor, were a sea of red and gold. The coaches and players were brought out in convertibles to incredible ovations. You couldn't hear yourself think in there.

The post-championship parade, attended by an estimated 700,000 fans in downtown Houston, was unforgettable. Gaynell and I were riding on top of a fire truck, 30 feet in the air, with all those fans cheering for us ... that's when I knew I had made it. What a feeling of appreciation from the city of Houston.

**GAYNELL DREXLER:** Clyde was very moved by the reception he got. It brought back memories of him being a boy and having to catch the bus to do whatever little boys do when they go downtown. To have this happen in the same city ... he was almost in tears. And I think I was in tears.

# CHAPTER 17

# REALIZING MY DREAM

Life was a little different after winning a championship. Pro athletes always receive their share of attention, but champions are in the eye of the storm. I appeared on *The Tonight Show* with Jay Leno on a night when his guests included Sylvester Stallone and Lisa Kudrow. I did a lot of national sports talk radio shows and some magazine interviews, but mostly I wanted to relax. I went back to Portland to play some golf, unwind, spend quality time with my family and enjoy a very peaceful summer. We took some vacations and had fun; it was great to see the reaction from friends and fans. People were so happy for me and the Rockets. They would say things like, "Thank God you finally you got a ring." Some people made the analogy of Julius Erving playing for so long before he finally got a ring with Philadelphia in 1983.

I was getting more appearance and endorsement opportunities through my marketing rep, Steve Rosner. Steve and his partner, Frank Vuono, run 16-W Marketing out of New Jersey —

one of the best marketing firms in the country. Any athlete would be fortunate to be represented by 16-W.

I met Steve through Hakeem when I first came to the Rockets. We hit it off and became good friends. He was instrumental in putting together a lot of endorsement packages toward the end of my career. I always had some endorsements, but I was very picky about what I did. It wasn't about the money so much as the time constraints and what I would have to do for the money. Steve made it easy. If I'd had him 10 years earlier, it would have been nice.

I had always been recognized in public, but now, wherever I went, people were calling me "champ." I was accepting all kinds of accolades, and it was humbling.

**RUDY TOMJANOVICH:** Clyde always handled himself with class. He has a presence when he walks into a room. I just saw him at the Super Bowl, and he still stands out in a crowd.

**JIM NANTZ:** I always thought there was a special way in which Clyde carried himself on the floor. In my years covering the PGA, there were certain players — with their gait, the way they walked up the fairway — that exuded an aura, a magnetism that comes out of the way they move. The way Clyde moved around on a basketball floor, it was so beautiful to watch. It was absolutely graceful. You could tell the first time you laid eyes on him that there was something about him that went above and beyond the norm. He had a grace, a certain pride, a regal quality in the manner with which he carried himself that he still does to this day.

**RUDY TOMJANOVICH:** Clyde was very good to me. He did something that was amazing. During the championship season, he kept talking to the owner about giving me a contract extension. I couldn't believe what this guy was doing. He had just gotten to the team, and he kept on saying so many good things about me publicly, but also privately. It took me aback. I thought, "Boy, this guy is really something."

Rudy was a great coach. He was a player's coach. He was not a yeller or a hollerer. I loved Rudy from day one. The first day I came in, he said, "Clyde, we are going to make this thing work. If there is something you want, you tell me." He had a great defensive system. It all ended with Hakeem in the back. Our defense was stellar. That is really the reason we won games.

I didn't see any reason why the Rockets couldn't win another championship. We had virtually the same team back, and we added some role players, including my old teammate from Portland, forward Mark Bryant. And in November, I signed a two-year extension worth about $11 million that would carry me through the 1997-98 season. After which, I told a reporter, "I am 99 percent sure I will retire."

**CARROLL DAWSON:** We were playing golf that summer, and I said, "Clyde, you have at least one more contract in you." He said, "No, I told myself when this contract is up, this is it." I thought to myself, "Yeah, right. The way he is playing, he will never quit." But he was true to what he said. I was really surprised. He wasn't at the top of his game, but he hadn't slipped enough that I could tell it.

As NBA champions, we participated in the annual four-team international McDonalds Championship in London during our 1995-96 exhibition season. We beat Italy's Buckner Bologna 126-112 for the title, and I won the Drazen Petrovic Trophy as the tournament MVP. It was poignant, because Drazen had been a teammate of mine in Portland after establishing himself as one of Europe's great players. After making third-team All-NBA honors with the New Jersey Nets during the 1992-93 season, he died tragically in a car accident that summer.

We began the regular season on fire, winning 10 of our first 11 games. Soon we were 15-4, and I was off to a great start, averaging 21.7 points, 7.3 rebounds, 5.3 assists and 1.8 steals. Against Charlotte, I made 17 of 23 shots—sinking 13 straight at one point—en route to a 41-point explosion. Twice in a three-game span, I had 19-point quarters. There was a seven-game span where I was averaging 28.1 points and probably playing as well as I have ever played.

But I couldn't stay healthy. My knee was bothering me, and I had to have it drained, which took me out of only one game. Then I missed eight games from Dec. 21 to Jan. 3 due to a right shin contusion after Charles stepped in front of me to try to take a charge and I got blindsided.

When I got back in early January, we were 23-8 and leading the Midwest Division. From that point, we went 25-26 the rest of the regular season. It was a big-time struggle.

And just after the All-Star break — I participated in my ninth All-Star Game — I suffered a lateral meniscus tear of the right knee. I had arthroscopic surgery, sat out 20 games and didn't get back until early April.

Just about everybody missed games due to injury that season — Hakeem, Sam, Robert, Mario, Kenny. We were pretty healthy going into the playoffs, though. As the No. 5 seed in the West, we were facing the Lakers, the No. 4 seed. They had home-court advantage, but we figured we could do what we had done a year ago.

**CARROLL DAWSON**: Here is the biggest lie you will ever tell yourself: Lord, if you let me win just one championship, I will never have to do anything else. That is a crock. Once you win, it is so addictive, you never want to give up trying for another. We went almost three years without losing a playoff series. Once that happens, you crave more.

We won the all-important opener at The Forum 87-83 behind the 32 points of Hakeem. The Lakers evened the series by winning Game 2 104-94, but we knocked them off in Games 3 and 4 to advance to the second round against Seattle, the Pacific Division champion and No. 1 seed in the West with a 64-18 regular-season record.

Gary Payton, Shawn Kemp and Detlef Schrempf were in their prime, and the Sonics were a very difficult opponent. They swept us in four games. They blew us out in the opener 108-75, then beat us in three very close games in which we had a chance right down to the final seconds. We lost the last game in overtime after coming back from 20 points down in the fourth quarter. Rudy said we had shown the old Rocket heart, but it wasn't enough this time.

Houston management felt it had to shake things up that summer, and boy, did that happen. In August, the Rockets traded Sam Cassell, Robert Horry, Chucky Brown and Mark Bryant to Phoenix for Charles Barkley. On the same day, we also signed Kevin Willis, who would prove to be important as a backup at both the four and five spots, as a free agent.

**SAM CASSELL:** The only thing that ever disappointed me about Clyde was that he should have stood up for me when they decided to trade me in the Charles Barkley deal. He knew what I meant to him, and what he meant to me, and what I meant to that team. That's all. I was young, I didn't understand the business of basketball then. But Clyde is my guy. He always will be.

My loyalty is always with my teammates, especially if we have a winning team. I would have loved to have kept Sam and Robert. I thought they were the future of the franchise. Nothing against Charles, but the chemistry was good, we had a lot of success and those two guys were pretty good building blocks. As a player, though, you can't always go against what management is trying to do. They had mortgaged the future for the present by making that trade. It had worked with me, and it would have been hypocritical for me to say anything about it that time. It also would be foolish to think that my opinion alone would have changed things. Sam knows how I feel about him. He was my guy, too.

All the conjecture focused on whether the Big Three — Charles, Hakeem and myself — could get along on the basketball court. Were there were going to be enough shots for the three of us?

As a player, you never really know how the chemistry will be with certain players. I knew we were losing two darn good players in Sam and Robert. Charles was an exceptional player, but the question was, would we get the real Charles Barkley or a step-slower Charles? When he was healthy — especially his first year with the Rockets — he was the real Charles. But there was a lot of concern about sacrificing the future of your franchise by giving up your two most talented young players. Les Alexander took the approach that he wanted to win it again —right now. The trade for me had worked, and he thought it would do the same thing with Charles.

Charles had been a Dream Team teammate. I knew he could play. I had mixed emotions about the trade, because it is hard to lose teammates. Sam and Robert had been two of my favorite teammates. But we needed a true power forward, and Charles was one of the best in the game. The problem was, we had been a running team during the championship season, pushing the ball at every opportunity. If we set it up, we would go into Hakeem, but if we could get into the open court and force the action, we did. When Charles arrived, we became more of a halfcourt team, with both Charles and Hakeem down in the box. We became a stronger rebounding team, but a slower team. We had to set it up more and more, and there is only one basketball. We were lacking efficiency. The other negative was, at that stage of his career, Charles was not the help defender he once was, and that caused some breakdowns.

A lot was made in the media of a supposed feud between Charles and me during our two years together in Houston. We had no problems. Charles has a strong personality and so do I, but we were both trying to win games. We would joke with everyone. We were always having fun. We had great conversations, especially the first year. The second year, it was becoming more difficult to run, we were losing more games and there was some friction among all of us. It was Hakeem's team, no mistake about it. He carried that team. But to his credit, Charles was more than willing to share the ball.

It's true that Charles and I always argued. We argued about everything. We would argue in good times and in bad times, but we could always go get something to eat and smoke a cigar together afterward. The only time I didn't want to be around Charles was when he went on that binge where he was knocking people out. I am the one who bailed him out of jail when he had that incident with the unruly fan at a restaurant in Orlando. It messed up my whole night. I didn't get any sleep. I had to stay up until 6 a.m. to bail him out. For a month after that, he would ask me, "Where are we going to eat?" And I would say, "Charles where are you going?" And he would tell me a restaurant, and I would go the opposite way.

But I can honestly say that I enjoyed being his teammate. We had fun hanging out. Charles came to Houston to win a championship, and when that doesn't happen, there is always going to be perceived friction. But did we ever stop talking? No. Charles would say stuff to the media, and I wound up defending myself. Once, in response to one of his wisecracks about me, I said, "If Charles would put as much effort into playing basketball as he does running his mouth, we would be a lot better off." But with Charles, he says what he feels, I say what I feel, and it's over. I love guys like that. I always knew where I stood with him.

**CHARLES BARKLEY:** We got along pretty good as teammates. It was just unfortunate that we were just too old to win a title together. He is a good guy and was a terrific player. We were both at the end of our career when we got to play together. We had a good time together. I enjoyed playing with him. But we weren't going to win a title. Hakeem, Clyde and I were all past our primes. We were just too old.

For a while, it didn't look that way. With the three of us jelling together quickly, we were the best team in basketball during the first half of the 1996-97 season. In our opener, a 96-85 win over Sacramento, I had 25 points, 10 rebounds, 10 steals and nine assists. By one assist, I missed joining Hakeem, David Robinson, Alvin Robertson and Nate Thurmond as the only players to get a quadruple-double in an NBA game. We finished November with a 15-1 record, the franchise's best first-month record and one of the best in NBA history. We lost at, of all places, Toronto, then reeled off six more wins to improve to 21-2. The experiment was working.

**RUDY TOMJANOVICH:** When we brought in Charles, we were right on target to win another title. Charles, Hakeem and Clyde got along about as good as you can considering they were three great players. There was a mutual respect for each other. My life could have been misery if I would have had guys who didn't respect each other.

Every one of those guys was used to getting the ball a lot. I would go through a series of plays for different guys. If somebody got it going, I just stuck with him. Then I would go to whoever was next. Then we would go to the third guy. If somebody got it going, he could have been getting a lot of calls for a long time. They did a tremendous job of dealing with that. Charles was great. He was as unselfish a player as I have ever had. From the power forward position, he sometimes had several assists before he took his first shot. He and Clyde were both great at throwing a pass that allowed the receiver to find the open man for a basket. In hockey, it would have been another assist.

**SAM CASSELL:** I didn't think that adding Charles to that mix would work. Clyde was a laid-back guy and Charles wanted the spotlight. We already had a good team. With the addition of a good, big power forward like Kevin Willis, we would have been in the Finals again in 1996. They wound up with three go-to guys, and it is hard to make that work.

It would have been interesting to see what we could have done, if only we had stayed healthy. But I played with a sore left knee most of the season, strained a hamstring compensating for it, and sprained an ankle. The hamstring and ankle caused me to miss 20 games over the second half of the season. Charles missed 29 games, too, with hip and ankle injuries. With Charles, Hakeem and I in the lineup, our record was unbelievable. But it just didn't happen enough times.

I didn't get to play in the All-Star Game because of the bad hamstring, but I wasn't about to miss the weekend. They brought 47 of the top 50 players of all-time to Cleveland to honor us. It was a tremendous thrill to be included. Gaynell and I were there, and I brought my autograph book. It was fun to get a chance to hang out with Julius Erving. He had been my boyhood hero, and I enjoyed being around him.

During a special ceremony at halftime of the All-Star Game, each of us wore a leather jacket representing our team. It was a tough decision, but I wore a Rockets jacket. I had won the championship with them, and I was playing for them at the time, and it was my hometown.

We finished the regular season 57-25, good for second in the Midwest behind Utah. It gave us the No. 3 seed in the West playoffs and set us up for a first-round match up with Minnesota. We felt good about ourselves, because we had everybody healthy and had added two good pieces to our bench at midseason, Eddie Johnson and Sedale Threatt.

The Timberwolves had plenty of good young talent led by Kevin Garnett, Stephon Marbury and Tom Gugliotta, but we swept them 3-0.

The next opponent was Seattle, which had given Chicago all it could handle in the Finals the previous season and was the team that had swept us in the second round. We knew it was going to be a war, but revenge was on our minds.

The first two games were at The Summit. We won the opener 112-102, but they got us 106-101 in Game 2. We headed back to Seattle tied one game a piece in the series. We took control by winning Games 3 and 4 in Key Arena, 97-93 and 110-106 in overtime. We were ahead 3-1 with a chance to wrap up the series at home in Game 5.

We couldn't do it. The Sonics won 100-94, then won Game 6 in Seattle 99-96 in a hotly contested battle that sent us back to Houston for Game 7.

That was a scary game. We led by 14 points early in the fourth quarter, then saw the Sonics cut it down to two with 21.7 seconds left. I made only two of four free throws in the closing seconds, but we played good enough defense to hold them off, 96-91. I had a big game with 24 points, eight rebounds and eight assists. And we were in the conference finals against Utah.

The Jazz, on the top of their game, won the first two games at home. We were upset with John Stockton, who had set screens that resulted in Charles drawing several fouls. Stock would flop and Charles was on the bench in foul trouble.

The Jazz got away with a lot of flops. Stockton knew all the tricks of the trade. He would reach around your body and pull you to get himself open, or hold you on a back screen. He and Jeff Hornacek were both clever that way.

We evened the series at 2-2 with a pair of victories in The Summit. Eddie Johnson was the hero of both games, scoring 31 points in 28 minutes off the bench during Game 3, then sinking a 27-foot 3-pointer at the buzzer in a 95-92 win in Game 4.

Karl Malone took control of Game 5, scoring 29 points and holding Charles to 10 as the Jazz won 96-91 in Salt Lake City.

It was back to Houston for Game 6, and it was a terrific battle to the wire. I hit five threes and scored 33 points, but Stockton came through in the clutch, knocking down a 25-foot 3-pointer at the buzzer for a 103-100 Jazz victory. It was a stunning way to end the season on just a great shot by Stockton. On the final play, a pick-and-roll with Malone, Karl held me in a bear hug. He had both my arms tied and I couldn't move. I guess the referee didn't see it.

I had pretty much decided the 1997-98 season was going to be my last when I signed my final contract. I never wavered. I felt healthy. I wanted to leave on a good note.

The Rockets had our starting five back — Hakeem, Charles, myself, Mario Elie and point guard Matt Maloney — along with

Kevin Willis, Eddie Johnson and Matt Bullard off the bench. We had some very productive veterans who could get it done when it counted. I liked our chances — again, if we could stay healthy.

On Nov. 24, in a game at The Forum against the Lakers, I became the 23rd player to score 20,000 points. I was almost embarrassed by the standing ovation I got from the fans. It caught me a little by surprise.

After losing five of our first eight games, we went on an eight-game win streak to improve to 13-5, but it was our high-water mark that year. Hakeem was out half of the season after knee surgery. I missed 12 games because of hamstring and shoulder problems, and Charles missed 14 games with back, toe and groin injuries.

In March, I announced my retirement and that I was going to accept the job as head coach at the University of Houston for the 1998-99 season.

But we still had more basketball to play. We finished the regular season 41-41, sneaking into the playoffs as the No. 8 seed. That got us a first-round date with Utah and our old friends, Stockton and Malone.

We scared the Jazz at least, winning two of the first three games to go ahead 2-1 in the best-of-five series. We had two tries to close it out but couldn't do it. Utah won Game 4, 93-71, at what was now being called the Compaq Center in Houston, and Charles suffered a bicep injury that took him out of Game 5.

**RUDY TOMJANOVICH:** We had the Jazz by the throat until Charles got injured. Antoine Carr bumped into him and ripped his bicep. We lost the series right there. There is nothing you can do about an injury like that.

The Jazz beat us 84-70 in the finale at Salt Lake City. I was terrible in that game, going 1 for 13 from the field and 4 for 10 from the line. My tank was empty. It was the same way with the rest of the guys. We just didn't have anything left.

I had averaged 18.4 points, five rebounds and five assists a game through the regular season. I was still an All-Star, but it was time. On May 29, less than a month before my 36th birthday, my NBA career was over.

It was a good career, a complete career. At the University of Houston, I made two Finals Fours and was an All-American. In the NBA, I averaged 20.4 points, 6.1 rebounds and 5.8 assists in 1,086 regular-season games, finishing with 22,195 points in 15 seasons. I averaged 20.4 points, 6.9 rebounds and 6.3 assists in 145 playoff games. I was one of three players to total 20,000 points, 6,000 rebounds and 6,000 assists, joining Oscar Robertson and John Havlicek. That is pretty good company. I was fourth on the all-time steals list.

I made the postseason every year, which was as important as anything. Not many players can say that. It meant you were always in the running for a title. I made the NBA Finals three times. I won a championship. I won an Olympic gold medal. I was named as one of the top 50 players in history. I had my number retired four times — by the Raiders (of Sterling High), by the Cougars, by the Rockets and by the Trail Blazers. I also had a gym named after me (Clyde Drexler Gymnasium at Sterling High) and a street named after me (Drexler Drive leading up to the Rose Garden in Portland). I wouldn't have thought all that was possible, all the while enjoying the company of great teammates, getting married, having four children and traveling the world.

The biggest thing, though, was I had achieved my dream of playing in the NBA. The biggest thrill throughout that journey was putting on my NBA jersey for the first time. Not many kids get to realize their dream.

And now it was on to a new career.

# CHAPTER 18

# COACH DREXLER

I hadn't thought a whole lot about being a coach during my playing days. The idea had crossed my mind, though, and I always considered myself a student of the game. The opportunity to match wits with an opposing coach had kind of intrigued me, and I enjoyed the teaching part of the game.

I wouldn't have coached at any other place except the University of Houston, though. I felt a tremendous amount of loyalty to that school. Houston had an impressive basketball tradition, but had gone through a few down years. I wanted to see what I could do to change that.

The good thing about coaching there was that I wouldn't have to move my family. I took a pretty good-sized pay cut — $150,000 base salary, with incentives that could double that figure — but that wasn't important. I wanted to give back to a university that had meant a lot to me and at the same time bring the Cougars back to respectability.

Athletic director Chet Gladchuk and the sports information director, Rick Poulter, were great people to work with. They made my transition easy. Chet was instrumental in helping me make my decision to take the job. He was so easy to talk to and work with. He wouldn't just pay you lip service; he would actually get things done. He did everything he said he was going to do and more. My two years with Chet were outstanding, and he had a great staff. Everybody seemed pretty excited to have me there, too.

**RICK POULTER:** The day Clyde was hired, they carried the press conference live on every five o'clock TV broadcast in the city. It was also carried as part of ESPN's *SportsCenter* show. Our basketball program went from almost no national credibility to instant national attention right off the bat. Clyde still had to finish out the season with the Rockets, but he had hired a couple of assistants — George Walker, who had been on the coaching staff at UH during Clyde's playing days, and Reid Gettys, a college teammate. They kind of ran the program until Clyde's NBA season was complete.

His first week on the job, he came in and did a summer camp. We had every major publication in the country — *Sports Illustrated*, the works — there doing stuff with him. The theme for all the stories was along these lines: Why would an NBA All-Star want to do something like this?

The Cougars had losing seasons in four of the five previous years, going 11-16 in 1996-97 and 9-20 in 1997-98. I knew it was going to take a while, but I needed to establish a winning mentality. And I had to rekindle enthusiasm in the community for the program.

**RICK POULTER:** We went from averaging 2,484 fans a game at Hofheinz Pavilion the previous year to selling out the building over the summer. In Clyde's first season, we sold out the entire season — 8,479 per game. We took out some seats at the top of the arena, put in 24 luxury boxes and sold those for three-year commitments at $45,000 apiece. We increased our courtside seating from 64 to 240 and sold them out at $1,000 for the season.

For our opener against Texas at Hofheinz, which was also Rick Barnes's first game coaching the Longhorns, we were live nationally on ESPN, and every major publication covered the game, including *Sports Illustrated*, *Newsweek* and *ESPN The Magazine*.

The Texas game was a lot of fun. The atmosphere was electric. San Diego Padres owner John Moores was courtside. So was pro golfer Steve Elkington. Hakeem, Kenny Smith, Mario Elie and Moses Malone were there. We jumped out ahead, held off a Texas comeback and won 71-69. I used the word euphoria that night, and I felt it. I wish it could always have been that way.

**RICK POULTER:** A sports information director from another school told me when Clyde would go out recruiting, he would walk into a high school gym before a game and get a standing ovation. We had not signed a greater Houston area Player of the Year for many years, and we got one both of his years — George Williams out of Elkins High, and Alton Ford out of Milby High. Rashard Lewis, who had a relationship with our previous coach, Alvin Brooks, said we were the only school he really considered, and I would guess Clyde was at least a part of that. Clyde signed Gee Gervin, George's son, too. You go from serenity to almost non-stop acclaim. The public relations value that he brought to our program was astronomical from the beginning.

Hundreds of people would hang around after every game, trying to get Clyde's autograph. A lot of people said he never came into his office, but when he would come to the office, there would be 10 or 15 people waiting for him, wanting an audience for whatever reason. We got caught in a snowstorm in Chicago when we went to play DePaul and got stuck there for three days. I'll never forget watching Clyde stand outside as the snow came down — there was a line of people waiting for him to sign an autograph. It was unbelievable. At a tournament in Alaska, we came out of the locker room and there were 200 people waiting for him to sign. To his credit, he signed for 90 percent of them.

One thing I enjoyed about coaching — on every road trip I tried to make sure we had a group outing. In Memphis, I took the team to the Martin Luther King museum. When we went to Chicago, we ate dinner at Michael Jordan's restaurant. Michael was not there, but it was a big thrill for the players to see all the memorabilia. It was a chance to enlighten the kids, soak up some culture or just foster some camaraderie. I didn't want them to sit in their hotel rooms and play video games all day. That was part of my teaching to the younger generation. I enjoyed it, and I hope the players got something out of it.

**RICK POULTER:** It was hard for Clyde to get anything done because he got so much attention. That is what became part of the grind. Clyde didn't have normal business hours, and I never knew when exactly when he would show up. With requests for him, you had to have a window of time. When I had interview requests, I would tell the reporter, "Give me times you can do it. Can you be free from noon to two?" And Clyde would be good about it once he arrived. I always scheduled things after practice. He never turned an interview down that way. You kind of allowed yourself some flexibility, just like you would any celebrity. If I told him we had to do something, for the most part he would say yes.

He would come in after five o'clock a couple of nights a week and handle all the paperwork with his secretary. He would sign off for travel reports and funds for the basketball budget, that sort of thing. The coaches would meet as a staff after practice, and he would show up about an hour before practice. The normal stuff a coach would do in the office in the mornings, he'd handle at home.

There was a lot to do as a college coach. You have to do the scheduling, take care of the travel for everybody in your party, make sure the trainer has everything he needs, take care of the academic and tutoring situations, and a hundred other things. A lot of that stuff was not in place when I took over the job, so I set it up so we could get it done. I knew what the job description was. I was willing to work hard. I wanted to bring the University of Houston program back to prominence again.

**RICK POULTER:** Everybody's expectations were sky-high after the Texas victory. We went from a team that couldn't score to a team that could score in the 70s and 80s. We had a 6'8" shot blocker, William Stringfellow, and 6'9" forward Kenny Younger. Gee Gervin led Conference USA in scoring and assists. They were a pretty good trio.

We were competitive, but our talent base was pretty shallow. We finished the 1998-99 season 10-17 overall and 5-11 in conference play, which was good for sixth place. With Gervin hurt, we lost to UNC-Charlotte 75-51 in our conference tournament opener. And the season was over.

**BOB COOK:** At the end of the first year, Clyde told me he was not having much fun. "Step down," I said. "Why be there for five years and be miserable?"

"Guys I recruited are counting on me," he told me. That is why he stayed through the next year.

That was part of it. I wanted to show some loyalty to those kids I recruited. I wanted to get them started on their college careers, to spend some time with them and give them a chance to succeed. I wanted to be there for them. The problem was, I went right from my playing career into the job. I was in my UH office five days after my last game as a player. I probably needed to take a couple years off. It would be a perfect job for me after I turn 50, when my life is more settled and my kids are older and I would be better-equipped to put eight or nine-plus hours a day into the work. To say I was burned out is an understatement.

**RICK POULTER:** Clyde wanted to play the best opponents possible. His first year, we played at North Carolina State, California and New Mexico, and against Louisiana State and Texas at home. He signed two-year deals with

Connecticut and Georgetown, a four-year deal with LSU. He would play anybody.

Everything unraveled the second year. Stringfellow was declared ineligible. Younger struggled. We went from a two-dimensional offense to Gervin outside. Gee was the only thing that kept us going. George Williams made the All-Freshman team and had a good year, but Clyde had really beefed up our schedule. We beat Marquette in the first round of the conference tournament, but size killed us all year long. The team did not have an inside presence. We finished 9-22 overall and 2-14 in conference play.

We felt like we were a year away. Clyde's recruiting was pointed toward that third year. Had he stayed for a third year, he would have had a great shot at getting Houston prep stars T.J. Ford, Daniel Ewing and Emeka Okafor. With 6'8" George Williams as a sophomore, 6'9" Alton Ford as a freshman and Okafor coming in, we were getting there. Clyde told me by George's junior year, we would hit the national map.

I fully believe that. Ford went to Texas, Ewing to North Carolina and Okafor to Connecticut and all had great careers. We had a great chance at recruiting all those guys; it was a matter of finishing the job. If I had stayed, I think we would have gotten them. We would have gotten some prep All-Americans and built a national program.

But I was proud of what we accomplished. We raised a lot of money that the university did not previously have. We sold out Hofheinz for the season for the first time ever. We added 25 luxury boxes at $45,000 apiece and sold out. We had corporate sponsorship for the first time. We endowed scholarships that had never been endowed. We had alumni donating money to the university in record numbers. School enrollment was up. We got good press on a national scale, something that hadn't happened since just before Guy Lewis retired.

We restored interest in the program, which is the most significant contribution I have made in my retirement. And I enjoyed the craft of coaching. It was easy. I have always known a lot about the Xs and Os of the game. I had thoughts throughout my playing career about how I would have done things. To be able to put in my own offense and defense was fun. Of course, I didn't quite have the talent to do exactly what I wanted, but I lived with that.

I had taken over a last-place team for whom the two best players were graduating seniors. I had a depleted last-place team. I took the job in March, when the recruiting season was over. Rashard Lewis had signed with the previous regime, but he decided to go pro, so we didn't get him, either. We had only one recruited athlete and no chance to recruit more. Others had to understand the enormity of the challenge I was faced with.

The program was dead, and we had to revive it. The first year, we got six or seven walk-ons to fill out the squad. What I focused on was enhancing the talents of each individual. We worked hard on skill development every day in practice, and eventually our players got better and we were able to compete with the good teams and beat some of them. That was a tremendous accomplishment. Our last victory the second year was over Marquette in the conference tournament. Two years later, Marquette was in the Final Four.

My intention when I took the job was to get the turnaround started. Chet understood that. I did what I was supposed to do. Then I took some time off for my family.

**RICK POULTER:** Clyde's resignation was huge. It seemed like it came overnight. He came to the gym and was watching the guys work out in a pickup game and was gone the next day, literally. We went from national attention to nobody talking to us at all. We went from guys lining up to come here to nobody wanting to come here. It was tough.

But having Clyde as a coach was fun for me, no question. Those were two of the most fun years of my life. Getting national attention, talking to people we had not talked to before, having all those national people calling you — that was great. Clyde was fun-loving, nice and cordial. When I was around him, he treated me in a professional way. I enjoyed working with him.

Rick took his job seriously and was a great guy. He made my coaching experience at UH much better. So did the other employees I worked with. I had a good staff and everybody worked extremely hard.

But I was burned out. I needed to hit the beach. I needed to spend more time with my wife and kids. I left for very simple reasons. I haven't regretted resigning. I never regretted taking the job, either. I enjoyed what we were able to give back to the university.

# CHAPTER 19

# CRASHING THE HALL OF FAME

**A**fter I left the University of Houston. I took a little time off in order to spend more time with my family, play some golf, travel and just enjoy life. I focused on some on my non-basketball business interests, and I was in touch with Kiki Vandeweghe, my old friend and teammate who had taken over as general manager of the Denver Nuggets.

Kiki and I have always been close, and we have always thought of basketball in pretty much the same terms. And when he asked me to join him as special assistant to the general manager for the 2000-01 season, it sounded like a good opportunity.

**KIKI VANDEWEGHE:** Clyde has great basketball knowledge. We were putting together a team in Denver in a totally different way than was done before. It was really a mess. Clyde was a guy I could trust implicitly. Clyde served in the position for a year, and he was great. A lot of the things he added were invaluable. Had he wanted to, he could have been an NBA general manager or a coach. But after all he has done, he deserved his time off.

I would spend a few days a month in Denver, but I was basically in an advisory capacity to Kiki and was able to spend the majority of my time in Houston. Midway through the sason, the Nuggets fired Dan Issel and hired Mike Evans as interim head coach, and I served as an assistant coach on the bench under him the rest of the season. I enjoyed the teaching part of it, and working with the players, but not the travel. An NBA team is on the road so much, and I had done that for 15 years. It was not for me at that point in my life.

I decided not to come back for the 2002-03 season. I told Kiki I would continue to consult if he needed me — come into Denver for a few days and brainstorm. Kiki called a few times and I helped out some, but was able to spend more time at home with my family.

Over the last couple of years, I have allowed myself the freedom of living without a job. It is great to wake up in the morning and say, "Let's see, what would I like to do today?" For so many years, my life was on a preset schedule for eight, nine months of the year. I don't want a job where I have to be there day to day. I still do a little consulting work for the Nuggets, but other than that, I am retired. It is hard to play golf in Denver in the winter.

And golf is one of my passions. In Houston, I am a member of the exclusive Lochinvar Country Club — which counts President Bush as one of its 200 members — and I try to play golf four or five times a week when I am in town. I also am a member at Waverley Country Club in Portland, where we still maintain a home and spend a good part of our summers. I am about a four handicap now.

**BOB COOK:** It isn't like the old days, when Clyde didn't know where the ball was going. He is a good golfer now, and when he is in Portland we try to get out. We play a little buck-a-hole game, and it is as competitive as when he was trying to win an NBA championship. There is some action on every shot.

**CARROLL DAWSON:** I knew Clyde had strong hands the first time I watched him play golf. He hit the ball like Tiger Woods.

**LES ALEXANDER:** Clyde hits the ball farther than anybody I have ever seen. It is great to have him as a partner in a scramble. To have a 170-yard second shot on a 500-yard par-five is something I am not used to.

**JULIUS ERVING:** Clyde and I both really like golf. It is a way of getting the competitive juices flowing in a friendlier environment than trying to go out and beat someone on a basketball court. Clyde's game is a little stronger than mine, though I have had a breakthrough recently. There is a solid four-stroke difference in our game, though some days I can get the best of a better player. As Clyde gets older, his handicap is going to come up and mine is going to come down.

I am also a member at The Houstonian, a health and fitness club where I try to play tennis twice a week and lift weights two times a week. And I run in a park in the area by my home at least a couple of times I week, so I stay pretty fit. I am at 232 pounds, about two pounds over my playing weight.

On December 30, 2003, Gaynell and I celebrated our 15th anniversary. We live in Houston with our three children — 14-year-old Austin, 13-year-old Elise, and 11-year-old Adam. My other daughter, Erica, 17, lives in Houston and is off to college this fall.

**GAYNELL DREXLER:** After our marriage, the most profound adjustment for me was leaving a law career and friends behind in New York and moving to Oregon, basically starting from scratch and shadowing my husband's career. It was an entirely different sort of life. Initially, the experience was euphoric. Clyde had a different sort of career than me, and there was a great deal of limelight and excitement that went along with that. But so much of me was lost in the process. I was fortunate to have good friends and family to keep my life in perspective.

After we decided to start our family and I got into the swing of being a full-time mom, I found that I absolutely loved it. Even though it is challenging, I would say it has truly completed my life. Some people feel parenting is grueling. I find it fulfilling. It is the most rewarding thing that I have ever done. We have neat kids. I am particularly close to my children. They have given me great joy.

I have worked for the past two years with the state of Texas and Harris County. I am currently working for Harris County writing policy for one of the county agencies. I am hoping I can have a life beyond carpooling eventually, and this is a step in the right direction. Some days I feel like I have bitten off more than I can handle. I am the primary caretaker of the children, but I feel it is important that I give this to myself. In 10 years, I want to have a purposeful career, if not a lucrative one. But my children will always take precedent.

People tend to lump wives of well-paid athletes into one category — women who want to be taken care of. That was the last thing I was looking for when I met Clyde. I grew up with a solid work ethic. I've worked since I was 13. I had summer jobs, and I worked two jobs to put myself through law school. I've always had a very strong desire to be independent, and it didn't quite turn out that way for me. My marriage afforded me the luxury to stay home with my children, which I took advantage of. But at the end of the day, I don't feel good having someone else take care of me. It doesn't do much for a person's self-esteem. You compromise a lot of yourself, whether you realize it or not, when someone is taking care of you. It is my single most significant regret to have shelved a potentially lucrative career.

Gaynell was a superstar in her own profession. She took a lot of pride in that. Her whole family is well educated. When she married me and took time off to have kids, in her mind she felt like she wasn't fulfilling her duties. She knows she is welcome to work at any time, but as far as making our family go, she is the best mom in the world. She is totally devoted to the kids. She doesn't pass on her motherly duties to anyone else. She does everything herself every day, whether it is fixing meals for the kids, setting up dental or doctor appointments, helping the kids with school assignments or projects, getting them to their activities and so on. If a teacher doesn't show up at school, she has even volunteered at times to teach a class. She has been an awesome caretaker of our kids.

I have a ton of respect for Gaynell. She is very intelligent. Before we met, she had a career and was making six figures annually. If she had continued in the law field, she would be making a whole lot more by now. A certain part of her self-esteem is tied to her ability to work and generate a living for herself. She is very independent, and it says a lot about her. She has been a great wife, mother, and daughter. She has always been there to support me. She is caring, nurturing. When I am on the road, I never worry that she won't be able to handle things at home. Let that be a lesson learned for the young players who are choosing significant others in their lives — make sure to choose someone who is responsible and can get things done in their absence. A player is on the road so often, their significant other will have to take in quite a lot without them.

**GAYNELL DREXLER:** Clyde hasn't changed a whole lot since I first met him. He is very much a free spirit. He likes to enjoy life. We have matured in a very different fashion, though we are on the same page most of the time.

I wasn't prepared for the type of attention Clyde receives. It was not in my circle of experience. When I practiced law, my circle of familiarity was academics — people who were highly successful, but not celebrities. There isn't any resentment on my part that Clyde is a celebrity, but I am often amazed that people don't see beyond the surface when they look at celebrities. They are worshipped like gods, but celebrities are actually very human. That part has startled me. There is a lot of madness that goes along with being married to a celebrity.

When he was playing, there was quite a bit of inappropriate attention from women. For instance, a woman would come up to Clyde and want him to autograph her breast. If he complied, when we got home, naturally we were going to have a row. It felt as if he had placed his celebrity status above the marriage. At least in my realm of thought and ethics, that is something that shouldn't happen. It is up to that particular celebrity to decide how far he will or will not go. I have been for the most part silent, but sometimes I have been moved to go home and cry.

I truly believe it is Clyde's duty to make the appropriate stand in my honor when inappropriate things occur, but it has always been hard for Clyde to say no. He thought it would be easier for me to digest than for him to offend somebody who is buying season tickets to watch him play. That is the price you pay when you marry someone famous. That has been part and parcel of my marriage.

The kids have paid the price, too. For example, Clyde would show up for a soccer game for one of the children, and he would be beseiged by autograph seekers and entirely miss the game, or miss that winning goal that one of our children made. This is the only life we know. We are all very proud of Clyde, but our lives have been far from normal.

People are always so nice when they come up to you. I never have been able to turn people down if they ask for an autograph, regardless of the situation. If I am out in the public and someone comes over and wants me to sign an autograph and hear one of their stories, I feel like it is my obligation to listen. They have good intentions, they respect what my teammates or I have done, and they just want to share it with me. I have to be a real prick not to cooperate with that. The guys who treat fans rudely don't have the right perspective. I have always believed it is an honor when people approach me for an autograph or just to tell me how much they respect me. I love hearing those stories, because I lived them. When other people appreciate it too, that is a nice thing.

And for the record: I never signed any breasts.

Gaynell and I have shared a lot, including the lives of our children. I have already told you about my oldest daughter, Erika, who is now in college. I would like to tell you a little about my other three kids.

Austin, 14, is the epitome of a good kid. I love the way he cares about other people, assumes his responsibilities and works hard at them. Begrudgingly, he is an athlete, but he prefers more of the extreme sports like skateboarding, snowboarding and surfing. He loves video games, enjoys writing and creating video game characters and would eventually like to do that for a living.

Elise, 13, is extremely intelligent, smart, hard-working, driven, tough-minded and a go-getter. She plays volleyball and softball and is a good little basketball player. She is very active in school, runs with a pack of girls and always has a full itinerary on weekends for her mom, and sometimes her dad.

Adam, 11, is the quintessential never-had-a-bad-day type of kid. He is full of energy and loves to play anything and everything. He is probably my most competitive child and is a very good athlete for his age. Doctors say he could grow to be 6'8" or 6'9", so college coaches, watch out. He reminds me a little of myself at that age. He will hop on his bicycle and jump a few ramps and curbs on his way to his buddy's house. He is a very active kid.

We have enjoyed traveling, both by ourselves and with the kids. One of our favorite destinations is Paris — the Louvre.

Gaynell is very interested in the arts. When we lived at River Oaks, we put on a benefit at our home that raised a record $55,000 for Project Row House, a Third Ward art group. About 225 guests attended an evening of wining, dining and music. Gaynell received plenty of attention for her interior design of our home.

In the last year, since leaving my coaching and playing career behind, I have been able to be home more often and do things with my children. For instance, I brought my boys with me for a weekend trip to Portland. They went snowboarding on Mount Hood and chukar hunting in Wasco County with a party that included Bob Cook. The boys found out that chukar hunting is hard work. Walking up and down through those canyons is pretty physical. But we had a great time.

I have devoted much of my energy toward renovation of our restaurant, Drexler's World-Famous Barbecue, which is truly a family operation and has been since 1967 when my uncle opened it for business. It is run by my mom, brother James, sisters Debra, Denise, Virginia, and Lynn, and my nephew, Eric.

The original Drexler's Barbecue was a small mom-and-pop operation that served great food and catered to regulars in downtown Houston. Now we have moved kitty-corner from its old spot to a new building on Pierce Street just off highways 59, 45 and 288.

The new place is an impressive state-of-the-art eatery that opened in June 2003 after two years of construction. It was built by Drexler Custom Homes, which is run by Denise and Virginia. It covers 16,000 square feet — the old place was about 1,000 square feet, so you can imagine the difference — and can serve several hundred patrons. The 22 Bar is one of the best in the city and the Drexler Room and Phi Slama Jama Room play host to private dining, group meetings and banquets. There is a stage where bands play on the weekends, and an adjustable hoop for kids or would-be superstars to try their hand at a shot or two.

Drexler's Barbecue is a veritable sports museum, with artifacts and memorabilia of both Houston and national sports figures decorating the facility. There are a ton of things from my playing days displayed. My family deserves all the credit. I don't do anything except assist in decision making and visit there often to eat my favorite item, the barbecue beef sandwich, which is the best in the world. The place is like a big party room for me, with so many good memories covering the walls. It is a labor of love for my family, and business has been good. In January 2004, I opened a second Drexler's Barbecue, along with two partners, at Bush International Airport in Houston. I also have a percentage of ownership in retail concessions at several shops at the airport.

One of my major endeavors now is helping out with charities and benefits. I have worked with the National Cancer Institute and National Multiple Sclerosis Society, among others. In Houston, I played in a benefit that raised $500,000 for the Andre Agassi Charitable Foundation, which provides recreational and educational opportunities for at-risk youths. I teamed with Andy Roddick in a doubles match with Andre Agassi and Dr. Phil. I have always liked Andre — a very normal guy who happens to be great at his craft. (We lost. Hey, Dr. Phil can play.)

I love attending the major sporting events — Super Bowls, Final Fours, NBA Finals, championship fights. I am a true sports fan. That will never change. I read the sports section in the newspaper every day. Some people follow sports casually. I have never been just a casual fan. But don't get the wrong idea. I don't bet on anything. I am not a betting man. I don't like to lose, so I don't gamble.

In March of 2004, I learned that I had been selected for induction into the Naismith Basketball Hall of Fame. It's a compliment just to make the ballot. To be voted in on the first ballot is like the ultimate compliment to a player's career. It doesn't get any better than that. I felt great that people in the know had acknowledged my accomplishments.

The people at the Naismith Hall of Fame are well organized and on top of things. I flew to Springfield, Massachussetts, in May of 2004 to attend a sponsors dinner with a group of legends that included Julius Erving, Bill Walton, K.C. Jones, Jo Jo White and Robert Parish. We had a wonderful time. There were an awful lot of good stories told.

Making the Hall of Fame is right up there with anything I've ever accomplished. As a team accomplishment, winning the NBA title was the ultimate. As an individual, the Hall of Fame is the ultimate.

The honor is a reflection of the coaches I have played for and the players I have played with along the way. Coaches such as Guy Lewis, Jack Ramsay, Rick Adelman and Rudy Tomjanovich deserve thanks. Teammates such as Hakeem Olajuwon, Terry Porter, Buck Williams, Jerome Kersey, Cliff Robinson, Steve Johnson, Kenny Carr, Darnell Valentine, Kevin Duckworth, Kiki Vandeweghe, Mychal Thompson, Kenny Smith, Robert Horry, Mario Elie, and Sam Cassell deserve praise. I have been lucky to have great coaches and great teammates. It has been an unbelievable run, and I thank every one of them.

Hall of Fame rules stipulate that inductees enter the shrine representing themselves and are not affiliated with the team or teams they played for. The plaques at the Hall do not show the player in any specific uniform. That prevented me from making a tough decision. When I was named as one of the top 50 players ever in 1997, I wore a Rockets jacket to the ceremony. If I had to make a choice for the Hall of Fame, though, I would have gone in as a Portland Trail Blazer. I was with Portland for 11 1/2 seasons. I was a Rocket for only three and a half seasons. Portland was the team that drafted me. To put their faith and their future in my hands says a lot. I respect that.

But no matter what I accomplish, I always go back to my roots. That means family. I grew up with the best one I could have had. All of us remain close. We all still live in the Houston area.

**DENISE PINK:** Everyone outside the family knows him as Clyde the Glide, No. 22 — a great basketball star. We know him as simply Clyde. Nothing has changed. He is still the nice, happy, fun type of guy we knew growing up. He has never gotten a big head. He is still a giving person to everybody — strangers, friends, and family. I have never really come to grips with the fact that I am Clyde the Glide's sister. At first, it was like, no big deal, so what? I guess I am kind of proud of it now. Yeah, that is my brother.

**VIRGINIA SCOTT-WESTBROOKS:** I am not just saying it because he is my brother, but he is one of the nicest guys you could ever know in your life. I have seen him from the inside, dealing with good people and bad people and bad situations, and there are not many people like him. He is a genuinely good person. There is never an ulterior motive. He gets taken advantage of a lot of times because of that, but he never complains. He comes at you with sincerity.

**DEBRA MATHEWS:** Clyde has made millions, but he hasn't changed one bit. Money changes a lot of people. They think they are better than others. He wasn't like that in the beginning, and he is not like that now. I look at him now, at what he has done with his life, and it is amazing. I just want to cry.

# CHAPTER 20

# REFLECTIONS ON A BLESSED LIFE

**S**o many people have touched my life, all the way back to my childhood in Houston, that I could never mention them all. But I want to talk about a few.

Julius Erving was the basketball player I most admired growing up. When I first met him, I was awestruck. He spoke at our annual Blazer Boosters banquet in 1992, and I got to introduce him. I don't know if our management knew how I felt about him when they chose him as our speaker, but they certainly did after I gave my introduction. The amazing thing is, since that time, Julius has become one of my best friends. There is so much depth to him. He is very intelligent and one of the best human beings you will ever meet. He has become like a big brother to me.

**JULIUS ERVING:** I remember that banquet, and the nice things Clyde said about me, like it was yesterday. It was very special. We have been able to hang out a lot over the last couple of years, and our friendship has grown. We talked about how he felt about me as a kid, and it very much parallels how I felt about Bill Russell when I was young. When I am around Clyde, I know what he is feeling and what he is experiencing, because I experience that when I am around Bill Russell.

Clyde is a quality individual, a very intelligent and caring person. We definitely share a lot of qualities, and we share the experiences we have gone through. He is still going through that transition, the period before you go into the Hall of Fame. Things change a little after you get recognized as a Hall of Famer. Your legacy becomes totally assured at that time, so there is a passing that occurs that allows you to truly be recognized as a legend of the sport. Not that it is necessarily going to make a difference on an everyday basis, but it is a recognition that is significant, and you have to discover how that is going to play out and what role it will have in your life. Some people want to rest on it, and others want to take it and run with it. I have chosen to run with it over the years. It has been 17 years since I retired, but in terms of recognition of my name or face, there seems to be a lasting respect. My career has had a lasting effect on a lot of people. With a lot of my peers, it hasn't been the same.

Clyde has the potential to have his name and legacy live on for a long time, or it might be relegated to the markets in which he played. But having been in places such as New York and China and Mexico with him, I think the former is going to happen. People are going to remember Clyde the Glide, and remember him as second only to Michael Jordan during the era they played. I can relate, because I was probably second to Kareem. And I have to say, people probably like me better than Kareem today.

I knew Clyde was an automatic for the Hall of Fame because of his consistency, the level of success his teams enjoyed and what he brought to the game every night. Clyde represented all that was good about the era and what being a pro athlete is all about. He makes the Hall of Fame better by being there. It is not a gift. He earned it. He needed to go through the front door on the first ballot.

I put Clyde in a very exclusive group of players who have shown the most creativity throughout their careers, alongside myself, Connie Hawkins, Elgin Baylor, Michael Jordan and George Gervin — and Vince Carter is knocking at the door. When I played, I always had the attitude that the game was not life and death. There is nothing wrong with daring to be great. Like me, Clyde's game was airborne, and he was willing to try things, to make decisions in the air, not knowing what he was going to do until he was up there. Yeah, it is important to stick with certain fundamentals, but fans appreciate innovation. This guy had the ability to go beyond the fundamentals, to use his talent and imagination to make things happen.

How do you find the daylight and space to project yourself differently than someone who is not as creative as you? A player who is not creative moves in columns — forward, left and right. The innovative player utilizes all the angles. It is impossible to stay in front of a guy like that. You are blessed if you have the ball-handling ability and the size to get to anywhere you want to go on the court. Only a few who have played the game can do that. Clyde was one. You don't have a nickname like "The Glide" otherwise. He would bring a big game to the court every night. That is why he became a champion.

Clyde and I went to China in August 2003 as goodwill ambassadors on behalf of the NBA. Clyde had a contact who asked him to go, and he extended an invitation to me. We helped the Chinese government eradicate a lot of the fear about the SARS epidemic, enhanced their desire to let the world know they are serious about the 2008 Olympic Games and the sport of basketball, and just had fun. I had too much fun. We were treated royally.

When I have introduced Clyde to people, they always come away very impressed with his cool — because he is cool — and the sincerity within him. He is pretty much a straight shooter. He is not afraid to let his hair down, but I have never seen him get crazy or out of control. He conserves his energy for the things he is really interested in. There is room on the planet for more guys like that.

I have listened to classical music for a long time. It helps me relax and think. I remember teammates getting into my car and checking out my stereo, and when they saw I had a classical tape, they would crack up laughing. They thought I was playing with them, but that's my music. It is music you can drive and think with. Since we have been together, Gaynell and I have enjoyed going to the symphony. When we were in Portland, the Oregon Symphony was lucky enough to have one of the top conductors in the world, James DePreist.

**JAMES DePREIST:** I started as conductor of the Oregon Symphony in 1980, but it was 1983 or 1984 when we really got our feet wet living there for any period of time. That was when Clyde was drafted and came to town, and I was aware of him just as anybody is aware of the biggest star of the town. George Rickles, who worked for the Blazers, was on our board of directors, and one day he said, "Come to a Blazers game." I did, and like everyone else, I was impressed with the grace and the athletic excellence of Clyde. Then every time I saw any public utterance of his, it was classy. He seemed like a person of great character.

One night in about 1986, Clyde came to a concert. I didn't know he was there until he came backstage afterward. Somebody had gotten him a ticket and brought him backstage. Even all of these musicians were caught up in the moment. You would have thought the president of the United States was on hand. Subsequently, we had a soloist, Kathleen Battle, an opera diva, and she and Clyde's wife were friends. Clyde and Gaynell came to the concert and the five of us had supper afterward.

To have someone with the kind of talent James possessed in the city of Portland was a treat for all of us who loved symphony. James and Ginette, his wife, are two of the nicest people.

**JAMES DePREIST:** As time went on, I got to know Clyde a little better, and we just enjoyed each other's company. After he was traded to Houston in 1995, I spent some time conducting the Houston Symphony. I called him during the playoffs that year, not knowing he was on the road. I left a message, and he called me back two hours before the game. I couldn't believe that. He left a message saying he was sorry he wasn't there, but we should go to his mother's barbecue place, which we didn't get a chance to do.

There is something so endearing about Clyde. On my 12th anniversary with the Oregon Symphony in 1992, they had a video tribute and Clyde was in the film they showed. What they showed just before Clyde spoke was a clip of him stealing the ball at one end of the court and moving through traffic all the way down the court and then dunking the ball, all set to a section of the 1812 Overture, prerecorded by the symphony. That was perfect. It was one of the greatest pieces of sports film set to music I have seen. Everybody at the Hilton ballroom loved it, the climax of the piece coming with Clyde's resounding dunk.

That piece was beautifully done, as was everything touched by James DePriest and the Oregon Symphony. I was honored to be a part of it. Whenever I attended any of their programs with DePriest conducting, I always knew I was witnessing perfection and would be greatly entertained.

**JAMES DePREIST:** Before my farewell dinner in 2003, Clyde was living in Houston. And the question was, who did I want at my table, aside from big donors of the orchestra who are friends? I said, "There is Clyde Drexler, and then there's everybody else. If you can get Clyde, I will be happy and you don't need anybody else." Clyde was available and came and spoke and we had a wonderful time. I am deeply indebted to him for that. He talks about me being his hero, but everything he has done, the way he conducts himself on and off the court, the type of human being he is, has always been an inspiration to me.

I have always liked basketball, but I must admit, my interest in the sport was piqued only after I had seen him play. Sometimes with people who are as good as Clyde is in every way, when you get to meet them, there is something about them that disappoints you. There has been nothing like that with Clyde. You can't say that about a lot of people. He is genuine and tremendously generous.

Not everyone was as fun to be around as James DePreist. My final half-season in Portland, Bob Whitsitt took over as president and general manager. As I said earlier in the book, I appreciate the fact that he saw to it that I was traded to Houston. But as I have watched what he did to the Trail Blazers franchise over the years, I have looked at him with disdain.

You have to understand, the Blazers and their fans had a unique relationship. I'm not sure there has ever been a love affair between an NBA team and its fan base like we had. Buck Williams, Terry Porter, Jerome Kersey, Kevin Duckworth ... they were beloved members of the community. We sold out Memorial Coliseum for something like 11 straight years. We had good players and good citizens, and I am very thankful to have spent so many seasons playing in that type of environment.

After Whitsitt arrived, the Blazers' decision makers changed their tactics. They brought in some players of questionable character. Soon they were known nationwide as the "Jail Blazers." It was embarrassing — not only for the fans, but for us former players who had cherished the relationship we had with our followers.

Whitsitt resigned after the 2002-03 season, to the relief of most of the fans. I don't believe in kicking people after they have been fired, but I do believe Whitsitt alienated the fans of Portland. He did not do what was in the best interest of that community. I don't know how much Paul Allen had to do with that, but whatever the case was, it was not a good fit. They didn't cater to the Portland community. They didn't cater to the sponsors. I don't think they thought about the Portland fan base and how strong it truly was, and they didn't involve the fans in the process. That was their downfall.

The Whitsitt regime was a comedy of errors. It gave off a condescending attitude, and people picked up on it. Over a period of time, the fans lost interest. When I was there, Portland was an exemplary franchise. It was a rare case if a player made a mistake. For a while during the Whitsitt era, the Blazers probably had more drug arrests than some small cities. Think about that. The players have not been good role models for the kids in that city.

For some reason, Whitsitt tried to distance himself from the Portland teams and players of the early '90s. At one point, he made a comparison to me and Isaiah Rider. I didn't appreciate that. And I started understanding what Whitsitt was about.

After Mike Dunleavy was fired, I was interested in coaching the Blazers. As had been the case with the University of Houston, it was one of the few coaching jobs I would be interested in. I left a message for Bob, and he never called me back. I was amazed by that.

I had to set Bob straight a couple of times. One thing about me — if I say something, it is with conviction. I don't ever look to talk bad about anybody. If I do, it has probably been festering for a long time.

I have to be truthful, folks — I wouldn't trust Bob Whitsitt as far as I could throw him, and I know I can't throw him too far. It is a crime what has happened to the franchise. I am encouraged with the steps Steve Patterson and John Nash have taken to get things back in the right direction. I am a Blazer at heart, and I want those fans to have something good to cheer for.

But to get back to my time as a player, I'd like to address a few things that people said about me. Most people thought I was a pretty good passer in my day. But apparently, my methods were unorthodox — something about dribbling with my head down?

**MYCHAL THOMPSON:** Clyde was a very underrated passer. I don't know how he saw his teammates with that turtle vision of his, but he had the best peripheral vision. I said, "Clyde, how could you see anybody when you are looking at the floor or the ball?" I guess he had his head down but his eyeballs up.

**CALDWELL JONES:** I used to call him Mr. Entertainment. Sometimes he would try to do a little too much and get out of rhythm. I would always say, "Well, well, well, Mr. Entertainment." Clyde would be laughing at himself. He would say, "Why did I do that?" He would dribble the ball straight upcourt, high bounces, his head down, and he would travel or lose the ball. One time he said, "Couldn't stop." And I said, "No brakes, huh? No brakes."

**JACK RAMSAY:** Clyde had very good floor vision. While it appeared he was looking only at the ball, he had such great peripheral vision that he could find the open guys.

**WAYNE COOPER:** Clyde could do everything wrong, but he always got the right results. He would dribble down the court with his head down, but he would always find the open guy.

**TERRY PORTER:** You didn't think he would see you, because he would be dribbling with his head down, but if you missed one of his passes, you would hear about it. He would say, "Come on, Judge, I am always looking. Keep your eyes open."

**GEOFF PETRIE:** Clyde never really got enough credit for his passing skills. He was an absolutely fabulous passer. If there was a 2-on-1 or 3-on-2 break, we would score every time. He had an uncanny knack of delivering the ball at the right time. You didn't even think he was looking at the guy. He could do that at full speed, which was pretty fast, with his head down. Bing! The ball was right there. Unbelievable.

**DANNY AINGE:** He had a reputation for not passing; but that guy made more passes to me with his head down, dribbling up the court, than I could ever imagine.

**ROBERT HORRY:** The first couple of days he was with us, he had me puzzled. Most guys dribble with their heads up. Clyde dribbled with his head down. I would stop running, and sometimes he would zing a pass out there ahead of me. One time he said, "Why did you stop running?" I said, "Who are you talking to? You saw me?" He said, "Yeah, I saw you." It was crazy. It took a little while for me to get used to him.

**CARROLL DAWSON:** He had eyes on the top of his head. He would put that head down and dribble upcourt and never run over anybody but make the passes he had to.

It may have looked like my head was down. Everyone seemed to think it was. And really, I guess it was. But the way I gathered speed on a fast break was to get low and take off. If someone was immediately open, I would pass it ahead. If not, I was on my jets. But even with my head down, I was able to see the court in full view and was always looking to make the pass. If a defender didn't cut me off by the free throw line I knew what I was going to do — dunk the ball.

I was pretty fast back in the day, and there was some story that got started about me racing the world's fastest man in the late '80s.

**JOHN WETZEL:** Clyde was always great at one-upsmanship. Whenever someone else had done something, he would always do it better. Supposedly he and Carl Lewis had this sprint race, and he beat Carl. I think Clyde even believed it. When he told it, everybody just fell down laughing.

**RICK ADELMAN:** Clyde had great stories to tell Buck and the other guys about his athletic prowess. He was telling all those guys he had beaten Carl Lewis in a sprint at the University of Houston. The story grew through Buck and Terry that Clyde was running in his street shoes. He was always the best at everything and could do just about anything. He could have been an Olympic gold medalist in the 100 meters.

**TERRY PORTER:** Haven't you heard about the race Clyde had with Carl Lewis? He said he used to work out with Carl in Houston in the summertime. Once they had a race, and Clyde ran in his basketball shoes, and Carl barely beat him.

**MYCHAL THOMPSON:** Clyde said one day they were working out in Houston, and they ran a 40-yard dash, and Carl beat him by a step. I said, "Clyde, come on. By a step?" Maybe Carl was running backward. I never asked him that.

**TIM HANEY:** According to Clyde's version, it was stride for stride, Clyde and Carl.

**BUCK WILLIAMS:** Clyde is such a dreamer. Yeah, he had stories, that he beat Arthur Ashe in tennis, and I think John McEnroe several times. He handled Wilt Chamberlain in his prime one on one, too, if I remember right. He has this imagination that is off the charts. It's tied into the fact that he has such confidence in himself. Sometimes he gets a little carried away.

**CALDWELL JONES:** The word was Clyde was a step or so behind Carl Lewis at the finish line. I said, "If you were a step behind Carl, that's not bad." I know one thing — Clyde had great closing speed. He ran as fast as he needed to. By his first step with the ball, he could be wide open. He would be full speed on his first step. For a guy that tall, I was amazed at his speed.

Truth of the matter was, we never raced. On an NBA team, I sometimes had to spend more hours with my teammates than I did with my family. I had to find ways to amuse myself and them. That was my way of sparking big debates and humorous stories. I would call it "jock talk."

The player I was compared with most often during my career was Michael Jordan.

**JOHN WETZEL:** I don't think there was a whole lot of difference between the two. Clyde was a different kind of player than Michael, but had the same kind of talents. He probably was not so much about scoring from the outside as Michael, but he was all about doing things on the floor to help his team win.

**RICK ADELMAN:** There was always that competiveness between Clyde and Michael. Clyde was the guy for us. Michael was the guy for Chicago. Jordan was winning championships and was the best perimeter player. Clyde was second only to him. There was that pressure of wanting to show he could compete with him, that he was just as good. It was a factor whenever the teams played. Clyde always wanted to measure himself against Michael. I think sometimes he tried too hard. It is human nature. We had a great chance when we played them in '92, but they proved they were the better team. When they beat us it was their bench more than Jordan. Clyde was right there with Jordan during those years. If you want to look for two class shooting guards, they are Jordan and Drexler.

**STEVE JONES:** They were 1 and 1a. Clyde was a better passer and rebounder than Michael. Michael may have been a bigger big-moment player, but Clyde was a big-moment player, too. He was right there with Michael.

**CHARLES BARKLEY:** Clyde had a great career. He was a very good player. He was up there with guys like Patrick Ewing, Gary Payton, Karl Malone, players like that. He wasn't Michael. Don't get silly. Michael was better than anybody else. Clyde is right there atop the next group of players, and that is pretty damn good.

**BILL WALTON:** Clyde was one of the most spectacular players ever. The only problem with Clyde is he was not as good as Michael Jordan; really, that is the ultimate compliment. If your only limitations are that you don't measure up to Michael, you have done pretty well. Clyde did it all.

I respected Michael's game. He was a fabulous player. I enjoyed playing against him whenever the opportunity presented itself, just as I enjoyed competing against Magic, Julius, Bird, Rolando Blackman, Joe Dumars and Isiah Thomas. Any time I got a chance to compete against the bigger names, I knew it would be a fun game — win or lose. The fun is in competing. Those are the games I lived for. I wish every night could have been a big game like that.

People always said, "Clyde is right there with Michael," which I took as a huge compliment. But I never tried to be like Mike; I was Clyde the Glide. As much as I respected and admired Michal's game, when I played against him I was never intimidated. I always thought I could match up with him, and I always knew I could keep him under 60 points.

After games in which we played the Bulls, Michael's father would catch me in the hallway and we would chat about the game. Mr. Jordan was like one of the guys. The only thing I ever envied about Michael Jordan was that he had a father who was at most of his games.

I enjoyed my transformation from a rookie to a champion. I learned a lot along the way, both about myself as a player and about myself as a person.

**BILL WALTON:** Clyde was a pillar of the community in Portland and in Houston, an outstanding leader who enjoyed a career marked with consistency and durability. Here was a guy who benefited greatly from the stability of two great franchises and brilliant coaches, starting with Jack Ramsay and moving through Rick Adelman and Rudy Tomjanovich. They did a wonderful job challenging Clyde to get him to a level that was not just based on his unparalleled athleticism. He was a player who could fly through the air, but he became an accurate perimiter shooter, an especially skilled and proficient ballhandler, and a very good defender.

I was there the night they retired his number in Portland. It was so great to be there and watch the highlight footage him delivering on the break, pulling up for his jumpers, making remarkable passes and steals and dunking over people. You tend to get numb to the brilliance of the greatest of NBA stars, but the cutting edge was always defined by Clyde Drexler.

**RICK ADELMAN:** Clyde really matured as a person during his time in Portland. It was good to see him as a young player, who came into the league as a very strong-willed individual, and as he went on, he got married, had kids, matured, moved on into other things and became a well-rounded person. It was the development of a genuinely good guy. We still have a warm relationship. It makes you feel good when an ex-player like Clyde always taken the time to say hello.

You always hope to have a group like we had in Portland. Clyde was like a lot of guys on that team. I saw many of the same things in Terry Porter and Buck Williams — married, solid family, still have the same wife. That was a great group of individuals. They were all different in their own way, and Clyde was the strongest personality of the bunch.

**BOB COOK:**  With his integrity, I am afraid Clyde is a dinosaur in this day and age of the NBA. He is a bright guy who has made the most of his business decisions, unlike a lot of guys who trusted agents who have proved to be untrustworthy or unscrupulous. And with some of his teammates who had a little misfortune financially along the way, he has reached out to those guys. It is a rare day goes by when somebody doesn't ask me about him — that is how well he is thought of in Portland.

**DARNELL VALENTINE:** As flamboyant as he was on the court with his athletic ability, Clyde is a very down-to-earth, knowledgeable, conservative person. One thing I have always admired is he honors players who played before him and those in the game now.

I have truly been blessed. First with a great family that was supportive and a mother who showed me the right way. Then with coaches, teammates and friends who have encouraged and enhanced both my life and my career. I have never felt alone. I could not have accomplished what I did without them. In some strange way, it's those around you that shape your destiny.

When I look back at my career, one of the most rewarding things has been my relationship with fans. It is always hard for me to imagine how a professional athlete wouldn't fully appreciate those people who are so supportive and, in reality, pay their salary. I have a problem with athletes who don't extend fans the simple courtesies of an autograph, a handshake or a smile. Those guys just don't get it. The fans have always been great to me. Maybe it is because they see me as a guy who is pretty normal and wants to give back.

Well, I appreciate them. They make what we do a lot more fun. Those years in Portland, the Blazermaniacs set all those NBA records for consecutive sellouts, and they turned Memorial Coliseum into a house of chaos. I couldn't walk on the streets of Portland for more than a block or two without getting a "hello" or an autograph request from someone. In Houston, the pandemonium over the Rockets' second straight championship in 1995 almost took fan support to another level. I honestly feel I could not have accomplished what I did throughout my career without the fans. A tip of my golf cap to all of you.

The players in the NBA take a lot of criticism, but I have found them to be mostly good people. There are some guys who need to grow up a little bit, but it has always been that way. When I was a young player with the Trail Blazers, we made a lot of mistakes. It is different now, though, because there is much more media attention; players today live under more scrutiny than the players that came before them.

I am not going to say today's NBA athlete is spoiled. It does seem as the average salary creeps up toward $5 million a year, the average player gives less of himself to the community and to the fans. It should go the other way. You should want to give more. I operate by the creed, "To whom much is given, much more is expected." You have to own up to that responsibility, but some of the guys don't.

My teammates and reporters always used to kid me about the political correctness of my answers in interviews. I plead guilty, but it is because I am never looking to say anything bad about anybody. The game is hard enough; no one needs the extra pressure of being ripped in the media. It just wasn't in my demeanor to do that. Besides, there's no need to give anybody an advantage by jabbering. I just never saw the beauty in that.

I had what I felt was an excellent relationship with the media throughout my career. I want to thank them for all the wonderful stories they wrote through the years to introduce me to the public. Without the media, our fans would never get to know about the athletes. The media has a great place in our game, and in sports in general. I have made some life-long friends with reporters who have covered me, and I am appreciative of those relationships.

Today's NBA players are playing extremely hard and have kept the game pretty entertaining. That doesn't mean there isn't room for a few suggestions to improve things.

The game has slowed down over the years. The average scoring total has dropped from 110 to 120 points a game in the 1980s to 80 to 90 today. Part of the reason for that drop is a greater emphasis being placed on defense and the sophistication of scouting. But we need to speed up the pace of play and get back to the fast-break game that the NBA was known for. When I attend an NBA game, I want to see something I don't see at a college game. NBA players should have an extra-special level of skill that can be displayed every night. That isn't happening as often as it should.

I would lower the shot clock to 18 seconds. That would force players to play at more of an up-tempo pace. Critics will say that we would see more rushed shots. But even with the 24-second clock, you still get a lot of rushed shots. I truly believe coaches are slowing the game down so they can have more control. They want to control every possession and make sure they get a good shot every time down; it is hard to do that and still score at a rapid pace. A faster game is fun for both the fans and the players; what we have now in the NBA more closely resembles a college game than at any time in history. Again, I have nothing against college basketball, but the NBA has the best players and athletes in the world. Let's let them show it.

I say outlaw the zone defense. The zone has no place in the NBA. Teams are too smart to let it affect them. They will find a way to get around that. It is part of the reason the game has slowed down so much, and it condenses the paint area.

If you keep the zone, you have to widen the paint. I think you should widen it, anyway. Guys are too big now.

I endorse raising the rim to 10 feet, five inches. Five additional inches would make a big difference. It would force big men to work on their skills. Now, they think they can just turn around and dunk. I am not saying that dunking is not a skill — I don't bite the hand that feeds me — but they need to work on their all-around game, too. I would also love to see a bigger court area to give the players more room to work with. Players are so much bigger than they were 50 years ago; they need more room to operate. I understand the cost of all these changes would be enormous; in a perfect world, just do it. The changes wouldn't alter the game that dramatically, but they would help speed the game up, make it faster and more fun for everybody.

I am proud to call David Stern a friend. Under the leadership and guidance of Stern as NBA commissioner and the very capable Russ Granik as deputy commissioner, the game has flourished unlike anyone thought it could when he took over almost

20 years ago. He has gone about his job in a first-class manner. He doesn't make decisions unilaterally. He forms committees, he puts together people with knowledge, he listens and then he makes informed decisions. Some of the players may say disturbing things about our commissioner, but this player thinks he has been awesome. We are blessed to have had him as commissioner for as long as we have. One player last season foolishly accused him of exploiting NBA players; any time David wants to exploit me when I am making $17 million, have at it.

I grew up as a Southern Baptist. It was an important part of my upbringing. I am not a Bible thumper, but I am in touch with my spiritual side. I think about God every day. I go to church. My kids have been raised Catholic. I go to mass with them, and I also go to my Baptist church. The Lord has a presence in our house.

One of my favorite bible verses is Psalms, chapter 23: "The Lord is my shepherd; I shall not want. He makes me lie down in green pastures; he leads me beside quiet waters; he restores my soul. He guides me in paths of righteousness for His name's sake. Even though I walk through the valley of the shadow of death, I will fear no evil, for You are with me. Your rod and your staff, they comfort me. You prepare a table before me in the presence of my enemies. You anoint my head with oil. My cup overflows. Surely goodness and mercy will follow me all the days of my life, and I will dwell in the house of the Lord forever."

That piece of scripture signifies my faith and is often in my thoughts. When times are rough, it is something I can lean upon.

I have a collection of quotes I enjoy referring to from time to time. One of the best is about success from the great Ralph Waldo Emerson: "To laugh often and much; to win the respect of intelligent people and the affection of children; to earn the appreciation of honest critics and endure the betrayal of false friends; to appreciate beauty, to find the best in others; to leave the world a bit better; whether be healthy child, a garden patch or a redeemed social condition; to know even one life has breathed easier because you have lived. This is to have succeeded."

In other words, try to make a difference. Don't just be a wallflower in the dance of life. Use your gifts for the benefit of others. I have had this saying on my refrigerators and in planners for the last 25 years. It is an inspirational piece I have gone back to 100 times.

Sometimes I sit back and wonder what I will be doing 20 years from now. My biggest challenge over the next decade is to continue to raise my kids and help them become mature, responsible adults. I want to continue to enjoy life and to give back for all the wonderful things I have gotten in my life.

I am not sure I want to coach again. I see myself working as a general manager or a president of an NBA club in the future if the opportunity should arise. I look forward to that challenge. My talents are best suited for the big picture.

I will continue to work with our restaurants and real estate investments. I want to keep improving my golf game, keep my body and mind in shape, and become a better father and husband. And I want to find a little more time to ride my Harley, which I keep down at Drexler's Barbecue. It is a fine ride, if I do say so myself.

What a wonderful world. Louis "Satchmo" Armstrong sang it, and it pretty much expresses the way I feel about my life. I have been truly blessed. So many people have enhanced my life and made it a great journey. So far, I say, because the journey continues. We constantly find ways to inspire and motivate ourselves to become better human beings. It is easy to get into a mundane grind, where you do the same things over and over. You need to continue to dream and aspire to achieve those dreams. I hope I will always do that. I hope you do, too.